CHARLES BUCHAN

CHARLES BUCHAN

A Lifetime in Football

With all good wishes from
Frances M. Klepp

Granddaughter of Charles Buchan

CHARLES BUCHAN

MAINSTREAM
PUBLISHING

EDINBURGH AND LONDON

-2011-

This edition published in Great Britain in 2010 by
MAINSTREAM PUBLISHING COMPANY
(EDINBURGH) LTD
7 Albany Street
Edinburgh EH1 3UG

ISBN 9781845966546

First published in 1955

All photos courtesy of the Estate of Charles Buchan

A catalogue record for this book is
available from the British Library

Typeset in Requiem and Sabon

Printed in Great Britain by
CPI Mackays, Chatham ME5 8TD

1 3 5 7 9 10 8 6 4 2

ACKNOWLEDGEMENTS

Sincere thanks are most certainly in order at this time, for without encouragement and support this significant book would have been unlikely ever to see the light of day again. Originally published in 1955, it needed to be re-presented in a contemporary fashion whilst, as far as possible, remaining faithful to the original. All this was undertaken by Michael D. Middleton, one who has grown to be a real friend but is a man who does not look for, or expect, personal accolades. It is he who painstakingly typed up the whole book, correcting a few printing errors or clarifying some misleading details that can arise when a book is written from a viewpoint of 1955. Without his enormous input this book would not be in your hands now.

To Mike, cousins, friends, colleagues and family members who have been supportive, I thank you all sincerely.

Needless to say, there are other people to be thanked, and they are the staff of Mainstream Publishing in Edinburgh, Scotland. My thanks go to Bill Campbell, Director of Mainstream, who was prepared to deal directly with me, the granddaughter of a man for whom he seemingly had great respect. It was he who allowed me to contact him directly in the early days of this undertaking when confidence was in short measure. It is one thing having a goal or inspiration, but it is quite another to be encouraged and supported by one who has both the willingness and the ability to ensure that it can be achieved.

Bill it was who understood why a Scottish publishing house was so appropriate for Charles Murray Buchan, an Englishman by birth but born of Scottish parents, natives of Aberdeen. From **Ellon** and **Logie** Buchan, the family at present (for further research is always possible) can be traced to 1758 and further back as part of the Comyn Clan. Proud my grandfather was of his Scottish heritage, as was his daughter Joan – and so am I, her daughter.

A sincere thanks is extended to all at Mainstream, especially Lindsay Ankers, Graeme Blaikie, Karyn Millar and Katie Robinson, who have been so encouraging and helpful in giving me the opportunity to re-present this significant gentleman to the world of today in the hope that his words, broadcast, will prove to be inspirational to those who read them.

Frances M. Klepp
Granddaughter of Charles Buchan Murray

CONTENTS

FOREWORD

One of the comments which I treasured most as a professional footballer appeared in the *News Chronicle* when I played for West Ham United. Their chief football reporter wrote: 'O'Farrell's first-time passes were models of accuracy.' Flattering indeed, especially as it came from the pen of Charles Buchan. This was a man who had embarked on a new career in journalism when his football career finished, a career in which he had played at the highest level for Sunderland, Arsenal and England.

After scoring 211 goals in 337 games for Sunderland between 1911 and 1925, he was transferred to Arsenal, where he made another 120 appearances and scored fifty-six goals. A further four goals in six internationals for England completed a remarkable record. What might he have achieved if the World War from 1914 to 1918 had not disrupted his career, as well as so many others?

In 1927, the year I was born, Buchan captained Arsenal in the F.A. Cup final, a simple goalkeeping error giving Cardiff City the goal that saw the Cup going out of England for the first, and only, time. Buchan retired at the end of the following season at the age of thirty-six. He still scored sixteen goals in his final campaign. He became a football journalist with the *News Chronicle*, as well as broadcasting for the B.B.C.

Then, in 1951, he edited his own publication, *Charles Buchan's Football Monthly*, ably assisted by John Thompson, Joe Sarl and Pat Collins, commissioning articles by top sportswriters of the day, like John MacAdam, Clifford Webb, Peter Morris, Leslie Yates and others. It was an instant success. There were ghostwritten articles by top players, coverage of football at all levels, letters from fans and (what seemed like an extravagance at the time) lots of coloured pictures of teams and players. I remember my club,

9

Preston North End, made it on to the centre pages in the 1957 to 1958 season. I still have that copy.

The words 'legend' and 'giant' are overused these days, often applied to personalities who don't remotely deserve them. In my opinion, Charles Murray Buchan was both a legend and a giant of the game and I look forward to learning even more about him from this book.

Frank O'Farrell

INTRODUCTION

Charles Murray Buchan was a man who appeared to be known to, but not *by*, millions. There are those who could relate all the known, recorded facts about the professional footballer, the journalist and the man from the B.B.C., yet how many could claim to have known not only about the man, but also the man himself? Few indeed could make such a claim today. One would have had to have been a mere child in the fifties to have survived him to this day; and how many children would have been likely to have been in close contact with him unless they were his own offspring? His teaching days were well over and, therefore, his contact with young pupils was an activity of the past, by at least a quarter of a century. There are only two of us who can say that we knew him as a grandfather and are pleased to be able to re-present him, through his own words, to a world that believes it knows him.

Meet him for the first time, or become re-acquainted with the man you thought you knew. Re-live the thrills and spills of the emerging 'superstar' whose upward journey was that of the seemingly ordinary man who strives to make something of his life, to make life better and safer for those entrusted to his care and who experienced the full gamut of emotions common to those of us who will admit to them. He was a man set apart by the life he lived to the full: a man of principle, a man of honour, a man of courage and a man humbled yet exalted in the world's eyes, a man who has made a real difference to the world of the 20th century, both during his life (tragically cut short) and since that time, through his extensive writing and foundations.

Charles Murray Buchan was a generous man, for he returned to the football pitch after the trench warfare of the First World War, during which he won the Military Medal for bravery, in order to support the widows and orphans of those who did not return. He did all that he could to make sure that those who returned, but were not really as fit as they needed to be to play professional football after their wartime experiences, did not lose their jobs. He ran under enemy fire to bring hot food to the men and, when commissioned in the field, gathered those who had lost their commanders to lead and protect them. He had a generosity of spirit that saw only the best in everyone (to quote from John MacAdam, a contemporary columnist of my grandfather), and that generosity enriched the lives of so many, myself included.

Significant gifts were received from the extensive travels he made as Sport Correspondent for the *News Chronicle*. His commentaries could be heard via his B.B.C. broadcasts on Saturdays, live from the matches he attended, and it was the B.B.C. on 25th June 1960 which announced his untimely death. A massive heart attack had robbed him of life during an evening's entertainment whilst on holiday with his wife, my 'Nana', on the French Riviera.

Therein lay a problem, for the airlines were on strike and repatriation of the body impossible. So it was that as soon as my mother could join my grandmother (not only for emotional support but for the translation of significant documents), a lengthy journey had to be undertaken. Imagine the scene: a procession speeding along the precipitous coastal road which winds its way mile after mile along the length of the Côte d'Azure. Noon arrived and with it a welcome break for the driver, an activity in which the widow felt unable and unprepared to participate despite the summer heat; that was just a halfway break. The remainder of the journey had still to be endured: a drive at speed to Marseille. There, and only there (for such places were far from commonplace in 1960s France), was a crematorium, albeit one that had not seen active service for many years. Service completed, the two bereaved ladies returned with grandfather's ashes in a transport plane, with an ill-fitting door through which the wind whistled. In his correspondence days I daresay that Grandad would not have taken exception to such a mode of transport, but his widow was most definitely unimpressed.

The formal recognition of Grandad's life's achievements took the form of a memorial service in St Bride's Church, Fleet Street, the 'journalists' church'. The church was full and the congregation, celebrities in their own rights, were deeply saddened, for Grandad was by no means an old man; he was only sixty-eight years of age and with a personality that was ageless.

His obituary can still be accessed and read in the *Times* Obituary for 25th June 1960. It rests in every library, as do his ashes in the chapel of rest at Golders Green Crematorium alongside his wife, neighbours and friends of many years.

At rest he may well be, but his words still ring out and wait to be read. He gave voice to so many youngsters, both in the literary sense and through their team skills, which he fostered. His Boys Club, which numbered 100,000 members, gave a sense of belonging to so many and encouraged them to write, a goodly number making writing their chosen profession. After all, wouldn't any youngster have been encouraged to write if it could earn him at least a 'golden guinea' for his efforts!

Charles Buchan founded his own publishing house in 1951 and then went on to have his own autobiography published in 1955. It seems high time, and a 'grand idea' (to use one of his seemingly favourite adjectives), to re-present his own account of his life to the world. There is so much genuine interest at present in nostalgia – in turning around to see what went before – to appreciate those who were the building blocks of a lifestyle that now overshadows the pitches. This autobiography gives voice to a man who was at the heart of his family, yet employed his 'people skills' to turn life around for so many people in a myriad of ways that deserve to be recognised and valued.

This year, 2010, is significant for it will mark fifty years since his death. It is just over 100 years since his football career really began to take shape, and 2010 is World Cup year, sixty years after he covered the matches of the 1950 World Cup for Fleet Street and the B.B.C.

A Lifetime in Football gives a background, setting the matches in a context that makes the whole affair seem real, for the descriptions are so sharp that it reads like a travelogue and an historic commentary on the first half of the twentieth century.

The privilege, I feel, it is to have been born into his family, to have been able to have been close to him, been treasured by him and had the time and emerging maturity to love him dearly. I trust that reading this book will give you the opportunity to imagine the actions described and offer you some inspiration for the future.

May the future for all of us be 'grand', as 'grand' as it can be.

Frances M. Klepp
Granddaughter of Charles Murray Buchan

CHAPTER I

HOW I BEGAN

WHEN BOYS WERE BROUGHT UP THE HARD WAY

As long as I can remember I have been either kicking a football or watching games being played. Right from the age of six, when I recall waiting for my mother to finish making a red football shirt so that I could go out and play in a game, football has been in the blood. It has never got out of it even now. Yet strangely, I did not come from a footballing family.

My father was first a soldier, a colour-sergeant in a Highland regiment and then a blacksmith in Woolwich Arsenal. A native of Aberdeen, he moved to London after leaving the Army. I was born in London, hence my qualification to play for England though of Scottish parentage. My father did not play football but my three brothers, Will and Tom, who were older, and Jack, four years younger, did. Tom did great service for Blackpool and Bolton Wanderers for a number of years. Many people, and I was among them, thought Tom a better forward than I ever was. Unfortunately, he had to go through cartilage operations that proved a handicap. He was a great utility player, giving a creditable show in all positions. Several times I played against him in League games. Once at Burnden Park, I got in trouble with the crowd for knocking him over with a hefty charge. The crowd evidently thought it unfair that a big chap like me (I was 6 ft and ¾in. tall at the time) should take advantage of his smaller, younger brother. Really he was two years my senior and it was part of the fun between us that we should charge one another whenever possible.

Jack, the younger brother, was a 'harum-scarum' lad who could never settle in one place long. He saw service with Bolton Wanderers and Charlton Athletic. Will, the eldest of the four, ran away from his apprenticeship as an upholsterer to join the Royal Navy. He had shown promise of developing into a useful outside-right.

Much of my early soccer was played with my brothers and, of course, at school. My first team was my school team, High Street, Plumstead. I was the centre-forward and easily the smallest boy in the side. We played most of the games on Plumstead Common, a vast expanse of stone and gravel without a blade of grass. It was the manoeuvring ground of the Royal Horse Artillery. Covered with stones, it was not really a fit place for schoolboys to play football. But it was handy and as long as we could either kick a ball about or play matches there we did not mind. It taught us many things, the chief one how to fall lightly without getting hurt too badly. Like an acrobat on the stage who knows how to tumble, so we learned the hard way to dodge injuries other than cuts and grazes.

My next school was Bloomfield Road, a higher grade school. There I was taught how to head a ball though I was still only a tiny tot. As often as possible we used to practise on a piece of waste ground. The teacher, Mr Swallow, coached us. He gave instructions to the wing forwards to cross the ball on my head. For hours I attempted to nod it past the goalkeeper.

It was at Bloomfield Road that I received my first medal. The school team won the Woolwich Schools Shield, winning the final on the Manor Field, home of Woolwich Arsenal at the time. I remember what a thrill it gave me to turn out on the League ground of my boyhood heroes. Certainly 'a dream come true'. A few days after the game, the team was to be photographed. When I took my place in the group, the photographer said to me: "You will have to do something about your shirt."

The brown and white striped shirt was so faded that it would have shown up white on the picture. So my colleagues and I spent quite a time pinning brown paper stripes on to the shirt. That photograph is still among my souvenirs.

From Bloomfield Road I moved on to Woolwich Polytechnic. My home was about two miles from the school buildings and it gave me the opportunity to improve my game considerably. It was the days of the old horse trams. They ran along the High Street, which was my way to school. So every morning I set off to beat the trams, running and walking in turn. I had not the money to pay the fare. Nine times out of ten I got to Beresford Square, where I took a different route, before the trams. The odd occasion was when I stopped to kick a tennis ball about. Always I carried some sort of a ball in my pocket. It did not stay there long. I used to run along the road, using the pavement edge as a colleague. I fear that in these days of heavy traffic, it would be impossible to carry out this sort of practice. But I thought nothing of it. I became so adept at pushing the ball against the pavement and taking the rebound that it did not impede my rate of progress.

When I first played for the Polytechnic, my position was left half-back. In one game I happened to score five goals. So I was immediately put into the forward line, where I remained for the rest of my playing days.

Then I had ambitions of becoming a centre-half, but I was too small for the position. Though I was big enough in later years, nobody seemed to fancy me as a pivot. At any rate, I never played in the position. Playing regularly for the school team was not enough to satisfy my appetite for the game. Every Saturday afternoon I went down to the Manor Field to see what I could of Arsenal's League and reserve sides. As my weekly pocket money was the princely sum of one penny, I could not pay the three-pence admission into the ground. I waited outside, listening to the roars and cheers of the crowd, until about ten minutes before the end when the big, wide gates were thrown open to allow the crowd to trek out. In I rushed with the other soccer-crazy boys to see the finish of the game. It was enough to get a glimpse of my heroes and to watch the way they played the game.

Among my favourites then were Bobby Templeton, Scottish international wing forward; big, burly Charlie Satterthwaite, an inside-left with a cannon-ball shot; Tim Coleman, a born humorist and inside-right whom, eventually, I succeeded at Sunderland; Percy Sands, the local schoolmaster centre-half; Roddy McEachrane, a consistently good left half-back and Jimmy Sharp, the youthful-looking full-back. They were the stars upon whom I tried to model my style. And there was no greater pleasure for me than to go, during the training month of August, and in the school holidays, to watch them kicking-in and sometimes retrieve the ball when it went behind the goal. At times, when they were out for a road walk, I followed, trying to keep pace all the time. Though it did not help me to grow, it certainly kept me fit and happy.

There was one occasion when Arsenal met Sunderland in a replayed F.A. Cup-tie at the Manor Field. Though it was on a Wednesday, I was determined to see the match. As I had not the necessary three pence, I sold one of my schoolbooks to raise the funds. I saw Arsenal win and was content, though I got into serious trouble from the headmaster when he found out what I had done.

In my mind I can still see that Sunderland forward line, which included players like Billy Hogg, Jimmy Gemmell, Alf Common and Arthur Bridgett, all great, husky fellows weighing something like 14 st. each. It is strange that my entire career was bound up with these two clubs. They are two of the best in the land.

In those far-off days, I thought nothing of playing two games each Saturday. In the morning, I played for my school. In the afternoon, I turned out for a senior team called Woolwich Polytechnic because they used the school for their headquarters. They were in the Kent Senior League and usually held a good place among professional opposition. It was an experience that served me very well later.

There were days when I played for my church team, Plumstead St Nicholas. We played on a hilly, sloping pitch at Bostall Heath. We had to carry the goal posts a long way up the hill to the ground. That did not curb our enthusiasm at all. We were only too glad of the opportunity. One Saturday, after my second game, I was asked to make up the number by a team which shared the ground. I eagerly accepted, making my third game that day. I never felt any after effects. Rather, I seemed to thrive on the exercise. The more football I got the better.

Sometimes, it was a bit difficult to raise funds to get to the away games played in various parts of London. My father came to the rescue though he must have denied himself many things to help me out. Often I went to him for half-a-crown. But what a lot could be done with that coin in those days. I recall after one Saturday game, I travelled by train from Plumstead to Charing Cross, had a very good meal at Gatti's, went to the variety show at the Tivoli (and saw a great artist like Wilkie Bard), bought a small packet of cigarettes, had a soft drink and finished up with a penny-halfpenny change out of my half-crown. But I must say that did not happen very often. Only after a special occasion that we wished to celebrate.

In those days young players were brought up the hard way, meeting all types of opposition from the sedate schoolboys to the boisterous, hard-tackling senior teams in the district. Against soldier, sailor or police the youngster had to learn to take care of himself. No quarter was asked or given. Nowadays, I fear he is nursed too carefully. He is taken in hand immediately after leaving school and usually allowed to play only one game a week – and that against opposition of his own class. He loses the benefit of the hardening process and takes years longer to mature. There are exceptions, of course, like the Manchester United boys, John Blanchflower, Denis Viollet, Eddie Lewis, David Pegg and Duncan Edwards, also Bobby Smith of Chelsea and Peter Broadbent of Wolves, who had won places in First Division sides before they were eighteen. But I wonder if we shall ever see again a young man like Arthur Brown, Sheffield United centre-forward, an England international at eighteen, or Arsenal's Cliff Bastin, who won every major honour in the game before he was twenty-one?

After leaving school, I assisted a local team called Plumstead, a nomadic side with no ground of its own. We used to play the best amateur sides in the Home Counties and won more games than we lost. I even played on Sunday mornings, for a North Woolwich team. I was so keen; I either ignored or forgot the F.A. ban on taking part in Sunday football. I was reminded of those Sunday mornings when I ran across Charlie Paynter, who served West Ham United as player (until he fractured a leg), trainer and manager for more than fifty years. Now he holds the unique appointment of West Ham's 'Ambassador at Large'. He represents the club all over the country and on the Continent. Paynter said to me: "Do you remember playing for Elder Tree one Sunday morning, on the public ground beside Boleyn Castle?"

"Yes," I replied, "and it was a tough game, too. I think we drew one-all that day."

"That's right. I was sent there to watch you. But you were so small and looked so frail I decided I would wait a year or two before thinking of signing you."

The strange part was I was just a tiny fellow then. My schoolfellows had nicknamed me 'Skip' because I had to be very lively to make up for my lack of height and weight. How I grew is another story I shall tell later.

It was whilst I was still at Woolwich Polytechnic, which I did not leave until I was seventeen as I wanted to become a schoolteacher, that Arsenal became interested. One day an official came to my home and asked me if I would like to play for Arsenal reserves in a South-Eastern League game with Croydon Common. They played at the Nest, now a goods yard, adjoining Selhurst Railway Station. But getting to Selhurst meant that I should have to take an afternoon off from school. That did not enter my mind at the time. I readily agreed to play; in fact, I thought it was a great honour. It would have taken a lot to stop me. So I played for Arsenal and we beat Croydon Common 3–1. Though I do not remember much of the opposition, I do recall that two of my colleagues were Johnny Dick, a grand Scotsman who put me at my ease before the start, and bow-legged Sammy Curle, an outside-right who told me exactly what to do. It so happened that I scored one of the goals. And one of the headlines in an evening paper read 'SCHOOLBOY SCORES FOR THE ARSENAL'. When I went to school the next day, the headmaster, Dr W. Bain, sent for me. When I could not explain my absence to his satisfaction, he produced the paper and showed it to me. The next few minutes were very uncomfortable though not as bad as I had expected or deserved. Many years later, I had the satisfaction of sending Dr Bain a couple of tickets for the Cup final between Arsenal and Cardiff City at Wembley. I felt that he wanted to see how his erring pupil had advanced with the years.

In all I played four games for Arsenal's second string in the 1909 to 1910 season. One of them was against West Ham United at Boleyn Castle. The left half-back opposed to me – a big chap called Bourne – played in spectacles. I shall never forget him, as apart from goalkeeper J. F. Mitchell, amateur international and Manchester City goalkeeper, I never played against another who wore glasses.

Arsenal must have been satisfied with my play for on two occasions I was chosen as reserve for the League team. Though it was a tribute to me really, I did not like it because it meant idle Saturday afternoons. After I had been a few weeks with the Arsenal, I put in an expenses account. I had played four games, trained two evenings a week at the Manor Field, and had paid my own fare to the away games. My bill was for eleven shillings. When I handed it to George Morrell, the secretary-manager, in his office on a bleak November day in 1909, he queried it. How could a youngster of eighteen spend such a sum on the club's business? After I had given a detailed statement of the account, there was an argument. Rather one-sided I must admit. I walked out of the office, very hurt and without the money. I did not play for Arsenal again for sixteen years – that is, until I was transferred to them from Sunderland in 1925.

This was the first of many arguments that seemed to dog me throughout the years. Though I was blessed with a placid temperament, I could not keep out of an argument where soccer was concerned. My friends say I will talk about it until I am 'black in the face'. I cannot deny they are right. In my early days, professional footballers were looked upon as a race apart. They had not reached the status of today. Whenever anybody spoke slighting them – and that was often – I 'took up the cudgels'. It landed me in all sorts of difficulties. The argument over expenses with the Arsenal manager was the first of many. It set me on the road to a professional career.

Previously, I had thought nothing about becoming a professional. I was keen to be a schoolmaster. But the following day, I signed for Northfleet, the Kent League club, as an amateur. I turned out for them the next Saturday. I did not wait to get my clearance from Woolwich Arsenal. That led to more trouble a few months later.

For the rest of the 1909 to 1910 season, I was Northfleet's inside-right. One of my colleagues was Gordon Hoare, the amateur international inside-left, and a great forward. We won all the competitions entered for that season, Kent Senior Cup, Kent Senior League and Thames and Medway Combination. I received three gold medals, the first of a big collection. But I regret to say I haven't got them now. Some enterprising burglar thought he had a better right to them or, at least, to most of them. As you can imagine, the Northfleet players, after these successes, were in great demand by League clubs. Seven of them signed professionally before the season had been over a month. They were Bill Jaques, a goalkeeper who gave good service to Tottenham Hotspur and Coventry City; Rogers and Quayle, the full-backs who went to Woolwich Arsenal; Nash, a half-back signed by Millwall; Williams, outside-right, transferred to nearby Dartford; and

Kennedy, a schoolteacher centre-forward. He scored a lot of goals for West Ham United in the next few years. I was the seventh and my signing for Leyton, then a professional club in the Southern League, was an accident.

The first to approach me was Bob Dunmore, who had been Woolwich Arsenal trainer but had joined Bury a week or two before. He had looked after me during my short spell with Woolwich Arsenal reserves. He offered me £3 per week to sign for Bury, then in the First Division. It was really a wonderful offer when you consider that the wages of a fully trained engineer, fitter and turner, or a carpenter were thirty-seven shillings and six pence. And they had to serve a five-year apprenticeship before they got it. There were many young men of my age earning less than £1 for a week's hard work. I did not accept the offer because, at the time, I still wanted to be a schoolteacher.

A few days later 'Punch' McEwen, Fulham scout, persuaded me to go to Craven Cottage for an interview with his directors, Mr Henry (later Sir Henry) Norris and Mr William Hall. When I entered the boardroom I had not long to wait before I received a blow to my pride. Mr Norris said: "We understand you want to be a teacher. We will find you a job where you can continue your training and pay you thirty shillings a week to sign professional forms for Fulham."

The idea of a job appealed to me but the scanty wage certainly did not. So I replied: "Thirty shillings? That's only half of what I've already been offered. Couldn't you make it a little more, say two pounds?"

The directors went outside for a consultation. When they returned I was told: "We think the job offered will be much better for you than a higher wage. Your future will be assured."

Naturally, I was disappointed and refused the offer. If they had raised the wage to £2 I would have signed and the whole pattern of my life would have been changed. Even more disappointed than I was 'Punch' McEwan, who had taken the trouble to get me the interview and had great faith in my ability to make good. Later, when I joined Arsenal at Highbury, McEwen was their chief scout. He often reminded me of that interview. He was one of the most lovable characters I met. Almost as broad as he was long, he was a great humorist. That's how he got the name 'Punch'. He was also a fine left-back and played for

Bury during their F.A. Cup-winning exploits early in the 20th century. I never played against him, of course, but I have often listened to his humorous stories of games in the 'good old days'. It was the same then as it is now. No player was as good as the star of yesteryear.

After the Fulham rebuff, I went back to my job. Then there arrived on the scene Micky Busby, a replica in build of McEwan, and with the same puckish humour. He was right-back for Leyton and did scouting work for them in his 'off' moments. He painted a vivid picture of life as it would be at Osbourne Road, the Leyton headquarters, at present the home of the Football League side Leyton Orient. Busby said to me: "Charlie, I want you to come over and sign for Leyton. I promise you we will take good care of you."

"What are the terms?" I asked.

"Three pounds a week from now till next May. You can live at home and train at Leyton three or four days a week."

As it was a journey of only seven miles from Plumstead, where I lived, to Leyton and the terms were good, I agreed to go for an interview with Dave Buchanan, the player-manager. He was the right half-back and a wonderfully consistent one too. He had one striking characteristic. He never appeared in public without wearing a black skullcap. You see he was completely bald, and very sensitive about it. He played in the cap too. Not once during the many games I saw him play was the cap knocked off his head, though he was an expert at heading the ball. He is the only player I met, except goalkeepers, who wore a cap through a League game. When I walked into the manager's office, he wasted no words.

"Well, young fellow, I want you to sign for Leyton. Mick Busby has told you the terms and you've had time to think about them. What's your decision?"

We discussed the matter for some minutes when suddenly he said: "Well, I can guarantee you a place in the first team for the opening games. No other manager can offer you that guarantee."

That made up my mind. I was not keen to turn professional but the prospects of a place in a League side were so tempting that I signed without any more delay. That was in May 1910.

During the summer months I stayed at work. Then I received notice to report for training at Osbourne Road the day after

August Bank Holiday. In those days the season opened on the first Saturday in September so the whole of August could be devoted to strenuous training. It also ended on the last Saturday in April. Since then the season has been extended and takes in the last week in August and the first week in May. I think this is one of the mistakes made by the ruling bodies. League football in cricket weather and on bone-hard grounds is neither good for the player or for the standard of play. It takes too much out of the player physically and mentally.

That August in 1910 was my first experience of systematic training. We trained twice each day and trained hard. Much harder than when I came back to London fifteen years later. Then, after the opening month, I went to the ground only once daily. Although present-day players have modern appliances to assist them, I still believe the 'old-timer' was more physically fit. Or I should rather say 'they were a tougher breed of men'.

As the opening day of the season approached, I grew more nervous. It did not help when, on the Thursday before the first game, my name appeared on the sheet posted in the dressing room at inside-right for the away game with Brighton. I could have run away with fright. But I had to conquer my nerves. Just as I thought I was getting the better of them, manager Buchanan, who had kept his word, said: "Charlie, I've some bad news. You've to attend a meeting of the League Management Committee, Arsenal want to make you a joint player. You can't play until they have decided the matter."

"A joint player?" I replied. "I don't understand. What's it all about?"

"Well, you signed an amateur form for Woolwich Arsenal didn't you? That made you their player until they agreed to release you. Evidently they don't want to do that. They want to have a claim on you."

I attended the meeting in London, but was not called in front of the Committee. They decided that as I had signed professional I was Leyton's player. Again Buchanan stuck to his bond. I was chosen as inside-right for the first home game, against Plymouth Argyle at Osbourne Road. But I had another disturbing shock before I was allowed to kick a ball. When I walked into the dressing room about an hour before the kick-off, George Ryder, our inside-left and father of Terry Ryder, now a professional, came up to me and said: "We're waiting for word that the players are to go on strike. Will you join the rest of the boys?"

Although I had not then joined the Players' Union, which was discussing the problem, I replied: "Yes, I'll do exactly as the others. In fact, I have no choice if the rest aren't going to turn out."

We spent anxious minutes waiting before the word came through that the strike was off. It had been settled in Manchester where those great players Charlie Roberts and Billy Meredith (who became great friends of mine later on) bore the brunt of the proceedings. I joined the Union the next week.

With shaking hands, I began to put on my kit. Sitting next to me was my partner Jimmie Durrant, who spoke a few kind words to put me at ease. Jimmie was an experienced hand at outside-right, almost of international class. He had taken part in an international trial. After brilliant service with Leicester Fosse (now City), and Luton Town, he had reached the twilight of his career. As we stood waiting to go out, Jimmie said to me: "Charlie, can you do a lot of running, and will you do exactly what I want?"

"Yes," I replied, "I'll run as much as you like. What do you want me to do?"

"When I get the ball, run to within about ten yards of me every time. Then I can give you the ball."

"What happens when I've got the ball?"

"If I shout, push it forward along the wing so I can run on to it. If I don't shout, do whatever you like."

I carried out these instructions to the letter. Though I thought I had done very little during the game, everybody seemed pleased with my display. The fact that I kept my place in the team meant that manager Dave Buchanan was satisfied too. That, as far as I was concerned, was the beginning of the triangular wing movement. Later, the right half-back was brought into the scheme of things and the trio completed. Very rarely is this move seen in present-day teamwork. I think that is because most forwards try it the wrong way round. The inside-forward pushes the ball to his partner, who in turn glides the ball along the wing for the inside-forward to collect. The result is that neither is in the final assault on the goal.

That was my first lesson. I'm sure it was the best of many I learned afterwards. But there was to be a second before the end of my first game. The Plymouth Argyle left half-back, directly opposed to me, was a big burly chap, inches taller than I, and a strong player. When our goalkeeper, Jack Whitbourne, was about to take a goal kick, the left-half sidled up to me and said: "I'll bet you a shilling you can't head this ball before me."

"You're on," I replied.

The kick came. I reached my highest and got my head to the ball. When I looked round, there was the left-half, about ten yards away, coolly trapping the ball at his leisure. When the next goal kick came along, again he said: "Let's make it double or quits. Two shillings to nothing you don't head the ball this time."

"Right, that's a deal."

The same thing happened: I headed the ball; he trapped it in his own time and set one of his forwards going with a lovely ground pass. Though I never got the two shillings, I am grateful to the Plymouth half-back. He taught me to think a move ahead and to study at a glance beforehand the positions of the other side. And never to take anything for granted on the field.

CHAPTER 2

I Meet Wonderful Harold Fleming

Listen to Billy Meredith, and move to Sunderland

Looking back over the years, I thank my lucky stars I joined Leyton and not a First Division club. Not because I had any conceit about my own play, but because I kept my place in the League side. It takes years before a youngster is capable of thinking things out for himself. He plays more or less instinctively, doing the first thing that enters his head. Sometimes it comes off, more often it doesn't. It is not until he has played several years in the top class, or until he is twenty-six or twenty-seven years old, that he can plan ahead and stick to a definite policy of his own. Club managers have lost several star players because they have not taken this into account. They introduce a youngster into the side, but because he either cannot play to instructions or make the most of his ability, he is discarded and later makes a big name with another club.

Jimmy Dunne, Irish international centre-forward, and Eph Dodds, a Scottish international centre-forward, are cases in point. Once they had got over what I call the instinctive period, they developed into grand, goal-scoring leaders. Playing in a League side gives a young player confidence. And confidence in yourself is half the battle in League soccer. You need it when you are up against the finest opposition in the country. And in those early days, many of the greatest were playing with Southern League teams.

One of the greatest of them all I met in the 1910 to 1911 season was Harold Fleming, the brilliant England and Swindon inside-right. Fleming, unorthodox and quick thinking, took a delight in shocking the critics. I have seen him beat man after man in a cross-field dribble that took him from his own position to outside-left and finish with a perfect centre. I have also seen him streak through a defence and score entirely on his own. His ball control with both feet was wonderful. He was, too, a great club man. Record offers were made for his transfer but he refused to leave Swindon. Fleming was deeply religious. He refused point-blank to play either on Christmas Day or on Good Friday, and was an excellent lay preacher. I attended a meeting with him recently and he spoke as he played, with strength, conviction and intelligence. He still runs a flourishing business in Swindon, not far from the County ground where he spent the whole of his playing career.

It was from Fleming I discovered that more than speed was required to beat an opponent. I frankly admit I copied one of his most successful tricks. It was to get an opponent on one foot by pretending to go one way with the ball, then suddenly changing direction and slipping past him on the other. I practised this move until I could do it, not as well as Fleming but good enough to get by most opponents.

Shortly after playing against Fleming, I wandered up to Plumstead Common one Saturday morning. That was an advantage of living at home; I could watch the schoolboys play in the morning before going across to Leyton in the afternoon. On this particular Saturday morning, I saw a schoolboy, not the height of six-pennyworth of coppers, weaving his way past the defenders like an electric eel. I watched fascinated. He ran with the ball to within a yard of the opponent, a much bigger chap, and feinted to kick the ball hard at him. Naturally the big fellow flinched and lost his balance slightly. As he did so the little fellow romped past him at full speed with the ball at his toes. I tried the move in the League game that afternoon. It worked. I continued to use it for many years and it seldom failed.

During the course of my apprenticeship with Leyton, I had another stroke of luck. About two months after the season started, the Rev. K. R. G. Hunt joined the club and played regularly behind me at right half-back. Only two years previously he had been right-half for Wolverhampton Wanderers when they unexpectedly defeated Newcastle United in the F.A. Cup final at Crystal Palace. The big, strong cleric was noted for his vigorous charging. He delighted in an honest shoulder charge, delivered with all the might of his powerful frame. He was an opponent not to be feared, as he never did an unfair thing in his life, but to be avoided if possible. Years afterwards I spoke to Billy Meredith, the great Welsh international outside-right, who played fifty-one times for his country. The name of Hunt cropped up. Meredith said: "I never ran up against a harder or fitter half-back. It was like running up against a brick when he charged you."

"But," I replied, "he was also a great player. He helped me a lot when I played in front of him."

"Oh, yes, his positioning was perfect. He seldom allowed you a yard of room in which to work. I'm glad I didn't have to meet him very often."

It was Hunt who instilled in me the art of positioning. In his quiet voice he would tell me where to go when he had the ball, or where to position myself when we were on the defensive. They are two of the most important assets of an inside-forward, who should be a link between attack and defence.

Another amateur in the Leyton side to whom I owed a lot was Sergeant McGibbon, the centre-forward. He was serving in the Royal Artillery at Woolwich, and one year saved Woolwich Arsenal from relegation from the First Division by scoring a hat-trick in a vital game. A six-footer, he was a born opportunist. His shouts of "Now" or "Through" taught me the tremendous value of timing a pass, without which no player can reach the top flight. Even a poor pass can be very useful when timed correctly. After each home game, I travelled to Woolwich with the sergeant. His comments on the game in general, and my play in particular, were enlightening, to say the least. Under his guidance my soccer education advanced rapidly.

So it did too, under Tommy Shanks, an Irish international inside-left, who joined us from Brentford after long service with Woolwich Arsenal. Tommy, of the brick-red face and pleasant smile, was a skilful ball player and one of the hardest shots at goal that I came across. He revelled in passing on his skill and knowledge to the young players. I spent hours with him in training. Tommy would say: "Now I'm going to show you how to place a ball accurately."

Then after about a quarter of an hour he would vary it with: "Now it's time you knew how to make a ball swerve. Use the outside of the foot and rub it along the inside of the ball. Like this."

Hours we spent together until he was satisfied with my work. He taught me things with a ball I should never have dreamed of myself.

Early in January 1911, I took part in my first F.A. Cup-tie. It was against Chelsea in a third round at Stamford Bridge. It was played in fog so thick you could not see half the field. And the ground was bone-hard with frost. We drew 0–0. Unluckily for me, I fell with a thump during the game and hurt my left shoulder. I was immediately taken to a specialist for examination. He told me I had slightly dislocated my shoulder and added: "You won't be able to play for three weeks. Keep the arm in a sling for about a week and you'll be as right as rain afterwards."

"But there's the Cup replay with Chelsea on Wednesday," I protested. "Can't I play then and take it easy afterwards?"

"Decidedly not. If you do, you run the risk of a permanent shoulder injury."

He put my arm in a sling and I left him. Two days later, I discarded that sling and played against Chelsea. We were beaten 2–0. Chelsea could see what they were doing this time and won quite comfortably. But the specialist was right. That shoulder gave me trouble right through the years and still does.

Two Chelsea forwards in that team were centre-forward George Hilsdon and Jimmy Windridge. George was not a stylist, but a natural 'goal-getter' who believed in hitting the ball hard for goal whenever he had the chance. He scored a hat-trick in his first representative game. Windridge was the clever type of inside-left who kept the attack moving with his clever passing and skilful footwork. He too played for England. In the Chelsea goal was big Jack Whitley, who afterwards became the club trainer and manager, taking over from Dave Calderhead, the Scottish international centre-half who had piloted the club through the trying period after their formation in 1905. He received the League's long-service medal for twenty-five years' service as manager. Whitley told me that following the Cup-ties, Chelsea wanted to get my transfer from Leyton. But they would not pay the £800 fee asked.

So my apprenticeship went on. I remained in the first team

without a break. In that I was indeed lucky. Great players like Jimmy Seed (Spurs), Jackie Carr (Middlesbrough), Leslie Compton (Arsenal) and Laurie Scott (Arsenal) all had to wait years before they secured a regular place in the side. And my apprenticeship was served with some of the finest players in the country. In those days the Southern League was a separate body from the Football League and, in my opinion, the standard of play was equal, at least, to the present Second Division.

Most of the players were recruited, when in their prime, from League clubs. No transfer fees were paid for men who went to Southern League clubs. If they were not satisfied with the pay or conditions with a League club they could, when their contract expired, throw in their lot with a Southern League club. But if they rejoined a League club, two transfer fees had to be paid, one to the original League club, the other to the Southern League team. Now, a professional player cannot go outside the League without permission from his club. If they wish to retain him, they can do so permanently. Yet the F.A. law relating to retained players has not been changed in any way. A different interpretation has been placed upon it, one that deprives the player of his only means of escape. It has always been a wonder to me that the Players' Union, a strong body nowadays, has not taken up this point. A return to the old system would, I am sure, be a blessing to a lot of the lesser-known players.

Well, as I say, my apprenticeship went on smoothly, until the beginning of March 1911. I was sitting on top of the world. I had been promised the maximum wage (£4 per week) by Dave Buchanan for the next season and I was planning a summer holiday when, like a bolt from the blue, the whole scene changed. On 10th March I was transferred to Sunderland. It came about so simply. We were due to play Southampton on the Saturday before. And Southampton made it widely known they were prepared to transfer two of their players, Frank Jefferies, inside-right, and Harry Trueman, left half-back. Managers from all over the country flocked to see the game. As it happened I had one of those matches in which everything went right. If the ball struck me on the shin, it went beautifully to my partner. I could do no wrong. In addition, I scored two of the four goals by which Leyton won. The result was the managers came for my transfer instead of the Southampton men.

Throughout the weekend, they visited the Leyton ground and my home at Woolwich. I told them all to interview my father, who put some of them off with the news that I would not leave home. The size of the transfer fee asked by Leyton put others off. Then on Tuesday I went to the Leyton ground. Manager Dave Buchanan told me I was wanted in the office. Bob Kyle, Sunderland manager, was waiting there. When I went in, he said: "How would you like to play for Sunderland in the First Division? You'll get maximum wages and a £10 signing-on fee."

To be perfectly frank I did not know exactly where Sunderland was. I knew it was on the north-east coast somewhere near Newcastle, but that was all. It seemed very far away from home. After talking the matter over, Kyle said: "You know, you'll never get a better chance. I can promise you a place in the first team for the rest of this season at least."

That settled the argument. I signed, received the £10 fee, and went in the dressing room to prepare for training. When Dave Buchanan heard I had signed he was the most disappointed man I met. He wanted me to go to Everton. The Sunderland manager came into the dressing room a minute or two afterwards and said: "Son, it's very cold up north, so I advise you to get an outfit of thick winter clothes. You'll need them."

I did. I bought a new lined overcoat (four pounds and four shillings), a tweed suit (two pounds and ten shillings), in fact a completely new outfit of what I thought would keep me warm in any climate. And the whole lot did not amount to the £10 signing fee. Today they would cost nearer £100. But within six months, they were no use to me whatever. I had grown right out of them.

Later that week I had instructions from Sunderland to report at the Fleetwood boat on Thursday night about ten o'clock. Sunderland were playing a friendly with Distillery in Belfast and I was to play inside-right.

Donning my new clothes, off I went to Fleetwood. I arrived there in plenty of time but when I tried to get on the boat, I was met with a polite 'youngsters are not allowed to collect autographs on board'. I must admit I looked a stripling but to be taken for a schoolboy was rather humiliating. As I stood disconsolately on the quayside, wondering what on earth I should do, along strolled manager Bob Kyle and Jackie Mordue, Sunderland outside-right. They took me on board and introduced me to the rest of the team, who looked at me with a puzzled air, which seemed to say, 'It's a shame to take a kid so far from home.'

This was my first meeting with Mordue, the best two-footed wing forward I ever met. He played both at outside-right and outside-left for England and could fill every position in the forward line with credit. He was incredibly fast off the mark for about ten yards. With short strides and shuffling gait, he was away in a flash. I never ran across anyone quite like him. Mordue was also champion of the world at 'hand-ball', a very popular game in the north, something like 'fives'. Jackie beat all-comers. The Sunderland players often won bets that he would beat his opponent with one arm strapped to his back. His speed off the mark and quick eye were unrivalled. Well, I played my first game for Sunderland in Belfast against Distillery and got on well with my new colleagues, scoring one of the five goals and hitting up an understanding with Mordue and the rest of the side. But straight after the game I went back to my home in Woolwich. We were to play Tottenham Hotspur at White Hart Lane the following Saturday.

It is, by the way, interesting to recall that Frank Jefferies, the Southampton inside-right, was later transferred to Everton and Harry Trueman, the left-half, to Sheffield United. The next time I ran across Jefferies, twelve months later, he was England's inside-right against Scotland at Hampden Park. I was reserve for England that day so I don't suppose Everton ever regretted that I did not go to them.

Another point about my transfer is that I did not receive a penny piece out of it, except, of course, the signing-on fee. A player was entitled in those days to ten per cent of the transfer fee, if he could get it, but I made no bargain with Leyton before I signed for Sunderland. When I approached the Leyton chairman and mentioned my share he said: "Sorry Charlie, the club is so badly off that I'm afraid we can't give you anything, much as we would like to."

He must have been right for within fifteen months Leyton ceased to exist as a League club. All the same, I felt aggrieved I had collected nothing from a fee of £1,200, which I believe was a record at the time. The biggest until then was the £1,000 paid by Sunderland for Alf Common in 1905. It was the players themselves who spoiled the transfer market as far as they were concerned.

Their demands grew to such an extent that one player, Joe Lane, a Sunderland colleague of mine, insisted he should get a third of the fee when he was transferred to Birmingham. The fee was £3,000 and Joe enriched himself to the tune of £1,000. Soon after, the club got together and the outcome was the players had to accept an accrued share of benefit, nothing more. That amounted, at the time, to £130 for every year of service.

After my second game against the Spurs, I packed up my kit and went to live in Sunderland. I shall never forget my arrival there. It never stopped snowing for the first four days and those thick clothes were a godsend.

Then came my first home game against Middlesbrough, meeting such players as Tim Williamson, England's goalkeeper, and George Elliott, a wonderful centre-forward. The ball ran in my favour and I had all the luck in the world. We won 3–0 and as we were walking off the field, big Jimmy Gemmell, our inside-left that day and a typically clever Scot, came up to me and said: "If you keep playing like that you'll be king of Sunderland."

Perhaps I was for a day, but the fact remains that for a long while after that, I did not produce anything like that form. In fact, I got 'the bird'!

CHAPTER 3

THEY WERE TOUGH
IN THOSE DAYS

AND I LEARN A VALUABLE LESSON

During my second home game for Sunderland I got another of those valuable lessons that were offered gratuitously by the great players in those days. It was in the early stages of the game with Notts County. The left-back opposed to me was a broad-shouldered, thickset fellow called Montgomery, only about 5 ft 5 in. in height, but as tough as the most solid British oak. The first time I got the ball, I slipped it past him on the outside, darted round him on the inside and finished with a pass to my partner. It was a trick I had seen Jackie Mordue bring off. It worked wonderfully well. But as I came back down the field, Montgomery said to me in a low voice: "Don't do that again, son."

Of course I took no notice. The next time I got the ball, I pushed it past him on the outside, but that was as far as I got. He hit me with the full force of his burly frame so hard that I finished up flat on my back only a yard from the fencing surrounding the pitch.

It was a perfectly fair shoulder charge that shook every bone in my body. As I slowly crept back on to the field, Montgomery came up to me and said: "I told you not to do it again."

I never did afterwards. I learned my lesson the painful way and never tried to beat an opponent twice running with the same trick. It made me think up new ways and was a very valuable lesson.

In this County team were the famous full-back partners, Morley, 6 ft 3 in., and Montgomery, nearly a foot shorter in height but twice as broad. 'Weary Willie and Tired Tim' they were nicknamed, after the well-known characters in a comic strip running at the time. They were the first pair to introduce the notorious offside trap. Morley would run forward *before* an opponent passed the ball, leaving Montgomery to guard the road to goal. As three defenders had to be between attackers and the goal *when* the ball was played, the forwards really did not have a chance. Later, Bill McCracken, Ireland and Newcastle United full-back, brought the system almost to perfection. The more intelligent the forwards opposed to him, the more easily they fell into the trap.

Games were becoming a procession of free kicks so the F.A. had to do something about it. Some years later, in 1925, they changed the offside law to two defenders instead of three. It saved the situation. There are people who would like a return to the old offside law. If that came about, the game would be ruined. Instead of one McCracken, there would be dozens to hold up the game and rob it of all spectacular appeal.

In a later game I played against Bradford City at Valley Parade. Only the previous April, City had won the F.A. Cup. They were a grand side, but we beat them 5–1 and I have never seen a better exhibition of inside-forward play than that given by George Holley, our inside-left. He scored a magnificent hat-trick, running nearly half the length of the field each time and coolly dribbling the ball around goalkeeper Jock Ewart before placing it in the net. Several times I have stood on the field spellbound, watching Holley bewilder the opposition. After one game, manager Bob Kyle said to me, when I went to draw the weekly wage-packet: "Do you think you've earned it?"

"No," I replied, "but I think George has earned it for all of us."

There was another occasion a year afterwards when I scored five goals against Kenneth Campbell, Scottish international goalkeeper, then playing for Liverpool. Four of them I just touched into the net. Holley had beaten the defence and even drawn Campbell out of position before giving me the goals on a plate.

One of the games that first season was against Preston North End at Deepdale. Tim Coleman, our inside-left that day, put on a thick black moustache and played throughout the first half with it stuck on his upper lip. During the interval he removed it and took the field with an innocent expression. The referee at once noticed the difference and spoke to Coleman about it. He thought we had put on a substitute. Coleman was an inveterate joker and a grand footballer who had played for England.

Well, that season came to an end quickly. I kept my place in the side for the eight games but I had no great cause for satisfaction. I had played one good game, the first, and a lot of moderate ones. I scored only one goal against Notts County. Even that 'ewe lamb' was a lucky one. Arthur Bridgett, our outside-left, took a corner kick. As the ball sailed high across the goal I shouted 'Right!' to our centre-forward. He made no attempt to play the ball, nor did Albert Iremonger, the 6 ft 5 in. County goalkeeper. I just nodded it into the net. The goalkeeper was dumbfounded when the referee allowed the goal. He chased him up field but it made no difference. Iremonger, a great goalkeeper with a tremendous reach, was an eccentric character. If anything upset him he did some extraordinary things, like sitting on the ball in the middle of the field and holding up the game until the referee firmly ordered him back to goal.

During the summer months, I played quite a lot of cricket, turning out for Kent Club and Ground. I also did a lot of thinking about my First Division experiences. The big difference from the play in the Southern League was in positioning. In the First Division opponents anticipated the next move and were always close enough to tackle quickly. And when they tackled, they used all their muscular powers. I can assure you they were tough in those days.

So I made up my mind that when I went back to Sunderland I would speed up my play and try to look two moves ahead instead of one. But when the next August arrived and I resumed training, nature took a hand. I started to grow at an alarming rate. I was 5 ft 9½ in., 10 st. 5 lb in weight during the first week in August. By the end of November (at which time I was twenty) I was 6 ft 0¾ in. and still 10 st. 5 lb. I was almost too weak to stand up straight. After every spell of training (I did not do many) and after every game, I was forced to lie on a couch for hours. It was too much of an effort to go outside the house. As you can imagine, my play was nothing to shout about. Only the faith of manager Bob Kyle kept me in the team. Trainer Billy Williams nursed me, he was a grand fellow, and Bob Kyle encouraged me week after week. It wasn't much use. The crowd began to barrack me and I must admit I deserved it. I asked to be dropped from the side but the manager would not listen. Finally, after one game in mid-November when the crowd had, with every reason, been noisily expressive about my play, I stormed into the dressing room and declared in a loud voice: "I'll never kick another ball for Sunderland."

Unfortunately, the local reporter heard me. In the evening paper there were bold headlines on my statement. On Monday morning there were more reports. Although I received hundreds of letters urging me to carry on, I packed up my bag and went home to Woolwich.

On the following Saturday, Sunderland were to play Woolwich Arsenal at the Manor Field, which was only about half a mile from my home. I did not expect to play. But two days before the game, manager Kyle came to the house and, after a talk with my father, persuaded me to turn out.

"Do your best to show the locals you can do it," he said, "and if you fail, we can talk about it afterwards."

I played, scored a couple of goals in a 3–1 win for Sunderland, and felt much better afterwards. I stayed the following week at home and somehow felt a lot stronger. That was the turning point. I returned to Sunderland and began to put on weight. I quickly ran up to 12 st. 8 lb (my playing weight for the rest of my days) and struck a little form. No longer did I get 'the bird' from the crowd. They were very kind to me, as they were for the fourteen and a half years I spent with the club. Up in the north-east, the crowd takes its football very seriously. They are strongly partisan and want their team to win every time. I think they know more about the game than Southern crowds. They certainly express their opinions more freely, but they are extremely loyal, good-hearted and have a keen sense of humour. Gradually I recovered confidence and began to pull my weight in the side. I started to score goals and for an inside-forward that is an important matter.

During this testing time I owed a debt of gratitude to trainer Billy Williams that I never repaid nor ever could repay. He looked after me like a father. If I got the slightest knock he came round to my house to attend to it at once. He also nursed me during training hours, saw that I did not overtax my strength and gave me tonics when he thought them necessary. At the time it was very often. After I had been a few weeks at Sunderland he noticed that I smoked quite a number of cigarettes during the day. Cigarettes were his pet aversion. One day he handed me a new pipe, a pouch full of tobacco and a box of matches.

"I want you to promise me that you will give this a fair trial and leave cigarettes alone," he said.

Taken by surprise, I gave him my promise. I smoked nothing but a pipe from that day until just over three years ago, when I parted company with my teeth.

Trainer Williams was a strict disciplinarian. One day I arrived a minute or two after the time we were due to report for duty. There he stood at the door waiting for me to enter. Without a word he pulled his watch from his pocket, looked at it, then put it back. I felt very guilty. A few seconds later he pulled out his watch again and repeated the performance. It made me feel so small that I vowed I would never be late for training again. I kept my vow. Whilst we were in the dressing rooms during training hours or on match days, smoking was strictly forbidden. If a club director came into the room smoking he was quickly ordered out. Williams was king of his own castle. In his young days, he had been the professional champion half-mile runner. He was 'as fit as a fiddle'. Often during our road walks he would outpace most of the players.

On the subject of punctuality, I was late only once in twenty years either for a train journey or for the matches. That was because I was too early. I arrived at Sunderland Station about half an hour before train time. Having, as I thought, time on my hands, I strolled up to the post office in the High Street, less than quarter of a mile away, and sent a telegram. When I got back to the station, the train had gone without me. As we travelled on the day before the match, it did not matter. I went by a later train and joined the rest of the team at the hotel. The match, I remember, was at Liverpool. We won the points so little was said about my delinquency.

Well, it was thanks to the great skill and devotion of trainer Williams that I survived my opening period at Sunderland. I would never let him down if I could help it. He nursed me back to health and strength. And with it came a return to form. So much so that at the beginning of 1912, about eighteen months after my arrival in Sunderland, the club received a letter from the Scottish F.A. asking them if they would release me if I were selected to play for Scotland in the next international. Manager Bob Kyle showed me the letter and said: "Well, what do you have to say in reply?"

I told him: "Both my parents are Aberdonians, born and bred there. But I happened to be born in Woolwich so I'm not eligible to play for Scotland."

He wrote back to that effect and with the letter I thought my chances of international honours had gone. Birth is the only qualification to play for a country in the international tournament. And this had brought some peculiar situations. For example, I recall Jocky Simpson, the great Falkirk outside-right, being denied several caps because, although of Scottish parentage, he was born in Manchester. His parents, both of Falkirk, were in Manchester only for a few months, during which Jocky was born. They went back to Falkirk with their son soon after the event. There is an unwritten law in F.A. circles that rules out the selection of players playing for teams outside the country. That kept Simpson out of England's team. And, as he was born south of the border, he could not play for Scotland. He had to wait until he was transferred to Blackburn Rovers (I think it was in 1911) before he received deserved recognition. Simpson was undoubtedly one of the best outside-rights of his generation. I have seldom seen a winger who could centre the ball so accurately while running at full speed. Several players with teams like Cardiff City and Swansea Town, and in Scotland, were left out of England's teams because they were outside the border.

One of the best half-backs I ever met was little Billy Hardy, the bald-headed Cardiff player. Yet he never played for England. He was so quick in tackling and so speedy in recovery that you never knew when you had him beaten. He was also a grand distributor of the ball, fast and accurate. Billy is now in Australia with his family and doing quite well I am told. But he has no international cap, which he well merited, to show for his years of brilliant service.

A few weeks after Sunderland had heard from the Scottish F.A., I was asked by the Football League to produce a birth certificate, I did so and soon had the gratification, much to my surprise, of learning that I had been chosen to play for the Football League against the Scottish League at Ayresome Park, Middlesbrough. The match was due to take place on 17th February 1912. Six days before that I went to bed with influenza. I was in a pretty bad way. On the Thursday Mr Fred Taylor, Sunderland chairman, called to see me in my bedroom. He asked me how I was getting on and whether he should let the League know that I was unfit to play.

"Oh no," I assured him, "I shall be all right by Saturday. I'm determined to play – I may not get another chance."

"All right," he said, "I'll send a car round for you at midday on Saturday. That will get you there in time."

Saturday came and I was driven the thirty miles to Middlesbrough. Though I was feeling a trifle light-headed, the meeting with such great stars as my partner, Charlie Wallace, Aston Villa ouside-right; Bert Freeman, Burnley centre-forward; Jimmy Fay of Bolton, for many years secretary of the Players' Union; Bob Crompton, Blackburn full-back, and his partner Jesse Pennington, of West Bromwich Albion, was a tonic in itself. But when the game started, I was all at sea. My head was fuzzy. After a few minutes, the left half-back opposed to me, big Jimmy Galt of Glasgow Rangers, caught me with an old-fashioned shoulder charge that hit me for six. When I picked myself up, all traces of the influenza had gone. I felt as fit as a fiddle and luck ran my way. Whatever I did came off. The ball, even if I mis-kicked, went in the right direction. I played a 'blinder' and we won 2–0. As we trooped off the field at the end, Pennington joined me and patted me on the back.

"A great show Charlie," he said, "one of the best I've seen. But don't be disappointed if you aren't in the England team for the next game, your turn will come."

It was a grand gesture from a great sportsman. He was right, too.

Some of the famous stars in the Scottish League team were Alex MacNair, Celtic left-back; Mercer, Hearts right-half; Alex Bennett, Rangers outside-right, and his partner Jimmy McMenemy, then with Celtic. It was McMenemy who drove home to me the value of 'making the ball do the work'. 'Napoleon' he was called because he dictated the course of a game with his accurate, timely passes. He walked through a game whereas I had been running about all the time. I studied him carefully and willingly admit I copied some of his methods. They were too good to miss.

With all those great players in one game, and others like Charlie Thomson, Sunderland centre-half, the immortal Steve Bloomer, Joe Smith, Billy Meredith, Charlie Roberts, George Holley and a host of others at the height of their powers, I was surprised to read in an annual at the end of the season these words: 'In a day when soccer personalities, especially on the professional side, are so few and far between, the continued fine play of Stephen Bloomer proves most refreshing to the football public.' How often are words with the same meaning written today? And how often is stressed the lack of personalities and players to compare with the old giants.

Bloomer, then in his thirty-seventh year, was undoubtedly a wonder. His thrustful dashes for goal and hard shooting were unequalled. The nearest approach to him I can think of is Stanley Mortensen, the Blackpool and England inside-right.

It was generally expected that Harold Fleming, the Swindon inside-right who had scored a hat-trick in the game with Ireland, would automatically get the England inside-right position against Scotland at Hampden Park. But the F.A. selectors sprang a big surprise by choosing Frank Jefferies of Everton. I was given the honour of travelling as reserve. I shall never forget my first visit to Hampden Park. The sight of the massed pipers, the crowd of 127,307 (the record for that time) packed round the vast amphitheatre, the enthusiasm of the Scottish folk, all filled me with awe. Nor shall I ever forget the wonderful duel that went on during the game between England right-back Bob Crompton and the Scottish outside-left Jimmy Quinn, of the Celtic. Quinn really was a dashing, tearaway centre-forward, who used his powerful physique and tremendous strength to the best advantage. He had been placed at outside-left, I'm sure, to pit his strength against the equally powerful Crompton. They went at it 'hammer-and-tongs' throughout the ninety minutes. It was an example of robust shoulder charging the like of which will never be seen again. It would not be allowed today. It ended with honour even. The score, too, was 1–1 so everybody seemed satisfied. I left the ground with my ears filled with the famous 'Hampden Roar', which had gone on ceaselessly throughout the remarkable game. Crompton, who ended his career with the record number of thirty-four England caps, was undoubtedly the outstanding full-back of his time. A commanding personality, he was the best kicker of a ball I ever ran across.

A month or so before, I received something of a shock. Sunderland had reached the third round, equivalent to the fifth round today, of the F.A. Cup. We were confidently expected to get to the final and a home draw with West Bromwich Albion increased our optimism. Roker Park that day was packed to overflowing. Indeed, the crowd encroached on to the field of play and were some five or six yards inside the touchlines in places. But the game went on. We were well and truly beaten by the Albion much to our surprise. Bob Pailor, now a big business man in West Hartlepool, scored two goals for the Albion and we got one through Arthur Bridgett. I can tell you, the result was a big blow to our pride. The late Fred Everiss, who served fifty years with Albion as player, secretary-manager and director, told me a story about the game. When he arrived at the ground with the Albion team he had difficulty in getting to the players' entrance door through the vast crowd that was massed outside. He eventually got to the door but was refused permission by the commissionaire.

"But I'm manager of the Albion and here are the team," said Everiss.

"That's a good one," was the reply, "you're the third Albion team that's tried it on so far!"

Eventually they got in and proceeded to bring about our downfall. I have never appreciated so much the play of Jesse Pennington, Albion left-back, as I did that afternoon.

There was another game that season that I have cause to remember. It was against Newcastle United at St James's Park. It had rained all the morning to such an extent that the ground was waterlogged. You can guess the ball got very heavy. Midway into the first half, I ran into that ball just as it was leaving the United full-back's foot. I received the full weight of the ball in the stomach and went down like a log. Trainer Billy Williams came on and brought me round with a sponge. The first words I heard came in a loud voice from the crowd: "Kick him again, he's breathing."

It was the first time I had heard that particular remark and I did not think it funny just then. I have laughed about it many times since. Most of the trouble was that I had eaten a good lunch before the game. Any hard knock after a meal may bring serious consequences, as I found. From that day onward I had nothing except tea and toast for lunch before a game. My advice to all players is to keep away from heavy food before the match. You can make up for it afterwards. Luckily, this was one of the most serious injuries I received during my career. Hard knocks I received in plenty but they were never on dangerous spots. My knees and ankles escaped real damage. Perhaps that was because my knees were so far from the ground and my ankles were big knobbly affairs.

Well, the 1911 to 1912 season drew on to a finish. Sunderland did not have a particularly successful season, finishing eighth in the League championship, won by Blackburn Rovers. I played in thirty-one of the thirty-eight League games and scored seven goals, not a bright performance. As soon as the last game had been played I made up my mind to have a holiday in Canada. Some friends of mine had emigrated to Hamilton, Ontario, about a year before and they invited me to spend the summer with them. I accepted. The boat I sailed on was the one following the ill-fated *Titanic*, which met with such a tragic disaster.

Whilst at Hamilton, I was asked to play soccer for a local team in the semi-finals and final of a cup competition. I played with a handkerchief tied around my head to stop getting sunstroke. The temperature was more than 100 degrees Fahrenheit. The games were played on Labour Day, or some such festival day in Canada. There were about 10,000 spectators. One of them brought me another spot of bother. He, or she, took a photograph of me in the black and yellow striped jersey enjoying myself in the sunshine. Copies of the photograph were sent to Sunderland and to the F.A. When I got back home, Bob Kyle asked me into the office and said: "Is this you?"

"Of course it is," I replied.

"Then you ought to know better than to play for a club during the close season. You stand a chance of being suspended."

Frankly, I did not know there was such a rule. I played thinking I was helping the deserving cause of charity. Then I received word from the F.A. I confessed my ignorance and promised not to break the law again. They let me off with a severe caution. It amazes me to think there are people who will sit down and write letters fully knowing they are bringing trouble to some unfortunate. I can understand the many who write to newspapers expressing some view of their own or even criticising a writer but for the life of me I cannot fathom the reason for trouble making. Everyone is entitled to express his own opinion. Few of the public get a chance to do so. Some take the opportunity of writing to get something off their minds and I do not blame them. But to get somebody into hot water deliberately is another matter. It is as bad as 'poison-pen' letters.

During my stay in Canada, I got very interested in baseball. Every day I wandered to the local ground at Hamilton to watch the League and friendly games there. Next to soccer and cricket, I think baseball is the greatest game. At least the way they play it in Canada and America. The crowds with their pungent remarks and atmosphere made it to me a very remarkably exciting entertainment. Whilst standing at the entrance to the baseball park one day, waiting for a friend, a stranger came up to me and said: "You look a big, strong chap, would you like a job? I can offer you £8 per week for five and a half days' work that would suit you."

Although the wage was about twice as much as I was getting at home, the offer did not appeal to me. I turned it down.

On several occasions I was offered jobs during my three months' holiday. I could have stayed with the team I played for, International Harvester Company, as coach and player. Somehow though the call of home was stronger. In fact, the biggest thrill I got was when the ship 'crossed the bar' at Liverpool on the homeward journey. It made me realise what an 'exile' feels on his return after years away from home and country.

Soccer in Canada then was in its infancy stage. It is improving by leaps and bounds and our touring teams nowadays have to play hard to keep an unbeaten record in their games. One thing I found was that the few games I played helped ball control to an extent. The grounds in Canada were stone hard, with little grass on them. If you could control a ball in these conditions, you ought to be able to on the luscious green League pitches.

Before I sailed for home, the team in Canada presented me with a gold ring as a memento. I could not accept one of those medals they had won in the competition as the man whose place I had taken had done more for the side than I had. This was their way of expressing thanks. And the experience did me a lot of good physically. I needed very little training when I got back to English football during August of that year.

It is strange how the most memorable moments of one's life often come unexpectedly. I have heard it said that we do not plan our destiny, and the saying is frequently proved by experience. It is certainly true of my personal recollections of the golden days of the season 1912 to 1913, which turned out to be the most successful and the most thrilling of my career. It opened on a dismal note. Sunderland began with practically the same team that had done quite well the previous season, but could not win a game. Of the first seven League games played, we lost five and drew two. Sunderland were at the bottom of the First Division table. Already there were gloomy prophecies that we would go down to the Second Division for the first time in the history of the club, something that actually has never happened to this day. Then came one of those strokes of genius that happen in the lives of all great managers. Bob Kyle went into the transfer market. He bought Charlie Gladwin, 6 ft 1 in., 14 st. Blackpool right-back, and Joe Butler, Stockport County goalkeeper. Local people thought he must have gone crazy to pay something like £3,000 for the two. In those days, when the record transfer fee was £1,850, paid by Blackburn Rovers to West Ham United for inside-right Danny Shea, it was a lot of money. Worth, I should say, ten times the amount today.

It was money well spent. From the moment Gladwin and Butler joined the side, Sunderland went ahead and became the finest team I ever played for, and one of the best I have ever seen. Not only did we win the League championship with a record number of points, but we nearly brought off the elusive League and Cup double, accomplished only by Preston North End and Aston Villa. We reached the F.A. Cup final, only to be beaten by Aston Villa at the Crystal Palace before a record crowd.

Joe Butler, short and sturdy, very like Bill Shortt, the Plymouth Argyle and Welsh international goalkeeper, was reliable rather than spectacular, but it was Gladwin who revitalised the side. There are people who say that no one player can make a poor side into a great one, and that there isn't one worth a £3,000 transfer fee. Gladwin proved they are wrong. He used his tremendous physique to the fullest advantage. Before a game he would say: "When there's a corner kick against us, all clear out of the penalty area. Leave it to me."

We invariably did. But one day Charlie Thomson, our captain and centre-half with the big, black flowing moustache, forgot the instruction. The ball came across the goal and Gladwin, as usual, got it and his mighty clearance struck Thomson full in the face. He went down like a log. That was just before half-time. Thompson was brought round in time to take his place after the interval, but when he came out he joined the other side and started to play against us. He was suffering from concussion.

Gladwin was one of those full-backs who never read a newspaper or knew whom he was playing against. He was a natural player who went for the ball, and usually got it. Before a game, a colleague would say to him: "You're up against Jocky Simpson today so you're for it!"

All Gladwin would say was: "Who's Jocky Simpson?"

At the time Simpson was as well known and as famous as Stanley Matthews is today. At other times one would say to Gladwin: "You must be on your best behaviour, 'Tityrus' is reporting the game!"

Now, 'Tityrus', the mighty atom Jimmy Catton, was the outstanding sports writer of the day and editor of the *Athletic News,* known then as the 'Footballers' Bible'. Yet Gladwin's only remark was: "Who's 'Tityrus'?"

Before every game, Gladwin pushed his finger down his throat and made himself sick! It was his way of conquering his nerves. Yet on the field he was one of the most uncompromising and fearless players I have known. He stabilised the defence and gave the wing half-backs, Frank Cuggy and Harry Low, the confidence to go up-field and join in attacking movements. Sunderland became a first-class team from the moment he joined the side. He was worth his weight in gold: yes, more than the £34,500 paid for Jackie Sewell.

With Gladwin and Butler consolidating the defence, Sunderland gradually crept up the League table until we knew we had a chance of winning the championship. There was only one team we feared – Aston Villa. At the same time we made progress in the F.A. Cup. In the first round, equivalent to the third round today, we beat Clapton Orient, then a Second Division team, 6–2 at Roker Park.

In the second round, Sunderland were drawn against Manchester City at the old Hyde Road ground. So eager were the locals to see this tie that the ground was filled to overflowing more than an hour before the kick-off. We had difficulty in getting into the ground. As we passed through one of our players said jokingly to the gatekeeper: "That little fellow isn't one of the team. Don't let him go through."

He pointed to our left-back, Albert Milton, 5 ft 6½ in. of solid manhood, with thighs like tree trunks and the courage of a lion. He was a grand player and a staunch colleague. The gateman would not let Milton through the gate. So without any fuss, Albert started to climb the wooden fence, about 8 ft high, surrounding the entrance. As he clambered up, a bulldog joined in the fun and seized hold of Milton's trousers. It seemed to enjoy the joke. We all did except the unfortunate Milton.

No sooner had the game started than the crowd began to encroach on the field. Before half-time they were three or four yards inside the tough lines. We were leading 1–0. Then, early in the second half, Jackie Mordue, our outside-right, added a second goal from the penalty kick. We looked to be safely through, but the crowd edged further and further on to the field until the referee was forced to abandon the game with about twenty-five minutes to play. There was a F.A. inquiry into the matter. The committee decided that the game should be replayed at Sunderland, and fined Manchester City £350, the biggest fine that had ever been inflicted on any club. We won the second game by the same score, 2–0. Again Mordue scored from a penalty kick. And after beating Swindon (with the great Harold Fleming in their ranks) 4–2 at Roker Park, we were drawn against Newcastle United, our nearest and sternest rivals, in the fourth round.

The first game, at Roker Park, was drawn 0–0. In the replay, at Newcastle, I headed a goal a few minutes before the end. As the ball entered the net I distinctly saw a vision of Crystal Palace, where the finals were played, as clear as a picture on the top of the cross-bar. There were only seconds to play when Newcastle were awarded a free kick about thirty yards from our goal. Colin Veitch, United skipper and one of the classiest players I met, slipped the ball a couple of yards to Wilf Low, United centre-half, and Wilf took a long speculative shot. As the ball neared goal, Charlie Gladwin made a lunge at it, intending to slash it well over the halfway line. The ball skidded off his foot into our net. The scores were level so we had to play extra time. That ended without any further score. We travelled the twelve miles home very disappointed men. On arrival at Sunderland I boarded a tramcar with Gladwin. It was so full that we had to stand on the conductor's platform. There were two workmen standing beside us. One of them said to the other: "I wonder how much Gladwin got for putting the ball through his own goal."

Without hesitation Gladwin hit the speaker on the chin and he toppled off the platform. The last I saw of him was his feet waving in the air as he lay in the roadway!

As there was a difference of opinion as to where the second replay should take place, the managers decided to toss a coin, the winner to choose the ground. Watt won the toss and naturally chose the United ground, St James's Park. It made no odds. Sunderland won this time 3–0, the second half being played in a snowstorm. So we entered the semi-final. We were drawn against Burnley at Bramall Lane, Sheffield. It was a terrible day, rain falling incessantly. I don't think either side would have scored if they had played for a week. The result, of course, was 0–0.

It was a different story in the replay at St Andrew, Birmingham. I consider this to be one of the finest games in which I ever played. We won by 3–2 after being a goal down twenty-five minutes from the end. Then Jackie Mordue equalised from a penalty kick and George Holley got the winning goal. But I can still picture Tommy Boyle, Burnley centre-half, a small chap physically though a giant on the field, and centre-forward Bert Freeman, striving their hardest to save the game.

We were in the final for the first time in the history of the club. When the players got back to Sunderland the next day they were mobbed by a huge crowd outside the station. The Sunderland supporters were so exuberant that I took refuge in a nearby tobacconist's shop. It was two hours before I was able to leave.

We knew by this time that our opponents at the Crystal Palace would be Aston Villa. And in the five dreary weeks waiting for the final, Villa slowly but surely whittled down our lead in the championship race. They were hot on our heels. By a curious trick of fate, we should have met Villa in the deciding League game at Villa Park on Cup final day. It was postponed until the following Wednesday. So we had to beat Villa twice in five days to bring off the League and Cup double. Villa had to do the same to us to repeat their 1897 triumph.

A week before the final we got a shock. George Holley, our great inside-left, received a severe ankle injury, which threatened to keep him out of the game. After a test on the morning of the final, it was decided to play him. It proved to be the most sensational of all the Crystal Palace finals. It was crowded with incidents, some of which are better forgotten.

First, there was the trouble between Charlie Thomson, our centre-half, and Harry Hampton, Villa's dynamic centre-forward, the terror of goalkeepers. It was Hampton who in 1913 won an international for England at Stamford Bridge by charging Browlie, the Scottish goalkeeper, with the ball in his arms into the net. Thomson and Hampton soon got at loggerheads and rather overstepped the mark in one particular episode. Though neither was sent off the field, they each received a month's suspension for the first month of the following season. There was also an injury to Villa goalkeeper, Sam Hardy, which kept him off the field for about twenty minutes. The game was held up for seven minutes, making it the longest final, apart from extra time, in the history of the event.

Hardy I consider the finest goalkeeper I played against. By uncanny anticipation and wonderful positional sense he seemed to act like a magnet to the ball. I never saw him dive full length to make a save. He advanced a yard or two and narrowed the shooting angle that forwards usually sent the ball straight at him.

When the game was resumed, with Villa centre-half Jim Harrop in goal, we peppered away at the Villa goal. We hit the upright twice, but simply could not get the ball into the net. Then, midway in this half, with Hardy back in goal, Villa forced a corner kick on the right. Charlie Wallace took it and sent the ball waist high somewhere about the penalty line, a bad kick really. Tom Barber, Villa right-half, dashed forward and got his head to the ball. As our defenders stood apparently spellbound the ball passed slowly between them into the corner of the net. This amazing goal was enough to give Villa the Cup – and made a dream come true for Clem Stephenson, Villa inside-left, of the stocky frame and north-country accent. When we were lined up for a throw-in soon after the game started, Clem said to me: "Charlie, we're going to beat you by a goal to nothing!"

"Oh," I replied, "what makes you think that?"

"I dreamed it last night," said Clem, "also that Tom Barber's going to score the winning goal."

I could not help but think of a song at the time, which had these words: 'Dreams very often come true.'

A great schemer and tactician, Clem brought the best out of his colleagues by his accurate, well-timed passes. He was by no means fast, but made the ball do the work. He was the general who led the brilliant Huddersfield team to three successive League championships.

Our hopes of the League and Cup double were dashed. There

was, however, the League game four days later when we could make partial atonement. Then came a blow for Sunderland. George Holley was unfit to play. His place was taken by Walter Tinsley, a clever inside-left who, in later years, did great service with Middlesbrough. The game began well for us. Tinsley scored in the first ten minutes. Our defenders played so well afterwards that I thought the game was won. But Villa equalised in the second half. The result was a 1–1 draw. It meant we had to get only two more points from the three remaining games to win the championship. We went to Bolton on the Saturday and got those points by beating the Wanderers 3–1.

On the last day of the season, though Sunderland had won the title, we needed two points to break the record aggregate; we met Bradford City, Cup winners a few years before, at Roker Park. Holley scored the goal that beat City 1–0 and so we set up a new League record with fifty-four points from thirty-eight games.

It was a wonderful season in every respect. The men who bore the brunt of it were Butler, goal; Gladwin, Milton and Ness, full-backs; Cuggy, Thomson and Low, half-backs; and Mordue, Buchan, Richardson, Holley and Martin, forwards. In reserve were such talented players as George Anderson, a goalkeeper who went to Aberdeen and is now managing director of Dundee; Billy Cringan, a Scottish international centre-half after he joined Glasgow Celtic; Bobby Best, a nippy outside-right; and Tommy Hall, an all-round forward of great ability.

CHAPTER 4

I WIN MY FIRST CAP

AND TWO STRIPES IN THE
GRENADIER GUARDS

The Sunderland team of those days was one of the best I ever saw or played against. It had, too, the physique and stamina to last through the hardest of seasons. And yet with all the reserve talent at command, it failed to bring off the League and Cup double, as it should have done. It made me wonder whether any team will ever do it again. West Bromwich Albion's vain bid last season may have proved my point.

Success in the Cup brings with it postponement of League games, which pile up towards the end of the season. Then every team is out to beat the prospective champions or Cup winners. They pull out the little extra that so often wins matches. And the regular players in the team lose that little enthusiasm in their play that means so much. It is more mental, I am sure, than physical. One match during Sunderland's run for the double illustrates what I mean. Against Manchester United in mid-week at Old Trafford, we were forced to bring in four players owing to injuries. Best and Cringan were among them. They pranced out onto the field like two year olds, anxious to give of their best and establish claims for a regular place. The rest of the team trooped out sedately, conserving their energy for the game. It was won by three goals to one, but the players who had borne the brunt of the hard season showed signs of feeling the strain.

In present-day soccer the pace has increased to such an extent that I think it is almost impossible to bring off the League and Cup double. It is too great a strain on the players. Just when they are showing signs of fatigue, they have to play several League games within a week or two; it is no wonder that they break down in either one or the other of the competitions. Nor do I think that special training helps a team to this desirable goal. When at Sunderland, trainer Billy Williams used to take us away for a fortnight in November to Southport, Saltburn, Buxton, for a change of air. His idea was that players would feel the benefit, not at the time of the special training, but a few months later towards the end of the season. It did not work out that way.

There is one thing that might help towards easing the 'end of the season tension'. That is longer intervals between the various rounds of the F.A. Cup and a shorter interval between the semi-finals and final, now either five or six weeks. Better spacing would ease matters all round. I am glad to note that the F.A. are now allowing three weeks between some of the rounds, but there is still that long, nerve-racking wait before the final. It should be reduced.

Well, that 1912 to 1913 season with Sunderland brought me most of my heart's desires. I played in most of the matches and scored thirty-one League goals. I also collected eleven medals during that wonderful nine months, one of them presented by the *Athletic News* to the best team of the season. Better than that, I not only played for the Football League against the Scottish, Irish and Southern Leagues but I got the biggest thrill of all, my first international cap for England! It was against Ireland at Belfast, on 15th February 1913. With me in the side were my colleagues, partner Jackie Mordue and right half-back Frank Cuggy, the nearest thing to perpetual motion I ever saw. The 'Sunderland triangle' it was called. It was good to have teammates at your side. I was not in strange company, as so many of our young players are in their first international.

It is the unaccustomed atmosphere that, I think, accounts for so many failures on a first appearance for England. The player is keyed up to such an extent that it is almost impossible for him to produce his normal game. That is why I consider that a youngster should be given more than one game before being discarded. If he is good enough for selection, he is good enough for a second chance.

Well, the result was a tremendous surprise. Ireland beat England 2–1, her first victory over her great rivals. The much-vaunted

England team, described as the greatest ever sent across the Irish Sea, were beaten by a fighting side that was not given a hundred to one chance before the game. Frankly, I thought that the right-wing triangle had a good game. I headed the England goal in the tenth minute, a grand start, and my colleagues got through a lot of good work. But everybody did not think the same for this was the last occasion a club triangle was chosen for a representative game for a very long time. Even today, F.A. selectors seem to be chary about including three players from one team.

The game in Belfast was really sensational. For one thing, it didn't go the full ninety minutes. About three minutes before time, Ireland were awarded a free kick. The wildly excited crowd, thinking it was the final whistle, surged on to the field and carried their players off the field in triumph. Another point is that both the Irish goals were deflected into the net by England defenders. Also, for most of the time, from shortly after I had put England ahead, Ireland played a man short. Their inside-left, McAuley of Huddersfield, had left the field with an injured knee. When I got into the dressing room, despondent at the defeat, I sat next to George Elliott, the free-scoring Middlesbrough centre-forward. On the other side of him was one of the linesmen. He passed some remarks to Elliott about the right wing, Mordue and myself, that I could not help overhearing and did not like. So with the hot-headedness of youth, I told him just what I thought about him. He turned out to be a member of the F.A. Selection Committee.

Just before the game in Belfast, I had another of those arguments about expenses that seemed to be my fate. When I was called in the room to be paid, the F.A. member in charge crossed out one of the items, the last on the list. It was for a cab from Sunderland station to my home, which I had included in advance. As I would not arrive in town until six o'clock on the Sunday morning, I thought I was entitled to the ride home. But the F.A. member said: "I can't allow this to pass. You must get home by tram. They run in Sunderland I suppose?"

"Yes," I replied, "But not on Sunday mornings." Before the First World War, the Sunday tram in Sunderland started off at midday.

Eventually he paid out with a very bad grace. I remember the bill, including the international fee, return travel from Sunderland and meals, amounted to £12 19s 10d. He handed me thirteen golden sovereigns and said: "Have you the twopence change?"

It was not an auspicious opening to an international career and, I think quite rightly, I never got another chance for seven (including the war) years. My consolation came in the international League games. The first was also in Belfast, against the Irish League in October 1912. My partner on this occasion was Jocky Simpson, who, a few months before, had been transferred from Falkirk to Blackburn Rovers for the then record fee of £1,750. Behind us at right half-back was a grand old-timer, Jack Brittleton of Sheffield Wednesday. Jack, an old international, was approaching the veteran stage but worth his place in any side. Despite the fact that Simpson had been scoring freely and that the Football League had a powerful attack, the Irish League held us down to a 0–0 draw. They were a much stronger team in those days than they are now. The trek across the Irish Sea had not begun in earnest. In fact there were many players from England in the Irish League sides.

My second inter-League game that season was against the Scottish League in Glasgow on 13th March. It was not very successful because we were beaten by four goals to one. But I shall always remember it vividly owing to the many outstanding players that took part. In the Scottish forward line were Bobby Walker, Heart of Midlothian inside-right, and outside-left Alex Smith of Glasgow Rangers. Walker, of the incomparable swerve, a movement that took him past opponents without loss of pace, proved to me just what could be done with a football; he almost made it talk. Smith, although he had been playing top-class football for nearly twenty years, sent across a stream of accurate centres that simply asked to be turned into goals. He put up a wonderful performance in his last representative game. On our side at inside-left was the immaculate amateur Vivian J. Woodward. It was the first time I had figured in the same team with this great sportsman and brilliant player. Woodward, rather frailly built although of average height, could play anywhere in the three inside-forward positions. He was the perfect example of a 'two-footed' player. Rarely have I seen another forward do as much with so little apparent effort. He made the ball do the work, opening up the play and finding his colleagues with beautifully timed passes. He seemed to stroll through the game yet was seldom out of position. He did his best to make the game easy for those who were playing around him. I could not tell, really, if he were fast or not. He seemed to have no concern with speed.

The third inter-League game in which I took part within four months was against the Southern League, at Manchester, where we won 2–1. That brought to an end the most successful season of my career. To wind it up, Sunderland took the teams on a Continental tour to Budapest and Vienna.

Continental trips in those days were more or less a picnic. You never had to worry much about being beaten; it was more a question of how many goals you could win by. It was my first trip abroad with a League side. We travelled straight to Budapest, spending thirty-six hours in the train, arriving about six o'clock on Saturday evening. Our first game was against the crack Hungarian team on the next day, Sunday. Our chairman talked to us when we arrived. He said: "Now boys, you're upholding Britain's reputation. You're up against the best team on the Continent, so I want every one of you to be in bed by ten o'clock. We have got to win tomorrow."

So off we went to our bedrooms. Half an hour later there were boots outside the players' doors but not one of them was in bed. Although we had pre-arranged matters, there was a complete reunion in the most famous nightclub in the city. We were given a dressing down next morning but promised to play our best. And we did to such an extent that we won 9–0. The British prestige soared. On the morning after the game, I came down to breakfast and sat next to Bill Hopkins, a reserve centre-half, who afterwards got a regular place in the side. Eventually he became trainer to Charlton Athletic and Grimsby Town. He was one of the biggest-hearted men I knew. As I sat down Bill said: "Charlie, there isn't any post yet, when do you think it will arrive?"

Jokingly I replied: "Who do you think's going to write to you, Bill?"

He answered quietly: "I know a lot of people who would like to write to me."

"Oh," I said, "and who are they?"

"Those in the cemetery," was his devastating reply.

Hopkins was our centre-half for the first month of the following season, 1913 to 1914. Scottish international Charlie Thompson had been suspended for a month for the Cup final incident the previous April.

It was an unlucky season. In the first game at Preston, my brilliant partner, Jackie Mordue, received a serious knee injury that kept him out of the game for the best part of the campaign. In fact, I never thought he was the same player after it. Sunderland did not do at all well. We finished seventh in the First Division and were knocked out in the fourth round of the F.A. Cup by Burnley.

One incident stands out in that unlucky season. It concerns Danny Shea, Blackburn Rovers inside-right, who, during the course of the game with us, brought off a feat that I had never previously seen, nor have seen since. He headed his own centre into our net. Shea got the ball wide of our goal near the junction of the penalty area and goal line. He scooped his centre high in the air, dashed forward and headed the ball past our goalkeeper. Danny at that time was the highest-priced player in the game. He had been transferred from West Ham United to the Rovers at a fee of £1,850. The stocky, fast and hard-shooting inside-right played a big part in helping Rovers to win the First Division championship that year.

Scarcely had the next season, 1914 to 1915, started when World War One broke out. It was my unhappiest season. I wanted to join up but, when the League decided that the competition should run until the following April, I was reminded that I had a contract to carry out. There was little interest in the League programme and the Sunderland players found it hard to concentrate on the game. Every weekday we went through military training, with broomsticks instead of rifles, from an Army instructor, preparing for the day when we could do our bit. That day came at last and I went to the recruiting office in Sunderland.

"You're big enough for the Grenadier Guards," said the sergeant in charge.

"That suits me," I replied.

"Then report at Caterham Barracks on Thursday evening," were his final words.

When I got there at about nine o'clock at night, I was smoking a pipe as usual. When I went to the guardroom to report the sergeant looked me up and down and greeted me with: "We don't tame lions here, we eat them!"

I found out why afterwards. From the guardroom I went to a hut in what was called 'Tin town'. When I got there I ran into another spot of bother. Someone asked me to join in a game of cards and before I knew where I was I was on the mat for playing cards after 'lights out'. Once I had settled down, I never got into any more trouble. The recruits' training was tough, but I know now it did me all the good in the world. I was proud to belong to the Grenadier Guards.

Of course it was not long before I was playing soccer for the Guards depot. In one game I fell on my shoulder, which brought a recurrence of the old injury. I was taken to the Medical Officer, who fixed the arm in a sling. But I was not allowed to miss a parade.

One Saturday, just as we had finished the morning parade, I was told that the Chelsea officials would like to see me. So I hurriedly dressed, met David Calderhead the manager and his trainer Jack Whitley, and a few minutes later I was on my way in a car to play for Chelsea. It was a wartime League they were in, and that season Chelsea had a wonderful side. An outstanding player was the Danish international Nils Middleboe, the centre-half. He was over 6 ft tall and sparely-built. But it was wonderful what he could do with his long legs. He could use the ball accurately either with his head or feet. It was the same Middleboe who gave one referee a bit of a shock. He captained the Chelsea team and after winning the toss decided that his team, instead of taking the choice of ends, would kick off. The referee argued that he could not do this, but Middleboe persisted and finally won his point. A captain has the right either of a choice of ends or the kick-off. Nobody seemed to have noticed it before.

Another great player in that side was little Bobby Thomson, the centre-forward. He had lost one eye through an accident when a boy, but it never worried him. He was so quick thinking and fast that you could hardly believe he had not the sight of both eyes. Thomson scored forty goals that season and I bagged thirty-nine. We beat Arsenal 10–0, and other clubs by almost as big a score. We won the London League championship quite easily. Among the forwards in that team were Harry Ford, a most progressive outside-right, W.H.O. Steer, the amateur international, and Jimmy Croal, the Scottish international inside-left.

One rather trying incident happened that year. I had been told during the week that Chelsea were to play Queens Park Rangers on the Saturday, so off I went to Kensal Rise. I thought it was the Rangers' ground but when I got there I discovered they had moved to Park Royal. A hurried dash in a cab got me to Park Royal just in time. All ended well as we won 8–0. Billy Steer, who afterwards played in the League for Rangers, scored four of the goals.

In one game with Clapton Orient at Millfield Road, I scored five of Chelsea's goals. But on the Sunday I was peeling potatoes on fatigue. I was not allowed to forget I was a soldier. After some months I was given two stripes to put on my arm – acting, unpaid, Lance Corporal Buchan – and I was sent to Manchester with a drill sergeant on a recruiting mission. I'm afraid I was not a great success. I did not get a single recruit and was recalled to barracks in a fortnight.

When the season was over, it was my turn for the draft to France. I paraded with the rest of my company, 'A' Company, Third Battalion Grenadier Guards, for medical inspection. When the M.O. got to me he scanned me very closely for a minute then told me to fall out. Later I reported to the Medical Officer's room. He told me my teeth were bad. I refused to have them out and found myself back with the rest of the boys in the draft. If I had agreed it would have meant I could have stayed in England and played for Chelsea the following season. But we were so keen at the time that all we wanted was to get out to France. A short spell in the trenches quickly changed my opinion, but I stayed there, with the exception of one leave of ten days, until March 1918, when I returned to England to take up a commission.

Out in France I could never escape from football; I did not want to. Rather, I was glad of an opportunity to play. My first game was behind the Somme front, just after the big push in July 1916, at our camp in Marie-court a little north of Albert. From the playing field we could see the spire of Arras church. Legend had it that when the statue of the Virgin Mary hanging at right angles fell, the war would end. We devoutly wished it would fall right then. No sooner had we started than the German shells began to drop perilously near the field. So we packed up and restarted on another pitch. The game had to go on!

We fielded a Grenadier Guards team and I had the job of getting the side together; I had been promoted to sergeant by this time. One of our officers was the outside-left. When I went to his tent to tell him about the game, he was not there so I spoke to his batman. He was our goalkeeper, Harry Jefferies, who played for Queens Park Rangers and Bristol City. I persuaded Harry to let me have one of the officer's shirts. Mine were in such a verminous state it was impossible to wear them. Just as I got the shirt I saw, through the top of the flap of the tent, the officer approaching. Hastily I tucked the shirt up the back of my tunic. I gave the officer the message and as I was going out he said: "Oh, Sergeant, you might tuck your shirt in, it looks unsightly."

The arm of the shirt was hanging down like a tail!

Our keen rivals were the Scots Guards. In their ranks were Sammy Chedgzoy and Billy Kirsopp who, before the war, had been Everton's right-wing in many League games. It was strange that later I partnered Chedgzoy in inter-League games against the Scottish League.

Well, I got through the Somme, Cambrai and Passchendaele battles without a scratch. Then I came home and was posted to an Officer's Cadet School at Catterick Camp for three months' training. Before going to Catterick, I spent a few weeks at Ripon waiting for a vacancy at the Cadet School. Needless to say, I had time for many soccer outings. Besides games with the Camp team, I also played for two professional clubs. The first was for Huddersfield Town against Birmingham. It was the first big game I had played in England for a couple of years, and I celebrated it by scoring a hat-trick from the inside-right position. During the game, the opposing left half-back got a bit tough. He wanted to fight me. I could not help saying: "I've had as much fighting as I want. If you fancy a scrap, join the Army."

He was working, and working very hard too, in a munitions factory.

Another game was for Leeds City against Nottingham Forest. This time I played outside-right with Clem Stephenson, my old Cup final opponent, as partner. Although we got on very well together, and won the game 2–0, I did not like playing on the wing. I seemed to be out of the game too much and often found myself wandering into the centre. And, being out of training, I had not the pace for a wing forward. Stephenson found my weak spot by giving me a wonderful service of the ball, really much more than I cared for. It was at this game I met Herbert Chapman for the first time. He was the manager of Leeds City, who had a very good team. Years later I was to become his close associate with Arsenal at Highbury.

Shortly after the war, Leeds City figured in one of the biggest sensations in the history of the game. The club was wiped out of existence by the F.A. because it was alleged they had made illegal payments to players. In October 1919, Leeds officials were asked to produce documents relating to players' payments. Because some of the men were guest players from other clubs, the officials refused to do so. After holding a Commission into the affair, the F.A. announced that 'Leeds City have ceased to exist.' Their record was expunged from the League Second Division and Port Vale took their place. The City's professional players were out of a job so the League Management Committee called a private meeting of the clubs and put the players up for auction. Well do I remember the outcry about this auction sale; 'SLAVE MARKET' and 'SELLING FLESH AND BLOOD' were two headlines.

Finally most of the players secured jobs with other clubs at prices ranging from £250 to £1,250. I wonder what the prices would be if a similar thing happened today. One of the £250 bargains was Bill Kirton. In less than twelve months he had secured a Cup-winner's medal with Aston Villa. In fact, he took part in the scoring of the winning goal during extra time against Huddersfield at Stamford Bridge. His header from a corner kick was inadvertently helped into the net by Huddersfield centre-half Tom Wilson.

A few weeks after the auction there was another sensation. It was given out that the Huddersfield directors, chief amongst them Mr Hilton-Crowther, wanted to move the Town team 'lock, stock and barrel' to Leeds. Huddersfield's gates had fallen almost to nothing and the club was losing money 'hand over fist'. The League had no objection to the 'transfer' but certain Huddersfield people had. Chief amongst them was Mr A. Brook-Hirst, really a rugby player, not a soccer enthusiast at the time. He raised sufficient support in the town to enable Huddersfield to carry on at Leeds Road, not Leeds City. The next April, Huddersfield reached the final of the F.A. Cup. Sir Amos Brook-Hirst is now Recorder of Huddersfield and Chairman of the Football Association, one of the wisest legislators in the game today. Before the next season, Leeds United, as they are now, came into being. They were straightaway admitted to the League.

Well, at last I was sent on to the Cadet School at Catterick Camp. When I got there, I found that my colleagues were mainly from Australia and New Zealand. Their game, of course, was rugby. Vainly I tried to get them interested in a round ball. My arguments were useless. In the end they turned the tables on me completely. They persuaded me to turn out with them. So I tried my apprentice hand at full-back. In my first effort, the ball came rolling along the ground to me so I hit it first time from just over the halfway line. The ball soared over the cross-bar between the posts. Mightily pleased with myself I asked: "What do you get for that?"

My joy quickly turned to gloom when the reply came: "Nothing, you forgot to pick the ball up first!"

I found that 'fly-kicking' in rugby was not viewed with any great favour. Yet I found it easier to kick a rugby ball somewhere into touch than it was to hit a soccer ball accurately at goal.

When I left Cadet School, I was posted to the Sherwood Foresters at Hylton Castle, near Sunderland. But as there was no football played at Roker Park during the war, the only play I got was with the battalion team. Then back I went to France but I got only as far as Calais before the Armistice was signed. I played a couple of games for the depot team, but shortly before Christmas my name was on the list for demobilisation.

The day before I was due to depart for England, the Commanding Officer of the depot sent for me to stay for a few days because the depot was due to play a team from Egypt who claimed an unbeaten record for years.

"We want our strongest team," said the C.O., "and I promise you will go home immediately after the game."

I played, but the game was so one-sided that I lost count at nine goals. It was four days thrown away. But I must say, we had a great side at the depot, mostly Scottish professionals and budding stars. I persuaded one of them to come to Sunderland and have a trial with the club. He was Jimmy Smith, a nephew of the famous Alex Smith of Rangers and Scotland fame; I thought him a great outside-left. But he did not do too well at Roker Park. Later he established a big reputation with Aberdeen and played for Scotland. Such is the luck of the game.

When I got back to Sunderland, I took up teaching at Cowan Terrace School. And Sunderland revived their team to play in

League and friendly games until the end of the season, April 1919. At this time I nearly became a Chelsea player. I had been offered a good job in London, which would have been far more lucrative than teaching or soccer. I decided to take the job and live in London until I could get my transfer to Chelsea. A few hours before train-time Bob Kyle, Sunderland manager, called at my home. He said: "I'm sorry Charlie, we will never agree to your transfer to Chelsea. You will remain a Sunderland player."

On reflection, I made up my mind to stay in Sunderland. After all, I would not be badly off, what with teaching and soccer.

There was not a lot of football for the first six months. A Victory League consisting of Newcastle United, Sunderland, South Shields, Scotswood and other clubs was formed in the north-east corner. The maximum wage paid was thirty shillings per week. They were hard games too. We were not trained and I am sure I worked harder for those thirty shillings than I did in later years when the maximum was raised to £9 per week. You see, when I came out of the Army, I weighed nearly 15 st. But a little training and several hard matches soon reduced me to what I termed my 'playing weight' of 13 st. 4 lb.

There was also a Victory Cup instituted among the clubs. Sunderland won the competition and that brought me the most embarrassing moments of my life. Messrs Black Bros., proprietors of a Sunderland theatre, presented a set a gold cuff links to each member of the winning team and a reserve. The presentation was made at Black's Theatre and I was talked into going to the stage to receive the dozen boxes. When I got them, the audience called for a speech. As I stepped forward to say a few words, the small boxes started to slip out of my hands. I grabbed at them and the audience grinned. After that had happened three or four times, and I became more and more confused, the audience howled with laughter. Finally I got off the stage very hot under the collar. As I walked into the wings, Talbot O'Farrell, the famous Irish comedian and singer, who was waiting to go on, said: "Sonny, if I could make them laugh like that I'd die happy."

I felt more like dying myself!

In August 1919, League football got going again. No summer wages had been paid to the players but they were to be given a maximum of £10 per week during the playing season. I was in a very unusual situation. When I joined the Army, I had a contract with Sunderland for three years and a benefit at the end. I agreed, before leaving, to accept half wages for the unexpired period. With the benefit money of £5000, they were to be paid when League football resumed. War service was allowed to count towards a player's service with a club, so before the end of that season 1919 to 1920, I had qualified for a second benefit. Sunderland behaved very generously, as they always did to me. I must be the only player in the history of the game who received two benefits within twelve months.

On the question of benefits, I am firmly of the opinion that a lot of unrest among players today would be wiped out if, after three years with a club, they were permitted to sign on for another three years with a guaranteed benefit at the end of it. At present, a player can sign on for twelve months or, if transferred during a season, for the remainder of that season and the following one. The maximum benefit paid now is £750 but that is worth nothing like the £650 paid several years ago. I think it should be increased to at least £1,000.

Before the season really got going, I played in several representative games. In one of them, at Goodison Park, my partner was Fanny Walden, the marvel of his age. He was only 5 ft 2½ in. in height and weighed less than 9 st., yet he was so bewilderingly clever that I pay him the compliment of comparing him with the great Stanley Matthews. Walden could beat his man in many ways and rarely wasted a ball. His twinkling feet took him past the biggest opponent like a flash. He helped to put Tottenham Hotspur right in the top flight and played a big part in the League and F.A. Cup triumphs during the early 1920s. Walden was also a county cricketer with Northamptonshire, a grand bat and a wonderful field.

Sunderland, of course, had been hard hit financially by the war. They had to cut down on expenses in a big way and the playing staff for the 1919 to 1920 season was kept down to a minimum. One of the players who was not re-signed was Jimmy Seed, the present Charlton Athletic manager. Jimmy had been slightly gassed during the war and it was a toss-up whether he or a left half-back named Thompson should be signed. Thompson was the choice. So Jimmy went down to South Wales and played there until he was discovered by manager Peter McWilliam and signed for the Spurs. He was inside-right during their palmy [prosperous] years, and also played for England several times. Seed was eventually transferred to Sheffield Wednesday when they were right at the bottom of the First Division. He not only helped them to avoid relegation but spurred them on to win the championship in the following two seasons. He was a great tactician and schemer. It was his guiding genius as manager that piloted Charlton from the Third Division South to the First Division in two seasons, 1934 to 1936.

Another player who was not retained by Sunderland was a half-back, Billy Cringan. He had been my best friend since I joined the club. Cringan afterwards put in some great work for Glasgow Celtic at centre-half, and also played for Scotland on several occasions.

Sunderland started the season with most of the 1915 men but, unhappily, the war had taken its toll of their stamina. Great players like Charlie Thomson, Frank Cuggy, Jackie Mordue and George Holley had slowed down so considerably that often I heard the remark form the terraces: "Go home and get a bike!"

One by one they disappeared from the scene and younger players took their places. It was not long before I was one of the only pre-war players in the League side.

Manager Bob Kyle had to go out and get new players. He created something like a sensation when, in 1921 to 1922, he paid £13,000 for Micky Gilhooley, centre-half from Hull City, Jock Paterson, Leicester City centre-forward, and Warney Cresswell, South Shields right-back. New discoveries like Bert Hobson, Bob Young, Arthur Andrews, Ernie England, Bobby Marshall and Billy Ellis also made their mark. In the course of a season or so the whole side was transformed. Though Sunderland did not set the world on fire during that first year, I had a good season. I had lost a little of the old confidence but tried to compensate for this by thinking more deeply about the game and relying upon positional play rather than speed.

Victory internationals were played that year and I had the pleasure of playing for England against Wales. My partner was Patsy Hendren, the famous England and Middlesex cricketer who was then outside-left for Brentford. He was a grand two-footed player equally at home on the left or right wing. I formed the impression that if he had not been such a top-class cricketer, he would have played more times for England at soccer.

All that season I carried on with teaching and playing. I applied for a job as Physical Education Officer for Sunderland and was in a short list of three to be interviewed. I went in front of the Committee straight from a match with Chelsea at Roker Park on a Wednesday evening. One of the questions put to me was 'did I think I could manage the double task of playing for Sunderland and looking after the physical training at school?' My reply, short and pithy, did not improve my prospects. I said: "I have taught all day, played against Chelsea, scored two of the goals in a 3–2 win, and now I'm standing here before you."

I lost the job by a vote.

I did find though that teaching and playing professional football did not mix. By the time Friday came round I could hardly talk to the class. I could not concentrate on both at the same time. League soccer is a full-time job. I believe it is because so many of the present players, particularly in Scotland, have other jobs as well that the standard of play has not yet got back to the old high standard.

During my teaching days, I had lots of opportunities for practice. Each class of the school had one half-day each week free for playing games on a local field. Because some of my fellow teachers were not strong in teaching outdoor sports, I got the job three or four times each week. I enjoyed myself cavorting around with the young lads. They were tremendously interested in the Sunderland team. Some of them used to wait after school hours, expecting me to give them a description of the games. One or two of them walked the best part of the way home with me, bombarding me with questions. One of them was the 'bad lad' of the class. Often I gave him a whipping – in those days you could use a cane heartily. Yet there he was, at the end of each day, waiting for me to expound the arts of the game to him.

One day whilst I was taking the class, a gentleman with a blue ribbon in his buttonhole walked into the room. After watching and listening for a few minutes – the subject was hygiene – he asked me what textbooks I used for the subject. Thinking he was a temperance man [campaigner against the use of alcohol] I said: "Oh, I just base my talks on the training I get with Sunderland. I have no books."

Without a word he turned round and walked out. Before long the headmaster came in and asked me what I had done with the visitor. He was a Government Inspector! Luckily for me I heard nothing more about the matter. Evidently he was content with my handling of the youngsters. I was told later that he gave the school a very good report. I was glad I had done nothing to spoil it.

At the end of the 1919 to 1920 season in May, I gave up teaching and, in partnership with a former professional cricketer, Amos Lowings, opened a sports outfitters business in Blanford Street, near the southern end of Sunderland railway station. Although it meant hard and continuous work, at least I could take time off for training at Roker Park ground. I did exactly the same training as the rest of the team. Each weekday morning and afternoon I reported at Roker Park. As soon as training was over I hurried away to my business, which improved rapidly each week. Even after a home match I went into the shop. It seemed that Saturday was 'a popular shopping day' for club secretaries. I played the match over again many times with them.

During the summer of 1924, when Newcastle United were Cup-holders, I borrowed the F.A. Cup for a week. I insured it heavily and placed it on show in the shop window. The crowds that came to see it on Saturday evenings were so dense that police were called to move them on. I think it was the first time the Cup had ever been in Sunderland. It went there again for a year after the 1937 final.

CHAPTER 5

THE STRUGGLE FOR BETTER PAY

AN EXPERIMENT IN HYPNOTISM; AND THE DIRECTOR WHO WAS LOCKED IN A BATHROOM

At the end of the first post-war season, 1919 to 1920, trouble broke out concerning players' wages. I was on the Players' Union Committee at the time and we wanted the weekly wage stabilised at £10 per week maximum. The League Management Committee, the mouthpiece of the clubs, proposed a reduction to £9 per week maximum. The Union held a delegates' meeting in Manchester at which it was unanimously decided to call a strike. The delegates were instructed to go back to their teams and vote 'yes or no' on strike action and come back to another meeting on the following Monday. In the meantime, however, several teams re-signed *en bloc*. So there could be no strike. The upshot was they had to accept the League's terms of £9 per week maximum.

Worse followed at the end of the following season, 1920 to 1921, when the wages were reduced to a maximum of £8 for the thirty-seven weeks playing season and £6 for the fifteen weeks close season. All the time, the Union were pressing for abolition of wage restrictions. They called for a 'no limit' wage but the clubs would have none of it. If the players had pressed their claims in the summer of 1920, I am sure they would have got the terms. As it was, they failed to get together as a body and were overruled.

Much the same is going on today. The Union are pressing for the abolition of the maximum wage and new contracts for players. They will never get them unless they work together in closer harmony. During the summer the League made what I consider the biggest mistake in their history. They formed the

Southern Section of the Third Division, consisting of the twenty-two Southern League clubs. It brought the League clubs to a total of sixty-six and, following the ravages of the war, there were not enough first-class players to go round. It was followed the next season by a Northern Section, which brought another twenty-two clubs into the League fold. That made the playing situation even more difficult. In my opinion, it was responsible for the deterioration in the standard of League play from which it has never fully recovered. Young players with little experience of League play were drafted into the teams. They had not been through the mill of tough, local football that knocked the rough edges off their game.

In pre-war seasons, the county leagues had been the happy hunting grounds for the professional club. Scouts had only to go to the north-east, the Birmingham area or any of the thickly populated districts to discover several players almost up to the top League standards. But in the next few years, these areas were practically drained of their promising material. The standard of play dropped in the counties. There was keen competition among the big clubs to get any promising young player that came along.

The shortfall of young talent is, I think, the main reason for the colossal increase in transfer fees for players. I am sure that if club officials were certain they could get hold of up-and-coming youngsters whom they thought were nearly ready for a League side, they would cut transfer fees to a minimum. But there is not enough young talent in the country to go round the clubs. Demand exceeds supply and until that is met there will be no great improvement in the playing standard. The quickest way to bring this about is to cut down the League clubs to three divisions of twenty clubs each. The remainder could go back to the county competitions, where they would increase local interest and bring on the future stars.

The formation of the Third Division also proved a disastrous move for the players. Previously they could, if they were dissatisfied with the terms offered at the end of their contract, join a Southern League club without a transfer fee having to be paid for them. Nowadays a player is tied to a club if they wish to retain him and offer him a wage of £332 per year. Several players, like Wilf Mannion, the clever Middlesbrough inside-left, and Alex James, the Scottish international inside-left of Arsenal fame, have tried to beat the system by refusing to sign at the end of the season, but the system and the clubs have won in the end. An outside league like the old Southern League was an outlet, and a blessing, to the lesser-known second-team men. We could do with one like it today.

During the 1919 to 1920 season, which was not too successful from Sunderland's point of view, I figured in one of the most extraordinary games in which I have ever played. It was a first-round Cup-tie at Roker Park on a cold, windy January day. Cardiff City, newly elected members of the Second Division, were our opponents. Their more-or-less unknown team was not given a chance against one of the crack First Division teams on a ground on which they had never previously played. But they proved the glorious uncertainty of the Cup by beating Sunderland by 1–0. That, after being penned in their own half for eighty-five of the ninety minutes. Sunderland, playing against the strong wind in the first half, more than held their own. At half-time there was no score. The second half was one-way traffic towards the Cardiff goal. Many times, the Sunderland forwards hit the woodwork of the Cardiff goal but the ball would not go into the net. Goalkeeper Kneeshaw, Fred Keenor, Billy Hardy and Charlie Brittan, their defenders, played the game of their lives. Then midway during this half, the Cardiff forwards broke away. It must have been the first time they crossed the halfway line. The ball went to the outside-right, little George Beare. He took a shot at goal from about twenty-five yards and the ball flew into the net. After that Sunderland bombarded the Cardiff goal. Yet we could not break down that gallant City defence. So we were beaten, a result that caused much consternation then, as did Walsall's defeat of Arsenal some twelve years afterwards.

The unexpected Cardiff win was the beginning of the great Welsh era in League soccer. They put the game on the map in South Wales and outrivalled their rugby neighbours. Ninian Park became as well known as the famous Arms Park, home of many great rugby internationals. Only a few months ago I had the experience of watching a game at Ninian Park and then, on my way to the B.B.C. to give an evening talk, hear the roars of the crowd in the struggle between the Welsh international rugby side and the South Africans.

There was one interesting character in the Cardiff City team in those days, a centre-half named Smith. He fancied himself as a hypnotist. The pranks the Cardiff players played on him were the most amusing incidents I have ever heard. Before one game, a Cardiff player asked me to join in the joke. I was to allow myself to be hypnotised by Smith during the game or at least to act as if I was in a trance. I am sorry to say my acting must have been really bad because Smith simply took no notice of me throughout the game. I must say though that he was a first-class player, almost up to international standard.

It was during this season that I saw one of the most peculiar goals ever scored. It was by Barney Travers, Sunderland centre-forward, against Sheffield United at Roker Park. We were attacking the United goal when the ball went to Milton, their left-back, about twenty-five yards from goal. Just as Milton kicked it hard, Travers, a big strong bustling player, put the sole of his boot up against it. The ball rebounded at such speed that it not only beat the United goalkeeper but also went right through the net, leaving a gaping hole! This was the only time I saw a net broken by the force of a ball.

During the 1920 to 1921 season Burnley set up the record League run of thirty games without defeat. They went from 6th September to 26th March before they were beaten 3–0 by Manchester City at Hyde Road. They won the championship of course. Yet they owed nothing to physique for they were one of the smallest teams that ever performed such great deeds. It was all done by teamwork and skill. Great players like goalkeeper Jerry Dawson, Tommy Boyle, Bob Kelly and the left wing of Lindley and Mosscrop were only of average build, but there were none better. The half-back line, Halley, Boyle and Watson, compared with any of the pre-1914 combinations. Kelly was usually England's inside-right. He had a remarkable burst of speed for about ten yards and his quick acceleration often left his opponents standing. His ball control too was wonderfully good.

England's team at this period was very unsettled. Many new players were tried and some made good. But, as in the present era, they were a long time in establishing themselves. The war had taken toll of the stars. They were difficult to replace, just like they are now after the Second World War. For example, England tried several goalkeepers, among them E.H. Coleman, the amateur from Dulwich Hamlet, Mew of Manchester United and Gough of

Sheffield United. Yet none of them became an automatic selection like Sam Hardy, of Aston Villa and Liverpool.

It was early in 1921 that I came back into favour with the F.A. selectors. I played in both international trial games, not in my customary position of inside-right but at centre-forward. The second of the trials, England against the North, was played on Monday at Turf Moor, Burnley. As Sunderland were playing in Manchester on the Saturday, I decided to spend the weekend in a Burnley hotel. Bob Kyle, the Sunderland manager, made all the arrangements for me. He telephoned the hotel manager and then said to me: "Everything is fixed, Charlie. The hotel manager will make you very comfortable. He has promised to bring down an armchair from his own private suite into the lounge for your own use."

So I made myself comfortable in the chair and enjoyed the time off until the Sunday afternoon when a member of the F.A. arrived and came into the lounge. Practically his first words to me were: "You will have to get out of that chair, Buchan, when Mr Lewis arrives."

That got my back up. Although I had made up my mind to go for a stroll during the afternoon, I got a book and dug myself in the chair. Eventually Mr Lewis arrived and I heard the words: "Buchan, here's Mr Lewis."

I took no notice but continued to read my book. It was just one of those things that hit me on the raw. I thought it disparaging to professional players as a whole and would have done anything rather than give up the seat.

The North beat England 6–1 that day and it brought the downfall of an England half-back line that had given wonderful service in many stirring struggles. Andy Ducat, Joe McCall and Arthur Grinsdell, after this rout, passed from the international scene. Joe McCall, medium-sized, swarthy centre-half, was classed amongst the great. His defence was superb and he changed defence into attack with one quick pass, usually a sweeping ball to the wings. Ducat, of course, was one of the few that have represented England both at soccer and at cricket. He was the academic type of player, never flurried and always placing the ball to advantage.

It was curious that I had seen, as a schoolboy, Ducat play his first game for Woolwich Arsenal at the Manor Field. He made a great start as a centre-forward, scoring a hat-trick against

Newcastle United. Later, he became one of the finest half-backs who ever wore England's colours.

Because they scored six goals against the England defence, I thought the North forward line would be chosen *en bloc* for the next international against Wales. But the selectors left out inside-right Billy Kirton and the line was not the same without him. As I had scored three of the North's goals, I was chosen as centre-forward. The inside-forwards were Bob Kelly of Burnley and Harry Chambers of Liverpool. I was made captain of the side. In the middle of the second half, a cloudburst hit Ninian Park. The game was abandoned for a few minutes and when it was resumed the ground was waterlogged. Neither side scored a goal. I must have been to blame in some way for I was left out of the side that played Scotland at Hampden Park.

In the Welsh game I first ran up against Moses Russell, the tough little bald-headed left-back from Plymouth Argyle. All 'wire and whipcord', he revelled in the fiercest exchanges. It did not pay to hold on to the ball whilst he was about. He was a great back and a trusty colleague.

A few days before the international, I had been the Football League centre-forward against the Scottish League at Highbury. I scored the only goal of the game in which there were, in the Scottish side, such outstanding personalities as Andy Cunningham and Alan Morton, of the Rangers, and Joe Cassidy, of Celtic. Morton, I thought, was one of the finest wing forwards in the game. Though on the small side, he had a wonderful way of slipping past the opposition and placing his centres perfectly. His was a very simple, but tremendously effective style.

Tottenham Hotspur were the team of the year 1921. The previous season they had won the Second Division championship with a record number of points. Now they played their way to a high position in the First Division. Four of their players, Bert Smith and Arthur Grimsdell, wing half-backs, and Bert Bliss and Jimmy Dimmock, the left wing, were chosen to play for England against Scotland. On the day the F.A. selectors announced the team, Sunderland were playing Spurs at White Hart Lane. I had the pleasure of walking into the dressing room and congratulating them.

At the end of the season I was again chosen as England's centre-forward. The match was against Belgium at Brussels. Soon after the game started, I noticed the Belgium goalkeeper always took three or four strides with the ball before making a clearance. So I awaited my opportunity and, as soon as he was about to kick clear, I put my foot in front of the ball. It rebounded quickly from the cross-bar and bounced clear. If the ball had gone into the net I think there would have been a riot. From that moment, the crowd roared every time I got the ball. You see, you are not supposed to go anywhere near a Continental goalkeeper even if he has the ball in his possession. It is the same now on the Continent. Perhaps there is some excuse for them as the grounds are so hard over there that a goalkeeper is likely to be seriously hurt if he takes a tumble.

It brings back to mind another incident in Vienna with a Continental goalkeeper. He was an enormous chap, inches taller than I was, and weighing about 15 st. I charged him when he had the ball in his arms. He went down like a log, although the charge was shoulder to shoulder and nothing out of the ordinary. Almost at once, a stretcher-bearer party appeared and carried him off. A substitute took his place before the game restarted. I came to the conclusion afterwards that the goalkeeper was not really hurt (he wasn't actually) but that the Viennese wanted a better goalkeeper in his place. Needless to say, I was not very popular after that charge. I thought there would be trouble before the game was over. There was! Nearing the end, our right half-back tackled an Austrian, who had the ball at his feet. He too went down apparently hurt. The crowd broke onto the field and the game finished abruptly. The crowd were demonstrative but, I am glad to say, not too pugnacious.

Now, with the British Associations back in the F.I.F.A., something may be done about the law relating to charging goalkeepers on the Continent. Our F.A. have had a booklet printed in various languages illustrating the law as it stands and it has been distributed widely abroad, but I fear that our interpretation will never be favourably received outside the British Isles.

There must be a ruling that will be carried out wherever soccer is played, a compromise that will be acceptable both to us and to those abroad. I suggest that it should be along the lines of allowing the goalkeeper undisputed possession in his own six-yard goal area. But it will be a long time before that comes into force. There is another defensive point that worries me too. It is the sliding tackle that is so prevalent nowadays and which, instead of being a last means of defence, is one of the main tricks in a defender's repertoire. In my opinion this tackle, which I first saw introduced by Dicky Downs, the sturdy Barnsley miner who afterwards went to Everton, has done more than anything else (except the change in the offside law in 1925) to alter the character of the game. It is because of this tackle, which of course comes within the laws, that the game has speeded up so much and consequently lost some of its accuracy. A player cannot pass a ball correctly if he has to do it hurriedly. It also puts an end to many promising movements. A defender sliding along the ground for a few yards, sometimes from behind, puts the ball into touch or out of play and what might have been a spectacular movement is brought to a sudden end. And when a forward is in front of goal, he always has the fear that he will be tackled from behind. So he shoots hurriedly and often wide of the mark. It brings more injuries to players too. Coming unexpectedly as it must do, it jars the ankles and the knees of the unfortunate victim. Sooner or later the player is hurt. Cartilage operations, more or less unknown in the early years of the century, are now commonplace.

Soccer in the old days was tougher and one got more 'hard shaking' from charges and strong tackles but serious injuries were fewer then than they are now. Once you were free of an opponent, there was little fear he would bring you down from behind. In fact, it was something of a 'cold war' in those far-off days. Players tried to frighten you off your game but their bark was much worse than their bite. I remember one game in Lancashire. As soon as the game started, the left-back came across to me and said: "If you come any of your tricks today, I'll kick you over the grandstand."

The left half-back who was standing near, overheard the remark and added: "Yes, and I'll go round the other side and kick you back on the field again!"

Yet during the game nothing unusual happened. They played the game fairly and, although they were beaten, never carried out anything like the threats. Sometimes, though, these tactics came off.

There were exceptions, but you soon got to know them. To be warned is to be forearmed and the clever player, without changing his style to any great extent, steered clear of the danger.

But in those days one had a little time, after beating an opponent, to study the next move. As there was no danger from the rear, he could place the ball where he wanted. Movements of four or five passes were carried out successfully. You do not see them often in these hectic days because one of the players is brought down by a sliding tackle.

Half-backs like Peter McWilliam, Scotland and Newcastle United, or Charlie Roberts of Manchester United and England, would never have dreamed of using this method. They relied upon clever positioning and timely interventions.

When the 1921 to 1922 season got into its stride, Sunderland still could not find a winning team. Many changes were made in the side but we could do no better than command a humble midway position. So manager Bob Kyle had, once again, to go into the transfer market. The first player he secured was Mick Gilhooley from Hull City. He was a Scottish international centre-half. If I remember rightly, the fee was somewhere about £4,500 and it turned out an unlucky deal. Gilhooley played only a few games before he broke a leg during a match, and although he recovered all right, he was never the same player afterwards.

Then Kyle broke all transfer records by paying South Shields £5,500 for Warney Cresswell, the fair-haired, stylish right-back. Before that, the English record stood at £4,600, the fee paid by Preston North End for Tom Hamilton, the Kilmarnock right-back and Scottish international. Falkirk, the Scottish League club, had, however, just a month or so before the transfer of Cresswell, given £5,000 to West Ham United for the signature of centre-forward Syd Puddefoot.

At the end of the season, Arsenal officials proposed that transfer fees should be limited to £1,650, but the League turned it down. So Arsenal joined the ranks of the spenders and helped to boost the highest fee ever, up to the £34,500 paid to Notts County by Sheffield Wednesday for Jackie Sewell.

It was strange that Cresswell never settled down with Sunderland. He had one bad fault in that, instead of tackling a wing forward, he would retreat before him and try and make him part with the ball. This brought a lot of extra work to the half-back and forwards in front of him. When I, as captain of the team, spoke to him about it he would say: "All right Charlie, I'll do my best to tackle quickly."

But he could not break the habit. Warney did not stay long with Sunderland. He went to Everton and there developed into the finest back of the between-wars period. It was a change from the right flank to the left that worked the trick. He became the complete defender, worthy to rank with the Howard Spencers, the Bob Cromptons and the Jesse Penningtons.

Despite the new recruits Sunderland had a disappointing season. They finished in a humble midway position in the League and were knocked out in the first round of the F.A. Cup by Liverpool. The first game at Roker Park ended in a 1–1 draw and we were beaten 5–0 in the replay at Anfield Road.

There was some excuse for the hiding we got at Anfield Road. There was an influenza epidemic raging in Sunderland and half the team were down with it during the few days before the match. There were not enough players on the staff who escaped trouble to make up a really fit team. When the game kicked off, there was a strong wind blowing and snow was falling. I lost the toss and, of course, Liverpool played with the wind and snow behind them. When we got to half-time only a goal down, I thought we had a chance. But when we turned out for the second half the wind and snow had changed right around! We had to play against the elements again in the last forty-five minutes. The team almost collapsed!

On the evening before, we had stayed in a Liverpool hotel. In the early hours of the morning I heard a terrific knocking that must have awakened everybody in the place. On investigation I found that one of our directors, Colonel Joe Prior, an inveterate practical joker, had locked one of his colleagues in a bathroom. He was not popular for the rest of the stay there.

Colonel Prior, however, was one of the characters of the game, a breed now fast dying out. Well over 6 ft in height and substantially built, he always dressed in Edwardian style with high collar and cravat and pipe-stem trousers. He was often called 'The Lord Lonsdale of the North-East'. He had a big contractors business in the town, but really enjoyed his football. The story is told of him that once, as a director of the club, he went to Glasgow to sign on a player, but came back with two horses! The facts are that, after watching the player, he did not think him good enough for Sunderland so he went to a nearby market and bought two horses for his business.

About this time there was another director who had recently joined the board. He did not know the players well then though he became a great favourite with them afterwards. At one game he attended at Roker Park against Sheffield United a fellow director arrived late at the ground. On asking his new colleague for the score he was told: "Oh, we're leading by three goals to nil."

Imagine his astonishment when he learned at half-time that Sunderland were three goals down and not three in front. You see, both United and Sunderland play in red and white striped jerseys and black shorts. Sunderland played in white shirts that day and the new director had not recognised his men!

CHAPTER 6

SNIPERS IN BELFAST

A GOAL IN A THOUSAND; AND THAT
£100-A-GOAL TRANSFER TO ARSENAL

In the 1921 to 1922 season I was again in favour with the Football League Selection Committee. I was picked to play against the Irish League in Belfast. There was a lot of trouble in Northern Ireland at the time. The League players were asked before the game whether they were willing to play because there were fears of riots. All agreed. On the evening before the match, I went with English McConnell, an Irish international centre-half, who had played for Sunderland, and lived in Belfast, to the scene of the disturbances. We went by tram. As we passed the end of one street, the conductor shouted: "Down on the floor!"

Without any question we fell flat on our faces. Luckily for us, no bullets passed our way, although I was told there were usually one or two from snipers perched on the neighbouring houses. The game passed off without trouble. It was a very close affair, which we won 1–0. It seemed that the Irishmen forgot their differences for the day and attended the game at Windsor Park in full force.

When the next season, 1922 to 1923, started, Sunderland's fortunes took a turn for the better. The inclusion of newcomers like Warney Cresswell, Charlie Parker, Jock Paterson and Alex Donaldson greatly strengthened the side and we made a bold bid for the First Division championship. For a long time we ran a neck-and-neck race with Liverpool. Unfortunately, we weakened in the final month of the season as Liverpool walked away with the title for the second year in succession by a margin of six points. There was no doubt they fully deserved the honour. They were a strong, all-round side without a weakness. Players like goalkeeper Elisha Scott, Eph Longworth, Don McKinlay, Walter Wadsworth, Dick Forshaw and Harry Chambers were all international class, and grand clubmen.

Scott still holds the record number of international caps for Ireland (thirty-one in all). At present he is a manager without a team. He still holds the office of manager of Belfast Celtic, but the team disbanded about three seasons ago. There is one story I like about Scott. He was walking down a Liverpool street when he met Bill ('Dixie') Dean, Everton centre-forward, renowned for the number of goals he scored with his head. As they were passing Dean nodded. Scott dived full length!

Despite the League successes, Sunderland could make little headway in the F.A. Cup. After beating Burnley in the first round, 3–1 at Roker Park, we were beaten 2–1 by West Bromwich Albion at the Hawthorns. I scored Sunderland's only goal. Whenever I go to see the Albion now, I am always greeted with: "Do you remember that goal you scored against Albion in the Cup-tie here?"

Yes, I remember it, one of those goals that come off once in a thousand times. The ball came across from the left about twenty-five yards from the Albion goal; it was knee high. As there was no colleague handy to whom I could pass the ball, I took a first-time kick at it, hitting and hoping it would go somewhere near the goal. The ball simply flew past Hubert Pearson, the Albion goalkeeper, before he could move. It might have gone anywhere. It was the sort of spectacular affair that people remember. But whenever I ask the questioners if they recall the goal I scored in a League game the week before on the same ground, the answer is invariably: "No." And yet it was a much better goal in every way, the result of a perfect movement in which all the Sunderland forwards had a part. My simple job at the end was to push the ball past the Albion goalkeeper from very close range.

Most of the onlookers usually remember the spectacular. That is why some of the players keep their reputations long after their active days are over. One can always recall the ball artists like Bobby Templeton, Harold Fleming, George Holley and Alex James when it is difficult to bring back to mind the dependable, consistent men who rarely played a poor game. For example, there was Clem Stephenson, the great Aston Villa and Huddersfield

Town inside-left who had a big hand in the successes of those two clubs. He was the schemer in chief, the tactician on whom the team's tactics were based.

Every week, Stephenson produced his best form. Yet he never stood out like Alex James. Despite his great work, he played for England only once during his career. He should have had a houseful of caps.

Another player, and a colleague of mine with Arsenal, who deserved a place in the list of famous players and yet one rarely hears mentioned nowadays, was Bob John, Welsh international left half-back. You could depend upon Bob in every game but this dapper player was not showy. He just got on with the job. John could play anywhere on the left flank with distinction. At full-back and forward, he could perform equally well. He was Arsenal's outside-left in the 1932 F.A. Cup final with Newcastle United and scored their goal in the first half. I have also seen him give many great displays at left-back.

It was during this season, March 1923, that I was again chosen by the Football League to play against the Scottish League at St James's Park, Newcastle. It was curious that whilst the League selectors looked on me with favour during this period, the F.A. selectors passed me over. Not that I had any cause for complaint. At the time Bob Kelly, the Burnley inside-right, was right at the peak of his form. He earned his place in any representative side of that time. Then the selectors of the international and Football League teams were separate bodies, not like they are today working together to produce a team good enough to beat any other side in the world. Apart from the games with the home countries, there was not the Continental opposition to think about seriously. Matches with teams abroad were really sidelines, not the main shows they are now.

The inter-League game at Newcastle was played on a pitch that was little better than a 'mud-heap'. I thought at the time that it was the worst ground I had ever seen. But after I saw Bristol Rovers play Newcastle United in a replayed F.A. Cup-tie at Eastville some time ago I changed my opinion. 'Ankle deep in mud' was a fitting description of the Eastville ground. I am glad for the players' sake that it has been remodelled. It was just too bad to be true. Some idea of the state of the Newcastle ground may be gathered from the fact that once during the game I received the ball near the halfway line. Several times I tried to pass the muddy ball to a colleague but could propel it only a few yards, just enough to beat the opponent nearest to me. After I had made five or six efforts like this, I found myself near the Scottish League goal with the ball at my feet. I hadn't the strength left to hit it past the goalkeeper. It must have looked to the spectators like a grand solo effort. Actually, I should have been only too pleased if I could have got rid of the darned ball!

My partner on the right wing was little Jacky Carr of Middlesbrough, one of the family of four brothers who did great work for the Tees-side club. Jacky was a born humorist who could see the funny side of any ticklish situation. He was also a ball artist who could 'dribble round a three-penny piece', something like Len Shackleton, the brilliant Sunderland forward. His brothers, Bill ('Pudden') and George were dour half-backs who carried the family spirit out on the field. If you charged one of them, you had to charge the pair sooner or later. And anyone who bumped 'little Jacky' could be sure of a share of attention from his sturdier brothers. Bill, by the way, was one of the few bow-legged footballers I ran across. He had the leg build of a first-class jockey.

On the other side of me at centre-forward was Norman Bullock of Bury, now manager of Leicester City. He was the studious type of leader, not a battering ram but beating defenders by positional play. He scored the first goal. The other, in a 2–1 victory, went to Harry Chambers, the big, forceful Liverpool inside-left. How he hit that heavy ball into the net from just outside the penalty area I do not know.

Opposed to me were two great Rangers players from Glasgow, inside-left Tommy Cairns and Tommy Muirhead, left half-back. The Scottish left wing of Cairns and Alan Morton, another Ranger, was easily the best at that time. Cairns is now Arsenal's chief scout in Scotland. He expects all his discoveries to reach his own high standards. Muirhead, after being manager of Preston North End for a time, is now a sports reporter with a Glasgow newspaper.

At the end of the season, just when I had given up hopes of ever playing for England again, I was chosen as captain of the England team to play France in Paris. It was the first time professionals had been picked for a game with France and as there were in the eleven such noted amateurs as inside-left Frank Hartley, who afterwards turned pro with Tottenham Hotspur, Lieutenant K.E. Hegan, Army and Corinthians outside-left, and F.N.S. Creek, a schoolmaster centre-forward, I was naturally proud of the honour. Our full back was Warney Cresswell, right-back at Sunderland with me, and we travelled down together to London to meet the rest of the team. My partner on the right wing was Frank Osbourne, Fulham outside-right. Frank is now the general manager of Fulham. He was an ideal colleague, always in position to help you out of any difficulties.

The blend of amateurs and professionals soon settled down together and gave a delightful exhibition. After half an hour's play, Hegan scored the first goal for England. As captain I was so delighted I ran across and shook Hegan's hand. Though I never thought about it for the rest of the game, I got a severe reprimand from the F.A. member in charge of the team after it was over. It seemed that hand shaking was one of those things that 'wasn't done'. Not long afterwards, Arsenal, through Mr Herbert Chapman, brought in a 'no congratulations to the scorer' order. It did not last long. It is only natural that players should let loose some of the pent-up excitement when one of their colleagues puts the ball into the net. What I don't like to see is the congratulations business carried to excess. It does the player no good when he is mobbed by his colleagues. The backslapping and enthusiasm takes toll of his stamina. As for kissing (which has been known), well – I think that a disgusting show of emotion.

Finally, although England had to play throughout the second half in Paris without Hartley, who injured his knee, we won by four goals to one. One of the outstanding players was Warney Cresswell. The French papers were full of the blond right-back, who strolled through the game and was such a contrast to the fast excitable Frenchmen. After the match, some of the professionals came to me and asked if they were to get their expenses and match fee that evening. They wanted to go shopping and, of course, to see the sights of Paris. So I went to the member in charge and put the matter before him. It got me into another of those spots of bother that seemed to dog me throughout the playing years. He refused point-blank to pay until we got on the boat for home the next day. I tried to make him see what I thought was reason but he said: "I'm determined that they shall go back with their money in their pockets."

Although we pooled our resources, I fear that some of the players had a thin evening on the boulevards.

Cresswell and I made the journey back to Sunderland together and I met with a most amazing coincidence. We had lunch on the train going northwards and left the dining car just as the train was pulling into Doncaster Station. Casually I glanced out of the window as I was making my way along the corridor. There I saw, to my amazement, my wife standing on the station. I had to look twice to make certain as I thought she was at home in Sunderland. So I grabbed my suitcase and left the train. She had been summoned hastily to Doncaster to see her brother, who had crashed on his motorcycle and was lying seriously injured in a Doncaster hospital. Knowing the time of the train on which I was travelling she took a chance and went to the station. It was a 100 to 1 chance that came off!

It was the end of a great season for me. I scored thirty League goals for Sunderland and had also played for England and the Football League. It also included another memorable incident. I was offered a bribe to lose a game: the first and only time. When I arrived at the Roker Park ground the Monday before the League game with Newcastle United at St James's Park, there was a letter waiting for me. I opened it and read with astonishment: 'You will be paid £1,000 if you lose the game at Newcastle.' The more I pondered over the letter, the more puzzling it seemed. Why offer a bribe to lose an away game with one of the best teams in the country? It did not make sense but it worried me. Though I said nothing to the Sunderland officials, I went to the Chief Constable of Sunderland, whom I knew, and asked him to investigate. I heard nothing more before the game. As it happened, Newcastle beat us by the odd goal after a grand, close match. No sign of the £1,000 was forthcoming during the following days, but on Wednesday I heard from the Chief Constable. He said over the phone: "Charlie, I've traced the sender of that letter."

"Oh," I asked, "who was it?"

"He's an inmate of an asylum at Bristol," he replied "so don't think you need to bother your head any more."

It was the only time anything like that ever happened to me, I am glad to say, and I was thankful that the incident had such a humorous ending.

Well, the following season, 1923 to 1924, Sunderland again threatened to win the First Division championship. After a great fight we were again at the top at the beginning of April. Once again we faded out in the last month and finished third behind Huddersfield Town and Cardiff City, who shared top place, Huddersfield winning the title on goal average. It was a thrilling wind-up. Cardiff had to win at Birmingham on the last day to finish a point ahead of Huddersfield, but they only drew. The galling part, from the Cardiff point of view, was that their centre-forward, Len Davies, failed with a penalty kick awarded when a Birmingham full-back saved a certain goal with his hands. Goalkeeper Dan Tremelling saved the kick.

The Easter Holiday programme really put an end to Sunderland's hopes. Sheffield United took four points from us in the two games and we were fighting a losing battle after that. We were disappointed in the League that season, and more so in the F.A. Cup. Sunderland lost 2–1 in the first round to Oldham Athletic, then in the Second Division, at Boundary Park. The man who, more than anybody, brought about our dismissal was J.E. Blair, an amateur centre-forward, who scored both Athletic goals.

What I consider my greatest honour, even better than a Cup-winner's medal (which of course I never got), came to me at the end of that season. I was chosen to play for England against Scotland in the first international between the two countries at Wembley. It was curious how I found out I was to play. Harry Chambers had been chosen as centre-forward but withdrew, because of injury, only a few days before the game. On the Thursday, I was walking home from business when a friend stopped me in the street.

"Congratulations Charlie," he said, "and may the ball run kindly for you."

Very surprised I asked him what it was all about.

"Don't you know?" he asked. "You're England's centre-forward at Wembley. I've just heard it over the air."

True enough, the first announcement had been made by radio. I boasted only a 'cat's whisker' set in those days and more often than not, it failed to work. So even my family knew nothing about it! Still, it gave me the greatest pleasure, and so did the game.

It was a great one, each side scoring once. Our goal came from Billy Walker, one of the finest inside-forwards of the period between the two World Wars. With Walker and David Jack on either side of me, and Billy Butler and Fred Tunstall on the wings, I suppose I should have got at least one goal. But Bill Harper, Scotland's goalkeeper, who became an Arsenal colleague of mine at Highbury, saw to it that I did not. In those days, professional players had the choice of a match fee or a gold medal. I chose the medal. I am glad I did, for it was the last time I ever played for England. After all, I was thirty-two years old and could not expect more caps.

Just about this time, I seemed to be getting a lot of extra attention from opposing half-backs. Wherever I walked about the field there was an opponent on my heels. In one game, at Roker Park, Harry Wilding, the six-foot Guardsman and Chelsea half-back, gave me no peace at all, I could not 'lose' him, no matter what I did. As we walked off the field together at the end of the game, a wag from the crowd shouted: "Why don't you take him home to tea, Charlie?"

There was another game at Newcastle in which Peter Mooney, the United half-back, was my shadow. Once I stopped near the touchline to tie up a bootlace. Mooney stood over me while I did so. I asked him why and he said: "I've been told not to leave you for a second; I'm not going to."

Mooney was one of the great figures of soccer. He met with a terrible accident during the first war yet, with great will-power, fought his way back to health, a place in the Newcastle League team and Cup-winning side, and an international cap.

When the following season began, I little thought that it was to be my last with Sunderland. It was not very inspiring as we did only moderately well in the League, finishing seventh, and were knocked out in the second round of the Cup 2–1 by Everton at Goodison Park after a 0–0 draw at Rocker Park. We did manage to beat Bury 3–0 in the first round at Gigg Lane. I have every reason for remembering that game. Sunderland had played Bury on the same ground in a League game the week before, and Bury beat us 3–0. I was centre-forward, up against 'Tiny' Bradshaw, the Scottish international centre-half, who later was a member of the Scottish 'Wembley Wizards', 5–1 conquerors of England.

I was experimenting with a pair of light football boots at the time. They were very similar to those tried by the England team for the World Cup games in South America in 1950. They were just what I was looking for, until it started to rain, then they were useless and I had to change into an ordinary pair at half-time. But whatever boots I wore, Bradshaw hardly let me have a kick at the ball.

As I had promised to spend the weekend with my brother Tom, who played for Bolton Wanderers at his home in Farnworth, I did not stop for a bath after the game but put on my clothes and hurriedly rushed to the station and caught a train for Bolton, only twenty minutes or so after the game ended. The compartment was filled with Bury supporters who had seen the game. I sat in a corner reading a newspaper and listening to the conversation. Most of it was about me, and what a bad game I had played. One of them remarked: "If that fellow's supposed to be a great player then 'Tiny' Bradshaw's a wonder!"

During the whole journey I heard only one complimentary remark. One chap said: "He did one thing that showed he's a player all right. Did you see how he trapped the ball with one foot and shot with the other, all in one movement?"

It was the same the following week, after the Cup-tie I caught an early train and again listened to the remarks, buried behind a newspaper. This time they took a different trend. To sum them up in the words of one disappointed Bury fan: "The big . . . wasn't trying last week."

It's rather curious that people should think this way, for it is much harder playing in a losing side that in a winning one. I had worked twice as hard to get away from Bradshaw in the game that we deservedly lost. At last, this uneventful season came to an end and I signed on, as usual, for the following twelve months.

All the time I had kept on the business as sports outfitter. Early in May I bought out my partner, Amos Lowing, and was sole proprietor. The business was flourishing and I thought I was settled for life in the town. At thirty-four years of age I could not reckon on many more playing years, but I was content. Then came a bolt from the blue. I was transferred to Arsenal, the club I had left sixteen years before. One day in May 1925, I was serving in my Sunderland shop when the great Herbert Chapman walked in. A few weeks before he had left Huddersfield Town to take over the managership of Arsenal. His first words on seeing me were: "I have come to sign you on for Arsenal."

"Yes," I replied, thinking he was joking, "shall we go into the back room and sign the forms?"

"I'm serious," was his answer, "I want you to come with me. Ring up Bob Kyle and he'll tell you!"

Still unbelieving, I phoned the Sunderland manager.

"Yes," he said, "we have given Arsenal permission to approach you."

"Do you want me to go?" I asked him.

"We are leaving that to you," he said. "Do what you think best for yourself. It's in your hands."

Slowly I put down the receiver. I was almost stunned by what I had heard. It had never crossed my mind that Sunderland would be prepared to part with me so easily. Mr Chapman just said one word: "Well?"

And all I could say at that moment was: "Give me time to think it over. Come back tomorrow and I will let you know one way or the other."

When I went home that evening I talked the matter over with the family. The thing that hurt most was that, after more than fourteen years with Sunderland, my services were so lightly regarded. Finally I made up my mind. The next morning Mr Chapman again called at the shop. I said to him: "I am prepared to sign for Arsenal, but I shan't do so until the end of July."

"Will you give me your word you'll sign then?" he asked, and when I replied, "Yes," we talked of other things. A lot of them concerned the Arsenal team and what I thought about them.

A few weeks later, a Sunderland director, Mr George Short, called on me at the shop. "What's all this about you leaving Sunderland?" he asked. When I told him he replied: "Then I shall resign!"

He kept his word. It seemed there were sharply divided opinions about my leaving, but the strange thing is that nobody asked me to change my mind. The summer went by, and then towards the end of July, Mr Chapman again visited me in Sunderland to complete the negotiations. It was arranged that I should go to London to talk with the Arsenal chairman, Sir Henry Norris, and a director, Mr William Hall. At the same time I was to look over houses similar to the one I had in Sunderland. As soon as the housing accommodation was settled (and that was not the difficult matter it is today) I met Mr Chapman again to sign the necessary forms.

Before doing so I asked him, as a matter of personal satisfaction, what was the transfer fee. After a little persuasion he gave me an answer. It was almost as big a shock as the transfer itself. He said: "Well, it's rather a peculiar one. We pay Sunderland cash down £2,000 and then we hand over £100 to them for every goal you score during your first season with Arsenal."

That rather intrigued me so I pressed for a reason for this unusual arrangement and he explained it to me. It seems that when Sir Henry Norris and Bob Kyle were discussing the possible transfer they could not agree on the amount to be paid. Sunderland, I understand, were asking for £4,000. Sir Henry was not prepared to go to that amount for a thirty-three-year-old player. In the course of the argument Bob Kyle said: "But he'll score twenty goals for you in the first season." As a matter of fact, I had averaged more than twenty for Sunderland during the post-First World War years.

"Are you prepared to back your argument?" countered Sir Henry. And when the Sunderland manager said he would, he proposed a £2,000 fee and £100 for every goal in the first season. Bob Kyle accepted these terms.

As it turned out, Sunderland got the better of the bargain, by £100. I scored nineteen League goals and two in F.A. Cup-ties, a total of twenty-one, which brought the amount paid by Arsenal to Sunderland to £4,100. I must say that at the time I never gave the matter of the transfer arrangements much thought. I signed for Arsenal and agreed to go to Highbury for training during the first week in August. But it caused quite a stir in the soccer world.

One of the most interested people was Leslie Knighton, former Arsenal manager, who later took over Chelsea. Some time afterwards Leslie told me that I had unwittingly led up to his resigning from the Arsenal job. He had offered Sunderland a record £7,000 for my transfer, which was at the time refused. He had made the offer without consulting Arsenal's chairman, who happened to be abroad at the time. Arsenal had just previously proposed a limitation on transfer fees, which the League clubs turned down. So he was hauled over the coals and resigned.

Let me say that the strange conditions of my transfer rarely bothered me whilst on the field. I had a few inward chuckles when I thought about it occasionally, in off moments, but whilst playing I concentrated so much on the game that there was no time for extraneous things such as transfers. That, I am sure, is the case with players like Eddie Quigley, Trevor Ford and Jackie Sewell, who were transferred for record fees, and each bore the label: 'the highest priced player'. During the week, I have no doubt they have wondered if they could justify the high price paid for them, but during the actual play it would rarely enter their minds.

I must admit, though, I did think about it once. It was the occasion of my first goal, a simple tap that made Sunderland £100 richer. It was about my fifth game for Arsenal. I did not make a good start and hadn't scored a goal until we met Liverpool at Highbury. Midway in the first half, Sammy Haden, our outside-left, got through and shot for goal. As the ball crossed the goalmouth I followed up. It looked as if it would go into the net, but then I saw Elisha Scott, Liverpool's goalkeeper with the record number of Irish caps, making a desperate effort to get at the ball. So I just tapped it with the side of my foot over the goal line to make sure. Just as easy as that!

It relieved my mind considerably. As I was travelling by tube to the game I sat next to two Arsenal supporters who were discussing the prospects and I heard one of them say: "Hundred pounds a goal! Why, that big fellow couldn't score if you gave him the Bank of England!"

CHAPTER 7

I AM CALLED A SAND DANCER

AND LEARN HOW TACTICAL MOVES ARE PLANNED

Let me say here that I made nothing out of my transfer from Sunderland to Arsenal. In fact I lost rather a lot of money through changing quarters like that. For only a few months after I joined Arsenal, the general strike broke out. Business fell away badly. With everything practically at a standstill, the workers had plenty of time to play games, but, although they needed equipment very urgently, they had no means of paying. I supplied many centres in the north-east without much hope of getting the money. Of course, I got my accrued share of benefit from the Sunderland club. They made no bones about it. If I remember rightly it was a little more than £500. But that was more than swallowed up by the losses in business. Although I kept the business going for several years after that, it never recovered from the strike. When I sold up eventually, I found I was much poorer for the experience.

Whilst with Arsenal during the early years, I used to drive up there every week by motorcar, up one day and down the next. The distance from London to Sunderland was 275 miles. It cured me of wanting to own and drive a car permanently. I have not had one for twenty years!

When I moved my home to London towards the end of July 1925, one of the first people I met was the late Jimmy Catton, former sports editor of the *Athletic News*, the greatest sporting paper of all. He was working free-lance in London. He called at my home for an interview and I was pleased so give it to him. It was an uncomfortable business though, because he arrived just as our furniture was being carried from a removal van into the house in Mayfield Gardens, Hendon. We sat on two packing cases in the bare room and talked.

Jimmy was a little tubby fellow, not 5 ft in height. He was, however, the greatest writer of his day, knowledgeable, benevolent and respected by all the soccer authorities. The first time I met him was just before my first international in Belfast. Though I knew him, he did not mince words about my play in general. After one game he called me a 'sand dancer'. I was inclined to take exception, remember I was very young at the time, but a Sunderland colleague, Tommy Tait, a very kindly fellow and a Scottish international, said to me: "Don't take any notice Charlie, and always remember this, whilst they write something about you, it doesn't matter what it is, you are somebody in the game. It's when they ignore you altogether you should begin to worry."

It was sound advice that every player should take to heart. Criticism can be helpful at times.

Shortly after the interview with Jimmy Catton I signed a contract to write a weekly article for a Sunday newspaper. From before the first war I had contributed weekly to Newcastle and Sunderland papers, so it was no new experience.

Then early in August, I reported for training at Highbury. Everything seemed different from conditions at Sunderland, and I took some time to settle down. Fortunately, I had nearly a month to get accustomed to the new surroundings. I always feel sorry for a player transferred to a new club during a season. Too much is expected from one who has just undergone a complete change. It is no wonder so many fail to produce their best form for several weeks. Within a few days of my arrival at Highbury, Mr Chapman called a meeting of the players. I was appointed captain. Although I did not want the job, I thought I would be of greater service as one of the 'rank and file', they insisted I should be in charge on the field.

One of the first things we did was to create a spirit of friendship among the whole staff. All were to be pals, working for the good of the club. We discussed matters from all sides, ironing out any 'bones of contention'. We soon became one hundred per cent Arsenal players. That, I think, is the secret of the team's unrivalled success over the years. The club comes first. Teamwork is not allowed to suffer from petty squabbling. Weekly meetings were instituted. On the eve of every match, big or small, the players, manager and trainer talked it over. We had no blackboards or plans of the field. It was a straightforward discussion with every player airing his point of view. We talked over moves for every basic part of the game, such as throws-in, corner kicks, free kicks and the strong and weak points of our own team as well as the opposition. We soon knew what every player was expected to do. It was an accepted principle that we never discussed any move that the opposition could interfere with. We concentrated on our own side; covering, backing up, calling for the ball and any point that we could work out for ourselves. Every player was made to talk. Some took a lot of persuading, but eventually all joined in, even the most self-conscious and the 'silent ones'.

One example will illustrate what I mean. Our goalkeeper, Dan Lewis, was not a talker. He preferred actions to words and gave many brilliant performances. At one meeting Dan said: "When we have a throw-in near to the corner flag, why doesn't the wing-half throw the ball to me?"

It had never been done before, at least as a planned affair. So another 'Arsenal move' was born.

It was during the summer of 1925 that the change in the offside law was made. It was the biggest upheaval in the game for many years and, in my opinion, altered it completely. It was necessary though. There were so many full-backs copying the example of Bill McCracken, Newcastle and Irish international full-back, known as the 'offside king', that the game was fast developing into a procession of free kicks for offside.

The change from three defenders to two between an attacker and the goal brought about a revision of tactics from the old spectacular passing movements and brilliant individualism to the thrilling 'three-kick' raids on goal and teamwork; from 'frills' to 'thrills'. Many people will say it was a change for the worse. But after all, it is what the public wants nowadays. They 'pay the piper' so they should 'call the tune'. The change certainly brought the end of the old style. New methods were required and Arsenal were the first to exploit them. They were at the beginning of their greatness in the 1930s.

It has many times been said that the change in law brought into operation the 'stopper' centre-half, but there were many such 'stoppers' long before that eventful day. We had at Sunderland Scottish international centre-half Charlie Thomson, a big, powerful fellow with a big, black, flowing moustache. He was a 'stopper' in every sense of the word. Then, Billy Wedlock (the 'India-rubber' man of Bristol City, only 5 ft 6½ in. in height) controlled the centre of the field. His wonderful powers of recovery enabled him to adopt a venturesome policy. The others like Joe McCall of Preston North End and Charlie Roberts, Manchester United, although complete players, excelled in defence of their goal. The only difference in the old-time centre-half and the modern is that the 'old-timer' was not just content to clear his lines. He placed the ball on every possible occasion, sometimes moving up field. He was always there though when danger threatened his goal.

When Arsenal held their meeting before the first League game of the season with Tottenham Hotspur at Highbury, I proposed that Jack Butler, our centre-half who really deserved, but did not get, an international cap, should take over a defensive role. I was overruled. We opened the programme with the old methods. We did not make a good start. Spurs beat us 1–0. I ran up against Arthur Grimsdell, one of the best all-round half-backs I ever met, in his finest form. He did not let me have many kicks at the ball. I did my best, but it was not good enough. Arthur was the master. At every meeting we held afterwards, I brought forward my proposal of a defensive centre-half, but without much support. We continued to play fairly well as a team, though we couldn't hit the winning track. Then one week-end, at the beginning of October, we had to play Newcastle United at St James's Park on the Saturday, and West Ham United at Upton Park two days later. These games turned Arsenal's fortunes.

At St James's Park we met Newcastle in their most brilliant mood. Hughie Gallacher, the wizard little Scottish international centre-forward; outside-left Stan Seymour, now chairman of the club; and inside-left Tom McDonald, made holes in our defensive plan. They outclassed us to the tune of seven goals to nil. After the game I said to Mr Chapman: "I would like to go back to Sunderland. I'm not of much use to Arsenal and I still have my business there."

I really thought about going back to the place where I had spent so many happy years. Mr Chapman replied: "Oh no, you're playing against West Ham on Monday. I know what you want and we'll have a special meeting to discuss it."

The meeting was held in the Newcastle hotel before we took the train back to London. Mr Chapman called upon me to outline the scheme I had in mind. I said I not only wanted a defensive centre-half but also a roving inside-forward, like a fly-half in rugby, to act as link between attack and defence. He was to take up such positions in midfield that any defender would be able to give him the ball without the chance of an opponent intercepting it. Of course, I had in mind that I would be the forward proposed for this job.

First we thrashed out the position of the centre-half. He was not to be a 'policeman' to the opposing centre-forward. He was given a beat of a certain area bordering the penalty line, which he was to guard. The other defenders were to arrange themselves around him according to the direction of play. It was the beginning of Arsenal's 'defence in depth' policy, brought to almost perfection by later teams. Then the roving forward was discussed. I got a surprise when I was told emphatically that I was not the man. Mr Chapman said: "We want you up in the attack scoring goals. You have the height and the stamina."

We talked about other players until Mr Chapman said: "Well, it's your plan Charlie, have you any suggestions to make?"

Then it occurred to me that I had seen, in practice games and playing for the second team, an inside-forward who was likely to fill the role. He was Andy Neil, a Scot who was getting on in years but who could 'kill' a ball instantly and pass accurately. So I said: "Yes, I suggest Andy Neil as the right man. He has a football brain and two good feet."

Finally, after a lot of argument, it was decided that Neil should be the first schemer-in-chief. And I must say he made a very good job of it for nearly the rest of that season. Thus the Arsenal plan was brought into existence. It has been copied by most clubs but many of them fail to carry it out successfully because the centre-half does not function properly. He should not be only a 'stopper'. He must be the dominating personality around his own goal. And he should not be content just to get the ball away anywhere but to send it, with head or feet, to the roving inside-forward.

Arsenal's 'smash and grab' raids, which often brought goals, were called 'lucky'. They were, however, carefully planned. A clearance from centre-half Herbert Roberts to roving forward Alex James, a long pass to either wing forward Joe Hulme or Cliff

Bastin, and Arsenal had scored with three or four kicks at the ball. Finally, to end the meeting, it was decided we should bring the plan into action against West Ham United the next day. It worked splendidly. We beat the United 4–0 and from that game Arsenal never looked back. They became a force in both the League and the F.A. Cup. The three busy 'Bs' (a half-back line consisting of Alf Baker, Jack Butler and Billy Blyth) were the backbone of the side. They compared with any of the old-time middle lines, like Duckworth, Roberts and Bell of Manchester United, or Veitch, Low and McWilliam of Newcastle.

Well, the novelty of Arsenal's new methods took the other League clubs by surprise. We began to win games with such regularity that by the turn of the year we were on top of the First Division and, it seemed, heading for the first championship success. Success followed in the F.A. Cup too. We beat Wolverhampton Wanderers in the third round 1–0 at Highbury, after a 1–1 draw at Molineux. The Wolves goal there was scored by centre-forward Tom Phillipson, who, some years later, became Mayor of Wolverhampton.

Then in the fourth round we defeated Blackburn Rovers at Highbury, 3–1, but before the next round came serious injuries that I consider lost us our chance of honours. Sammy Halden, outside-left, broke a leg during a League game; Sid Hoar, outside-right, had to undergo a cartilage operation; and Jack Rutherford, who had returned to the game, was taken ill.

With the wing forwards out of action, Mr Chapman was in great difficulty. He got out of it by persuading Dr James Paterson, Scottish international outside-left who had retired some two years before and had not kicked a ball since, to return. And included at outside-right, Bert Lawson, a youngster from Luton who had played only a few games in the reserve side.

We did well to draw 1–1 with Aston Villa in the fifth round of the Cup. We did better still to beat them 2–0 at Highbury in the replay. 'Doc' Paterson scored one of the greatest goals I have seen, a twenty-five yard, left-foot shot taken on the run, in the very first minute – greatly to my relief! You see I was nearly late for the kick-off. I left home with what I thought plenty of time to get to the ground in comfort, but the underground trains were so packed that, about twenty minutes before the starting time, I was jammed in the huge crowd in the passageway at Highbury (now Arsenal) station. Luckily, a policeman noticed me, helped me over the iron railing dividing the ingoing from the outgoing passengers, and enabled me to get to the dressing room with ten minutes to spare. Doc Paterson's goal was the tonic I needed to make me forget the incident. I was glad when we got through successfully.

We were not so lucky in the next round. We lost at Swansea, to the Town who the previous season had won promotion from the Third Division South to the Second Division. Although we had many chances that 'went a-begging', Swansea beat us deservedly 2–1. Our only goal was extraordinary. Right-back Alex Mackie, an Irish international, from his own half of the field kicked the ball high into the Swansea goalmouth. Big Jock Dennon, Town goalkeeper, took his eye off it and it went, second bounce, into the net. But Jock more than atoned with several great saves towards the end. And soon after the Cup defeat, our League chances went. We lacked scoring power on the wings.

My first season with Arsenal had its strange features besides the £100-a-goal business. There was the Christmas holiday time when we had to play Notts County twice. After the first game at Highbury I was taken ill on the journey to Nottingham. A doctor diagnosed tonsillitis and influenza. The annoying part of it was I had made arrangements to spend a few days, and the Boxing Day match, at Sunderland. Instead I spent four days in bed in a Nottingham hotel. On the Thursday, I struggled up to Sunderland with a great big turkey and a huge pineapple that were to have been part of the New Year celebrations. But on the following Friday I was recalled to London to play the following day against Tottenham Hotspur. It was a nightmare of a match. I did not know which way I was going. All I can remember is that, on one occasion, I did manage to get through the Spurs defenders but had not the strength to kick the ball past big Jack Nicholls, the Spurs goalkeeper.

Then there was another game early in February against Leeds United at Elland Road. During the week before the game, I had trouble with my foot. It seemed to be slightly poisoned. When I arrived at the station I could hardly put my foot to the ground, so Herbert Chapman sent for the club doctor to examine it. He lanced the foot in the railway carriage and I turned out the next day, but with a training shoe instead of a football boot on my right foot! I was told to play inside-left to save the damaged foot as much as possible. Jack Lambert, the big, stouthearted centre-forward, took my place at inside-right. I could not have been much of a success at inside-left, as I was never asked to play there again. During the following week I spent a lot of time nursing the foot, until one day I was advised to try an old-fashioned remedy called 'Dale's Plaster'. It worked so well that I was able to play the next Saturday.

At this time manager Herbert Chapman signed on Joe Hulme, the Blackburn Rovers flyer, at outside-right. He was not twenty-one, but as fast as anything I have seen on the field. From the start he showed sign of developing into a grand winger. He joined us before our match at Leeds. Before the game started I said to him: "Joe, if I call for the ball, give it to me straight at my feet." He agreed.

It was just the move I had carried out ever since my Leyton association with Jimmie Durrant; it had served me well for many years. Joe, however, did not understand straight away. The first time I called for the ball, he went haring up the field as fast as he could go. When I asked him why he had not given me the ball he said: "There was a player right on top of you. It would have been no use."

That was the whole point of the move. A player had been drawn out of position and if I had the ball at my feet, I could part with it to advantage. If I was clear of the opposition there was no point in having the ball. It took Joe some time to get used to Arsenal ways. Once he settled down though he soon became one of the outstanding outside-rights in the country. Within fifteen months of joining Arsenal, he received his first international cap. Hulme and I got on very well from the start. He was a humorist and kept us all amused with his wisecracks. When I retired, however, Joe had to adapt himself to quite a number of partners.

One day after a match that I had reported, I met Joe and had a talk. Almost his first words were: "Did you notice that partner of mine? When I give him the ball at his feet he never gives it back, the move is wasted."

"Give the lad a chance, Joe," I replied. "Remember, it took you about three months to work things properly. He'll come round to it in time."

Joe's partner was Ray Bowden, formerly with Plymouth Argyle, a great player with the ball. He dovetailed so well with Hulme later on that they formed England's right wing together. It is curious that, although Hulme was one of the fastest wing forwards in the game, he was not the fastest player on Arsenal's books whilst I was there. That distinction went to goalkeeper Dan Lewis. Many times we had sprint races on the Highbury track. Invariably the first man past the post was the Welsh international goalkeeper. I might add that I was never in the first three. Jack Lambert, the centre-forward, was usually within inches of the winner.

Big Jack, a Yorkshireman from Doncaster, was one of the most loyal servants Arsenal ever had. For several seasons he played in the reserve side without complaint. When he did eventually get a place in the first team, his robust dashing methods did not please everybody. Particularly Mr Chapman. Several times he went into the transfer market and bought centre-forwards, but after short stays in the senior side they were shelved and Lambert restored.

The first was Dave Halliday, the big Scot from Sunderland, then Tim Coleman from Grimsby Town and Jimmy Dunne from Sheffield. Between them they cost Arsenal something like £21,000 in transfer fees. Big money in those days. But it was the big-hearted Lambert who led Arsenal's attack in most of their triumphs. His forceful methods kept the opposing defenders on tenterhooks and allowed inside-forwards like David Jack and Alex James to play their normal games. Lambert was the effective foil for those two great inside men.

There was another Arsenal player that I must mention. A full-back named Ralph Robinson, who hailed from the north-east. He was with the club for seven seasons yet never once played in the Football League. Many times he was reserve and captained the second string for years without a grouse of any kind. He was the ideal club man, a pattern that could be followed with advantage by many modern players who, if they are dropped from the first team, immediately rush to the manager's office and ask to be put on the transfer list. After all, a club cannot play all its men in the senior ranks. A week or two in the reserves should make a player, more than ever, determined to win back his place in the senior team.

Not long after he had got Hulme, Chapman signed on, within a few months, Bill Harper, a Scottish international goalkeeper from Hibernian, and Tom Parker, the strong, fearless Southampton right-back. It was the beginning of Chapman's efforts to put Arsenal on top of the world. They were so successful that a few years later Arsenal became the most successful team of all time. When Harper arrived from Scotland he lived in a London hotel for a few days and then got a house near my home. One night, I received a telephone message from the Golders Green Police asking 'would I identify a stranger in the neighbourhood who had been detained by the police at midnight because he was carrying a big bundle of household goods?' He had told them he was Harper, the Arsenal goalkeeper. Once I had told them he was indeed Harper, he was allowed to go about his business. But I know this great goalkeeper, a blacksmith by trade, never forgot the incident. He was, of course, quite legitimately moving blankets from one place to another.

Parker figured in one F.A. Cup semi-final that has gone down in history. Whilst with Southampton and playing against Sheffield United, he first of all put through his own goal and then had the bad luck to miss a penalty kick. His team were beaten by an odd goal. He had sweet satisfaction though when in 1930 he captained Arsenal the day they won the Cup for the first time.

Soon after Hulme's arrival, we went to the top of the First Division. There were visions of the championship flag flying over Highbury for the first time. (The season 1925 to 1926 had been Arsenal's previous best, as runners-up to Huddersfield.) Our hopes rose when, about the middle of April, we beat Huddersfield Town, who were our chief rivals, 3–1. But those hopes finally crashed on my old ground Roker Park. Sunderland beat us 2–1 after a curious game. A few minutes had passed when Dan Lewis, our goalkeeper that day, and Dave Halliday, Sunderland centre-forward, got 'at loggerheads' and were sent off the field. I made the mistake of putting Joe Hulme in goal. He soon let a long centre from the wing curl over him into the net.

It was my first visit to the old ground, which I consider one of the best playing pitches in the country. It was one I shall never forget. On leading Arsenal onto the field I got a wonderful reception. It was like going home again. But at the end I was soundly booed off the field. There were only a few minutes to play when a ball came across the Sunderland goal. I went for it at the same time as Charlie Parker, their centre-half, gave him what I thought a fair shoulder charge, got the ball and just missed the goal with my shot. Parker fell rather awkwardly and was slightly hurt. He played on, but the crowd, as they do on occasions like this, expressed their disapproval strongly. I went off to the 'boos' and 'catcalls' of some of the onlookers. And yet I had done nothing that I had not done on many occasions when playing for Sunderland. I know I charged awkwardly, having to bend a little to make shoulder contact properly, though never unfairly, and the crowd usually laughed at my efforts.

Well, we lost the game and with it went our championship chance. Huddersfield Town won it with a margin of, I think, five points to spare. Arsenal were runners-up. It was the highest position ever occupied by the London club. Their total points (fifty-two) was the highest ever recorded by a southern team. It was a great triumph for Herbert Chapman. Arsenal, his new club, finished second. Huddersfield, the team he managed previously, won the championship for the third time running, a performance never before accomplished by any club, though it had been equalled since by Arsenal. Huddersfield were given a special Commemoration Shield to mark the occasion. They were a great side, with stars like Roy Goodall, Sam Wadsworth, Tom Wilson, Clem Stephenson and Billy Smith producing match-winning form whenever it was required.

There was another unusual experience during that first season. I had father and son as partners on the right wing! First there was Jack Rutherford, who returned to the game for a while and gave some grand displays at outside-right. Jack had lost most of his hair by this time but little of his skill. He was one of the best at centring the ball quickly from any angle. Then in one game against Bury I had his son, also named Jack, as partner. He was a most promising youth and could have made as big a name in the professional ranks as his father, but he preferred to remain an amateur.

We won the game 6–1. After it I was accused in some quarters of 'starving' young Jack out of the game. Of course, I had no intention of keeping the ball away from him, but as our left-wing was in grand form it was only natural that play should be concentrated on their side. The result justified our tactics. Some years later I recall there was an outcry that the wonderful Stanley Matthews was wilfully kept out of the game with Wales at Wembley. True, Stanley saw little of the ball. England, however, scored eight times mainly through pressing their attacks down the centre where the Welsh defence was weakest. That is the answer to such criticism.

Stanley did his job just by being there and keeping the Welsh defenders guessing. They dared not leave him unattended and that gave the other forwards their big chance.

Although I had left Sunderland for good, I followed their fortunes with keen interest. I was extremely glad they finished in third place that year, four points behind Arsenal. They owed a lot to the sharp shooting of Dave Halliday, a tall centre-forward secured from Dundee during the previous summer. Dave scored thirty-eight goals, a record for the club. It would have been a pleasure to play with him. He was such a grand chap. His short, shuffling stride got him over the ground very quickly and his trusty left foot surprised many goalkeepers. Halliday played for Arsenal for a short period, but he was not too successful in London. Now he is the manager of Aberdeen, the club that gave him his first opportunity.

On looking back over my first season with Arsenal, I have always been surprised that I got through so well. It was something different from what I was accustomed to. In Sunderland we trained twice a day. I had also my business to attend to. In London, however, Arsenal trained only once each day after the opening month of turning up and getting into trim had passed. I had plenty of time on my hands. So I joined the Hendon golf club and put in a lot of time each day on the course. I soon became quite useful at the game.

There is no doubt I was bitten, and bitten badly, by the golf bug. At every opportunity I was knocking the little white ball about. I had a willing confederate in Billy Blyth, our left half-back, and a good scratch player. Round after round we played. And when it was dark we would have the motor-car lights in the adjacent park turned on to the last green so that we could practise pitching and putting. Very soon I got down to a 4 handicap. One day Blyth said to me: "I have entered for the Middlesex Amateur Championship but my partner has scratched. Will you enter and take his place?"

After a lot of persuasion I agreed. There were two qualifying rounds of stroke play, the leading eight to play a knock-out tournament for the championship. By some stroke of luck, off a 4 handicap, I qualified for the final. Blyth, the scratch player, did not. And I went on to win my first big tournament.

In the semi-final at Crew's Hill, I met the former champion. There was a crowd of about three hundred people. On driving off the first tee, the head of my driver flew off and when I reached the tenth hole I was three down. The tenth green was near the clubhouse and the crowd melted away. Somehow or other, though, I struggled along and won on the last green, more by luck than judgement. The final was played at Hendon on my home course. A few days before it took place the Middlesex County secretary rang me up and asked me if I intended to play. My opponent had got into some trouble at his club and was prepared to stand down. I replied: "Yes, I'll play. I don't want to win the championship without playing off the final."

It turned out a foggy day and what with my knowledge of the course and the fact that my opponent was right off his game, I won comfortably. But I will be the first to admit that I was never a champion golfer. I had no pretensions to style, being quite satisfied to hit the ball in the most comfortable way. I think that to be a champion you must start the game when you are young.

All the time I was golfing I had the feeling I ought to have been at Highbury doing more work with football. Although a lot of the Sunderland training ideas had been instituted there, I never felt as fit as when I was beside the seaside at Roker. I am convinced that London teams need more training than those in towns situated along the coast. The players, I believe, should be kept fully occupied for the whole of the day. To a newcomer London can be a very lonely place; he should have something to occupy his time and his mind.

When the 1925 to 1926 season had ended I thought I would be able to go back to my business in Sunderland for the summer months. Mr Chapman had other ideas. He arranged for a Continental trip in which Arsenal were to play matches in Budapest, Vienna, Prague and Innsbruck. When I asked to be excused he said: "Sorry, Charlie, I have guaranteed to take a full League side. They especially asked for you."

Perhaps I did not need a lot of persuading. At any rate, I went along with the rest of the team. We started off with the journey to Paris, where we spent a night. Mr Chapman nearly spent that night in a Paris jail. There was some misunderstanding over a meal we had at a café and it ended with Mr Chapman being escorted by a gendarme to the nearby police station. He was allowed to depart after explanations.

From Paris we went to Budapest, a thirty-six hour train journey. We arrived there on Saturday night and the first game against the crack local team was on the following day. We played very well in the first half. At half-time we were leading by two goals to nil, then, when the teams were lined up for the second half I noticed a stranger opposite us at centre-forward. Jimmy Hogan, the man who has done more for Continental football than any other 'Britisher', was coach to the Hungarian team. He was standing beside the touchline, so I walked across and spoke to him.

"You have a new centre-forward Jimmy," I said.

"Oh, yes," he replied, "it's a common practice on the Continent to bring on new players at half-time."

"Are there any more besides the centre-forward?" I asked.

"Yes, there are five altogether. I want them to get some experience against a really good team."

What with the effects of the long journey and the introduction of fresh blood into the home team, we were not the same side afterwards. We managed to draw 2–2.

The question of substitutes in matches abroad has been the cause of a lot of controversy. It has also been responsible for quite a lot of the beating our teams have suffered out there. Surely it is time something definite was settled in the way of allowing substitutes in matches. We have our way of looking at the question and the Continentals, another. Some agreement has to be reached in internationals under the jurisdiction of the F.I.F.A. Now a substitute is allowed for an injured goalkeeper at any period during the match and for one injured player up to the forty-second minute. That, I think, is the best solution. Many games have been spoiled because a goalkeeper has had to leave the field in the early stages. It is, in my opinion, unfair to the onlookers that they should have their enjoyment marred because a man is hurt. Unlimited substitutes would, I know, lead to a lot of abuse. But in the case of a goalkeeper, a team naturally chooses its best man for the job and would not gain by changing him during the course of the game. As for the men in the field, I agree that a change could do a lot of good to the team, especially in the case of a defender who might be having a bad time against such a skilful opponent as Tom Finney or Nat Lofthouse. But there must be something introduced into the laws of the game about substitutes. As long as the law is the same all over the world I do not mind. As it is now, we do not know exactly where we are.

When the trip, a very enjoyable one, was over, I went back to my business in Sunderland. It was the year of the general strike. I spent a lot of my time arranging cricket matches between teams of footballers and the local sides in the mining districts. There were many good cricketer-footballers in Sunderland and I got together a useful team. Our visits usually attracted big attendances. There was no charge for admission, but a plate was taken round for the benefit of the local club.

I also played for East Boldon in the Durham Senior League. One Saturday we played Durham City. We got them out for a small score, something like one hundred if I remember rightly. After a cup of tea I lit my pipe, awaiting my turn to bat. As I was in first wicket down, I had not long to wait. I put my pipe down on the seat and went in to face Bill Sadler, a fast bowler who had played for Surrey. When I came out I picked up my pipe, sucked at it, and to my amazement found it still alight. I had been in and out before it had time to cool down!

The summer soon passed and I reported back at Highbury. There I discovered Arsenal had a new trainer, Tom Whittaker, the present Highbury boss. His playing days had been cut short by a knee injury received when touring with the F.A. party in Australia. He had spent the previous season as assistant to George Hardy, undergoing courses at a London hospital for massage, treatment for injury and radiotherapy and getting himself thoroughly equipped for the job.

Hardy went to Spurs as trainer and Whittaker took command of the Highbury dressing rooms. He soon had everyone working with him for the benefit of the side. Tom may not have been the greatest half-back in the world when he was a player, but I know of no man who can get more out of players either in the dressing room or on the field of play.

CHAPTER 8

THE SECRET OF HERBERT CHAPMAN'S GREATNESS

I PLAY IN A CUP FINAL AND MAKE A NERVE-RACKING BROADCAST

The 1926 to 1927 season did not promise to be the most exciting in the history of the Arsenal club. Yet it ended with our first appearance in the F.A. Cup final. From the start, we ran up against injuries and bad luck. We occupied a humble midway position in the League, averaging a point a match, with no distinguishing features except that the Arsenal plan was being licked into shape. Though we had no really outstanding stars, the teamwork was first class.

Just about Christmas time, both our left-wing forwards, Sammy Halden, happily recovered from a fractured leg, and Harold Peel, secured from Bradford, were on the injured list. Their deputies were also out of action. Herbert Chapman sent for me, the captain. After a little talk he said: "Have you any suggestions about the left-wing? I don't know what to do about it."

I replied: "I think we have a ready-made wing in the side in Billy Blyth and Sid Hoar."

Sturdy, humorous Blyth, a wholehearted player who never spared himself, had made a reputation as an inside-left with Manchester City before he joined Arsenal and developed into a top-class wing-half, whilst Hoar, fast and accurate with his centres, had frequently appeared at outside-left when with Luton. Mr Chapman listened to my suggestion and played them on the left wing in the next game. That, I think, was one of the secrets of his greatness. He would always listen to other people and take advantage of their ideas if he thought they would improve the team in any way.

The move came off. The team became settled and although it made no progress in the League, exceeded all expectations in the F.A. Cup-ties. Newcastle United won the championship that season. With clever, mercurial Hugh Gallacher, the Scottish international, at centre-forward; Stan Seymour, outside-left; Charlie Spencer, centre-half and Frank Hudspeth left-back, they were a great side. Second to Newcastle were Huddersfield Town. They came very near to winning the title for the fourth year running. Only the brilliance of Newcastle stopped them.

Early in January came our first Cup-tie, against Sheffield United in the third round at Bramall Lane. I had the satisfaction of scoring the third goal, as it proved to be the winner, in a 3–2 victory. The chief thing I recall about that game is the wonderful exhibition given by our goalkeeper, Dan Lewis, the Welsh international. In the closing minutes and with darkness falling rapidly, he brought off amazing saves. United forwards were inspired by one of the greatest left wings in the game, Billy Gillespie and Fred Tunstall. They ran us stiff, but Lewis came to our rescue.

It was in a match at Sunderland in which I played in 1914 that Gillespie suffered a compound fracture of the leg. It was thought he would never play again, yet here, some thirteen years later, he was the brains of the United side and captain of Ireland. There have not been many better inside-lefts.

Our opponents in the fourth round were Port Vale, then a prominent Second Division club, at Hanley. I shall not forget their dressing rooms in a hurry. They were converted stables in one corner of the ground! Nor shall I easily forget the big fight they gave us. They were leading 2–1 until about two minutes from the end when Jimmy Brain equalised and forced a replay. Brain was one of the fastest men off the mark I ever played with. For ten yards or so he was like a hare. He used his speed to the best advantage. Whenever an inside-forward had the ball, Brain would take the centre-half a few yards out of position and, when the pass came through a few yards to one side, would beat his opponent to the ball by the sheer quickness of his action. He did not make the mistake, as so many do, of slipping into an unmarked position. He left the space for his colleague to place the ball. Then he pounced on it. Brain regularly got about thirty goals each season I was with Arsenal.

My direct opponent in the Port Vale Cup-tie was James Oakes, a short, sturdy and bald-pated left-back. I could make little of him, so perfect was his positional play. Afterwards he did great work for Charlton Athletic in their promotion years.

In the replay at Highbury I had great satisfaction in scoring the only goal of the game, although I must confess it was a lucky effort. The ground was bone dry with frost, and play rather scrappy. Midway into the second half I got away from Oakes for once in a while. As I went through, Howard Matthews (Port Vale goalkeeper, who played several times for England) advanced to narrow the angle. As I got near him I shot. The ball passed through his legs and into the net. We went into the fifth round. This time we had a home draw against Liverpool, the team that a few years previously had won the League championship two seasons running. We won 2–0.

Another home game followed in the sixth round, with Wolverhampton Wanderers. They were beaten 2–1 and Arsenal were in the semi-final for the first time since 1907. The winning goal against Wolves was one of the most extraordinary I have seen. We were pressing their goal in the second half and our centre-half, Jack Butler, came up and joined the attack. The ball came across about fifteen yards from the goal. Running full tilt, Butler got his head to the ball and it simply flew past the Wolves' goalkeeper like a cannon-ball.

So we were in the semi-final with Southampton, Cardiff City and Reading. It was the first time since professionalism was legalised in 1885 that southern clubs had monopolised the semi-finals. Arsenal met Southampton at Stamford Bridge. It was a game featured by the brilliant work of my partner, outside-right Joe Hulme, the flyer. Though opposed to Mike Keeping, a big, strapping left-back, and one of the best in the land, Hulme gave a wonderful exhibition. He got the first goal and I got the second. It was on the strength of this performance that Joe won the first of his many caps for England. Hulme was a great favourite at Highbury. We often heard the chant from the crowd: "Give it to Joe!"

But I also heard it elsewhere: first at Bolton Wanderers' ground at Burnden Park. Whenever Ted Vizard, Wanderers' Welsh international outside-left, had the ball and neared the opposing goal, up went the cry: "Give it to Joe!"

Meaning inside-left Joe Smith. Smith was one of the hardest shots I ever met. He scored many wonderful goals with his trusty left foot, holding the scoring record for several years, with a total of thirty-eight in one season.

Although only a Second Division team, Southampton gave us a shaking in the Stamford Bridge semi-final. When we got a two-goal lead, I thought the game safe, but near the end Bill Rawlings netted for Southampton, and in the closing minutes they practically hemmed us in our own goal. One of the defenders who helped to keep them out was Tom Parker, Arsenal right-back, a former Southampton player. Bill Rawlings, by the way, was one of the few players capped for England when playing for a Third Division club. It was in 1922, the year Southampton won promotion from the Third Division South.

Well, Arsenal were in the final for the first time. Now followed the long wait for the great day at Wembley. Our opponents were to be Cardiff City, the only club that has taken the Cup out of England. Manager Chapman asked if we would like to go away to the seaside for special training, but we preferred to carry out the usual routine at Highbury. The weeks dragged by wearily. Wherever we went we could not get away from the excitement, nor the rush for tickets. Each player could have disposed of hundreds. All we were given were two each. No fear of a black market!

It has always been a wonder to me why the time between the semi-finals and final has not been cut down. It is a nerve-racking period and one of the reasons why the Wembley final so rarely produces a classic game. Despite the Easter holiday period, which usually intervenes, and the congestion of League fixtures, surely it could be so arranged that the period between the last two stages of the Cup be limited to three weeks.

Anyway, the great day had to arrive, and when it did the team reported at Hendon Hall, about four miles from Wembley, for a light lunch and a charabanc ride to the ground. We left the Hall nearly two hours before the kick-off for a journey that normally takes about a quarter of an hour, but we were nearly late for the start. Traffic on the way was so congested that with only three-quarters of an hour left we were a long way from the Stadium. Manager Chapman left the charabanc and sought police aid.

The F.A. Cup Final of 1913: Charlie Thomson leads the Sunderland team out at Crystal Palace. Butler is behind him, followed by Buchan.

Successful Trial: In an international trial match at Burnley in March 1921 England were beaten 6–1 by the North. Standing: Hillman (Burnley, trainer), Bamber (Liverpool), Cresswell (South Shields), Mew and Silcock (Manchester United), Wilson (Sheffield Wednesday), Bromilow (Liverpool). Seated: Chedgzoy (Everton), Kirton (Aston Villa), Buchan (Sunderland), Chambers (Liverpool) and Urwin (Middlesbrough).

Stripes – and Stripes: In the 1914 to 1915 season, Buchan, in common with the other Sunderland players, found it hard to concentrate on football. As soon as the season ended he joined the Grenadier Guards.

Picked for England: Buchan's part in the North's victory led to his being chosen for England against Wales at Cardiff. Standing: Wilson (Sheffield Wednesday), Bamber (Liverpool), Cresswell (South Shields), E.G.H. Coleman (Dulwich Hamlet), Silcock (Manchester United), Bromilow (Liverpool). Seated: Chedgzoy (Everton), Kelly (Burley), Buchan (Sunderland), Chambert (Liverpool) and Quantrill (Derby County).

Sunderland F.C. 1922 to 1923: The Sunderland team in the season in which they were runners-up to Liverpool in the League Championship. Standing: Ferguson, Cresswell, England, Robson, Hawes, Poole. Seated: R.H. Kyle (secretary), Donaldson, Buchan, Parker (captain), Paterson, Ellis and W. Williams (trainer).

Inter-League Match: Charles Buchan, playing for the Football League against the Scottish League at Highbury in 1923, leaps to avoid a tackle.

That £100-a-Goal Tag: In addition to the transfer fee, Arsenal undertook to pay Sunderland £100 for every goal Buchan scored for them in his first season. He netted nineteen in the League and two in the Cup, so it cost them £2,100! His first match at Highbury was against Spurs and he is seen nicely placing a header.

Fours and 'Fore!'
Above: Whilst on Wearside, Buchan played good enough cricket for East Boldon to be selected for Durham County.
Below: Later he became a keen golfer and in this picture is watching Lord Charles Hope drive off in the 1929 Amateur Golf Championship at Sandwich.

Greeted by the King: His Majesty King George V greets Charles Buchan. The other Arsenal players, from left to right, are Lewis, Brain and Kennedy.

Before the Kick-off: Buchan's second and last final was at Wembley in 1927, when he captained Arsenal against Cardiff City. He is shaking hands with Fred Keenor before the kick-off. The referee is I.W.F. Bunnell of Preston.

All Smiles: England captain Billy Wright (white shirt) and Hungarian captain Ferenc Puskas exchange bouquets of roses before the start of the return match between the two countries at the People's Stadium, Budapest on 23rd May 1954.

Buchan Shows the Youngsters: These boys knew how lucky they were to have an old England star to coach them. This was in 1930 when the F.A. organised instructional classes at Highbury.

Eventually, with a police escort, we arrived in the Stadium dressing room with half an hour to strip. It was enough. We stepped onto the lovely green turf in time to be presented to His Majesty King George V. It is a great honour, which every player appreciates, but it adds to the strain on the players' nerves. They need a few minutes to recover.

It must be admitted that the game that followed was not a great one. Neither side produced its best form. Cardiff won by a gift goal, one of the freaks that featured in the early Wednesday finals. Most of the honours went to the defenders. On the Cardiff City side, Jim Nelson, Fred Keenor and Billy Hardy, the best left half-back who never got a cap, put up the game of their lives. For Arsenal, Tom Parker, Alex Kennedy, Alf Baker, Jack Butler and Bob John were right on top form. I was right off. It looked as if neither side was going to score. Then seventeen minutes before the end, Dan Lewis, Arsenal goalkeeper, made the tragic slip that sent the Cup to Wales.

Hugh Ferguson, Cardiff centre-forward, received the ball about twenty yards from the goal. He shot a low ball that went at no great pace straight towards the goalkeeper. Lewis went down on one knee for safety. He gathered the ball in his arms but as he rose his knee hit the ball and sent it out of his grasp. In trying to retrieve it Lewis only knocked it further towards the goal. The ball, with Len Davies following up, trickled slowly but inexorably over the goal line with hardly enough strength to reach the net. It was a bitter setback.

Even after that Arsenal had a chance of pulling the game out of the fire. Outside-left Sid Hoar sent across a long, high centre. Tom Farquharson, Cardiff goalkeeper, rushed out to meet the danger. The ball dropped just beside the penalty spot and bounced high above his outstretched fingers. Jimmy Brain and I rushed forward together to head the ball into the empty goal. At the last moment Jimmy left it to me. I unfortunately left it to him! Between us we missed the golden opportunity of the game. Arsenal had no more chances after that. Cardiff's valiant defenders held all our desperate efforts, and Fred Keenor's boys brought off the best performance of their careers. There were stories that Dan Lewis, in his misery after the game, threw away his Cup medal. I can vouch they were not true. Dan, although silent and depressed, took the blow like the real sportsman he is. If we had won, I do not think Lewis would have exulted too much. He was never a great talker at the best of times.

After the game, Arsenal's players went silently away. Before I left I went into the Cardiff dressing room to toast their success. Of course, I was bitterly disappointed. It was the second time I had been at the losers' end in a Cup final, the first with Sunderland at the Crystal Palace in 1913, and now at Wembley! I realised too, that my chances of getting a winner's medal were pretty slim. I was thirty-five and a half years old and could not expect to go on much longer.

On the eve of the final, I had my first experience of broadcasting. It turned out a rather trying one too. It was at 2LO at Savoy Hill. The two captains, Fred Keenor and I, were to give a quarter of an hour's talk on the teams' prospects. At the last moment Keenor had to cry off so the announcer and I had to cover the full time. Somehow I got through, but it was worse than any football match. Though I have often been on the air since, I shall never forget that first talk at Savoy Hill. That was the climax to an eventful season. Arsenal had done something they had never done before and were beginning to be recognised as a power in the land. Their new methods were making the other teams take notice. Arsenal were no longer the Cinderellas of the First Division. They were setting a fashion that later on changed the whole complexion of the game.

At the opening of the next season, I did not anticipate it would be my last in League football. I thought I could go on for another two or three years, but luck took a hand. During the previous summer I had contracted with the *Daily News* [the *News Chronicle* at the date of writing] to write a series of articles, a hint-a-day to improve the youngsters' game. Before the season ended, I was asked to join the staff of the paper. As I was turned thirty-six I accepted. It was too good an opportunity to miss. I retired from football when my contract with Arsenal expired on 3rd May.

The season proved the most exciting and dramatic of the nineteen I had played with Leyton, Sunderland and Arsenal, not so much from my own point of view, but from the many tremendous events that happened. First, there was the extraordinary League position. Though Arsenal played no conspicuous part in either championships or relegation problems (they finished tenth with an average of a point per game) the First Division competition was without parallel. Everton won the championship by two points from Huddersfield Town, who had a great chance of capturing the elusive League and F.A. Cup double. They fell, however, 'between the two stools'. Two Cup semi-final replays with Sheffield United sapped their stamina to such an extent that they lost three of their last four games, *and* the championship. And they were beaten by Blackburn Rovers in the F.A. Cup final at Wembley.

There was a relegation situation without equal. No fewer than nine clubs were involved, and the two points covered them on the last day of the season. Sunderland, who have never played in any division but the First, had the narrowest of escapes. They had to win at Middlesbrough on the last day to avoid going down. They won 3–0. Tottenham Hotspur finished the season early with thirty-eight points. Thinking they were safe, they went on a Continental trip. Events turned so rapidly that they found themselves relegated, with Middlesbrough. It is a generally accepted principle that a club with thirty-four points is safe from relegation. This was the exception that proved the rule. Middlesbrough got thirty-seven points, Tottenham Hotspur thirty-eight, and both went down.

Then there was the display given by Scotland's international team at Wembley in April 1928. They trounced England by five goals to one. Their brilliance earned them the name of 'The Wembley Wizards'. Although I did not see the game, I was busy with Arsenal, those who did see it are positive that this was the best exhibition of forward play ever given by any international side. The Scots' forwards were small, but on a rain-soaked turf proved irresistible. The line was Jackson (Huddersfield), Dunn (Everton), Gallacher (Chelsea), James (Arsenal) and Morton (Rangers). Only Jackson of the five stood more than 5 ft 6 in. tall. People talk about that game to this day. I wish I could have seen it.

Though Arsenal had a very thin time in the League, they put up a great show in the Cup. We got to the semi-final, only to be beaten by Blackburn Rovers, the winners, at Leicester. It was in this season that the tag 'lucky Arsenal' was first applied. We were drawn at home in all four ties.

In the third round we beat West Bromwich Albion 2–0.

In the fourth we overcame Everton 4–3 after one of the greatest games it was my pleasure to play in. Despite heavy rain, which fell throughout the tie, it was a thriller from beginning to end. One of the greatest players that day was Everton full-back Warney Cresswell, who had been my colleague at Sunderland.

Then in the fifth round, Arsenal met their almost regular Cup opponents, Aston Villa. Villa were beaten 4–1 despite the great displays of Billy Walker and Frank Moss, the father of present Villa players Frank and Amos. Every time I watch Villa and see one of the Moss boys I am reminded of their father, a great-hearted player who served his club so well for many seasons.

The sixth round saw the defeat of a third Midland club, Stoke City, by four goals to one. Arsenal were in the semi-final for the second year running. I thought I had yet another chance, my last, of getting that winner's medal.

We were drawn against Blackburn Rovers on the City ground at Leicester and were made favourites. We should have won for we commanded a large share of the play. But we could not break down a Rovers defence in which the 14 st. right-back, burly Jock Hutton, centre-half Rankin, and international left-half 'Aussie' Campbell were right on top of their form. Midway in the second half, a tragic mistake led to a Rovers victory. Our left-back Horace Cope, an expert in offside tactics, moved forward to put the Blackburn forwards out of play. He mistimed the move and Blackburn centre-forward Jock Roscamp, a fast full-back, who had been converted into a dashing type of attacker, was given a clear field. He received the ball just over the halfway line with nobody between him and our goal. Maintaining perfect control, he ran on and steered the ball into the net.

Rovers were ahead, but we still pressed them hard and missed chances. Once, from a Joe Hulme corner kick, I headed the ball straight (as I thought) past Campbell, their goalkeeper. But centre-forward Jimmy Brain went for the ball. I tried to shout but the words stuck in my throat. Jimmy side-footed it straight into the arms of Campbell. So, try as we would, we failed to get an equalising goal. Rovers went on to beat the favourites Huddersfield Town in the final at Wembley, by three goals to one. It was Roscamp who set them on the road to victory. In the first minute, he charged goalkeeper Mercer and the ball rolled over the goal line for the first goal. It was the Rovers' sixth F.A. Cup success, equalled only by Aston Villa. Strange that neither of the two teams have won the Cup from that day until the writing of this in 1954 at least.

During the season, Arsenal 'discovered' two of the finest players who ever put on the red and white sleeved jersey. The first was left-back Eddie Hapgood. He was signed from Kettering, and whenever I came up against him in trial games, usually held at Highbury each Tuesday morning, I was impressed by his wonderful positional sense. I mentioned the matter to Herbert Chapman at one of our weekly meetings. He told me that Hapgood would have been in the first team had it not been for one serious flaw. Every time he headed the ball in one particular place, he fell to the ground unconscious! Usually, he took no further part in the game. So Arsenal could not take the risk of playing him in the First Division games. Hapgood was convinced that the fault was physical, due to a weak frame. He was sent to a farmhouse to build up his strength. Finally the weakness was cured and Eddie became one of the greatest left-backs of the 20th century. He played for England, including wartime games, no fewer than forty-three times. The F.A. presented him with a £100 testimonial and an illuminated address.

The second player was Herbie Roberts, who afterwards became the prince of 'stopper' centre-halves around whom the Arsenal 'defence in depth' plan was perfected. At the time, Roberts was a right-half, a clever ball player who practised for hours on end with a tennis ball. It was not until he took the place of Jack Butler and was given a definite job to do (to close the centre of the field) that he became the greatest centre-half of his generation. Whenever the Arsenal goal was in danger, the auburn-haired Roberts was there to guard the way. I think Herbie deserved many more than the one international cap he got. But our F.A. selectors frowned on the 'stopper' in those far-off days when attacking centre-halves like George Wilson of Sheffield Wednesday and, a little later, Jack Barker of Derby County, set the pattern.

It was shortly after Arsenal's F.A. Cup semi-final defeat at Leicester in March 1928 that I received the offer to join the *Daily News* staff. So I went to Herbert Chapman and told him I would not re-sign for the club. I was retiring from the game. He was rather upset at the news. He said: "You know Charlie, it will cost the club £10,000 to replace you."

"I'm sorry," I replied, "but I have had such a good offer I can't possibly turn it down. It may never come again."

After some discussion he accepted the situation and started to make plans to find my successor. Several young players were tried without satisfactory results. In the meantime, I was left out, quite rightly, from the League side.

Some months later, it was brought home to me what Chapman meant when he said I would cost the club £10,000. In October of that year, 1928, he signed David Jack, England and Bolton Wanderers' inside-right, at a transfer fee of £10,340, the first five-figure fee in the history of the game.

So the season dragged on to its end. The only game I took part in, until that very last day, was a friendly at Kettering. It was part of the Eddie Hapgood transfer bargain. It was strange playing on the sloping ground of the Southern League club. I'm afraid I did not produce anything like form although I was pleased to be in touch with the ball again. It is a long break like this which can upset a player's concentration. It takes weeks before he gets back to full confidence and his normal game. In recent years Wilf Mannion, the Middlesbrough and England forward, found this out when he was absent for several months. Neil Franklin, Stoke and England centre-half, never recovered his top form after his period in Bogota and the subsequent suspension.

On the last day I was brought back into the Arsenal team. It was to be my last game, against Everton, who had won the League championship. It was a farewell performance for me. It was more than that for 'Dixie' Dean. The Everton centre-forward needed to score three goals to break the record of fifty-nine goals in a season set up by George Camsell, the Middlesbrough centre-forward only the year before. Before the game, the Arsenal players presented me with a briefcase and a writing-set of fountain pen and pencil. It moved me more than anything else during my career. There are many who believe that Arsenal sat back and allowed Dean to get the three goals that broke the record. I can assure them that nothing is further from the truth. For myself, I wanted to go out on a winning note, just as I came in back in 1910. The Arsenal players wanted to help me in this by beating the champions.

It was a memorable day, one I shall remember as long as I live. The game was worthy of the occasion and ended in a 3–3 draw. And it was Dean who scored the three Everton goals. When he got the third, the Goodison Park crowd rose to him. It was a scene beyond description. Dean, tall, dark haired and magnificently built, was then at the height of his powers. His headwork was beautiful, so well timed that it seemed effortless. He headed two goals that day, one from well outside the goal area with just a nod of the head. Everton planned their game around Dean. A long, high ball up the middle to Dean's head, a clever deflection to the feet of an inside-forward and Everton's attack was in full cry for goal.

This day rivalled as a memory that of the Wembley Cup final the year before when the Arsenal team, before the game with Cardiff City, were presented to His Majesty King George V. I recall he said something to me about £100 a goal, but I was in such a state of nerves that I cannot remember the exact words.

When I got back from the game at Goodison Park, I took stock of my last season. I had played in thirty League games (scoring sixteen goals) and in all the Cup-ties. I made my mind up that I would never play another game. With soccer being in my blood I was afraid that if I ever did, I would want to make a 'come-back'. It was the hardest decision I have ever made but, in the face of tempting offers, I have kept to it. I have kicked a ball occasionally, though never once have I stripped for a game, much as I wanted to.

A few weeks after the season I received a cheque from Arsenal for £432; it was my accrued share of benefits for the three years I served with the club. There was no obligation on Arsenal's part to pay it. Like benefits and bonus money, clubs *may* pay these extras if they feel so inclined. It was a generous gesture on the part of Arsenal and Herbert Chapman. Though he must have been extremely disappointed at my retirement, Chapman was a sportsman. Later I was called to pay, I think it was £162, income tax on this gift from Arsenal. It *was* a gift for which I did not expect to pay anything, but the income-tax officials thought otherwise. I have never yet fathomed the reason why professional footballers have to pay tax on benefits or accrued share of benefits whilst a professional cricketer, whose reward soars into thousands of pounds compared with the footballers' hundreds, is exempt.

Before leaving the 1927 to 1928 season, there was another point that stands out. An amateur club tried to get into the Football League. Argonauts, who included many amateur internationals in the ranks and had powerful backing, sent an application for membership. It was turned down at the League's Annual General Meeting in June. The only thing against them was that if they were admitted, a professional club would have to drop out.

What I should like to see is some amateur club like Pegasus take over the mantle of the old Corinthians and join the League. I am sure they would be welcomed by all clubs, just as Queens Park are favourites in the Scottish League. Many people will recall the grand fights put up by the Corinthians in the F.A. Cup-ties in the early 1920s. Their games with Millwall provided tremendous thrills to big crowds and their gallant effort against Newcastle United at the Crystal Palace was a topic of interest for years. Recent Cup exploits of amateur clubs like Walthamstow Avenue, Finchley and Leytonstone suggest that the present amateur players are up to the Corinthian standard.

A representative amateur side would prove a big draw too, at grounds all over the country. People would love to see a tilt between the unpaid and the paid professors as they did in the days when the Dewar Shield was in existence and Corinthians trounced Bury, a First Division team, by something like ten goals to three. Amateur players would benefit from the experience with the professionals. And when the Olympic Games come along, there would be a team capable of holding its own with any other country in the world.

Within four weeks of finishing playing, I began work at the *Daily News* office. I was kept busy going to cricket matches and golf tournaments. I was very glad as it kept my mind away from football. As I had been writing weekly articles for many years, the job was not exactly new. Which reminds me that at one time the F.A. threatened to stop all players from writing in newspapers. It was after an article by Jack Cock, Chelsea centre-forward, in which he had criticised the foul play of opponents. It caused quite a stir, and the F.A. stepped in and banned all players' articles. When it was pointed out that some players, like Arthur Grimsdell and myself, had signed contracts for the season to write for papers, they compromised. Players could write, but they must not criticise players or officials in games in which they had taken part.

It was soon evident that my writing did not please quite a lot of the *Daily News* readers. Every day I received scores of letters telling me what they thought about my efforts. When those letters filled a large-sized drawer in my desk I began to get worried about them, so I spoke to the sports editor and asked him what I should do. His reply shook me. He said: "Why didn't you tell me about them before? It's proof that a lot of people are reading your stuff anyway!"

One of those letters was amusing. It covered four sheets of very intelligent comments on a cricket match that I had described. After reading through two and a half pages, I came across this sentence: "You know Charlie, you ought to be in here with me. My address is Clifton Mental Hospital!"

At last came the real test, the football season. It took weeks before I could get out of the old habits. It was a 'tea and toast lunch' before each game. I always arrived at the ground about an hour too soon; and I made straight for the players' entrance.

Gradually I got used to the change. Instead of 'playing' each game from the press box, I began to enjoy the skill of both sides. The number of goals I scored from my seat was phenomenal. Chances look so easy from a position high up in the stand. They are not so simple on the actual field. It is my firm conviction that every press box should be as near the play as possible. Then the reporters would see the things that are going on and would realise how difficult the game really is. Instead, at places like Hampden Park, Wembley Stadium, St James's Park, Newcastle, and Bramall Lane, Sheffield, reporters are perched high up in the roof of the grandstand. They get a bird's eye view of the game. They can see what a player should do with the ball before he makes a movement. It would be much better if they were right on top of the play as they are at Shepherds Bush, Queens Park Rangers ground, or the Baseball Ground, Derby, where only a few yards separate them from the field. In fact, if they were in seat just outside the touchline, they would get a better perspective.

Whenever I went to games in which my old clubs, Sunderland and Arsenal, were concerned, I got an extra thrill. I tried hard to give an unbiased view of their games. But I still got hundreds of letters from readers, one half of them accusing me of 'wearing red and white coloured glasses', the other half asking what Sunderland and Arsenal had done to me to make me so bitter against them.

There was one game at Sunderland, when Arsenal were their opponents, in which Eddie Hapgood, Arsenal left-back, chipped an anklebone and Sunderland won by four goals to one. After the game, I went into the boardroom by invitation, and when I ventured the remark that, although Sunderland won deservedly, Arsenal were rather unlucky to lose Hapgood at a critical period,

I was told that when I had more experience of the game I would know better than to say such a thing. I could not refrain from pointing out that I had fourteen and a half years' experience on the field at Roker Park and more with Leyton and Arsenal in other years.

It was strange that during this season I saw both Sunderland and Arsenal knocked out of the F.A. Cup. Sunderland were beaten by a last-minute goal by West Ham United at Upton Park in the third round. Arsenal went down before a record crowd, 1–0 to Aston Villa at Villa Park in the sixth round. In each case I thought, and wrote, that the better team had lost. That brought another shoal of letters from West Ham and Villa supporters. It was good to get both sides of the picture, although it did involve a lot of work answering the letters.

Sheffield Wednesday won the League championship that year with the low total of fifty-two points. It was a triumph for Jimmy Seed, who started his career as a colleague of mine at Sunderland. Wednesday were a well-balanced side with a great half-back line in Alf Strange, Tony Leach and Billy Marsden, and a dashing, goal-scoring centre-forward in Jack Allen.

It was during this season that I saw the shortest international career in the history of the game. Big Jim Barrett, 14 st. West Ham centre-half, played eight minutes for England, his only experience of international matches. It was against Ireland at Goodison Park. After eight minutes' play, Barrett received a knee injury that put him out of the game and brought a cartilage operation. He was never selected again.

A minute from the end, when the score was 1–1, Billy Dean, Everton centre-forward, caused a flutter in the press box by scoring the winning goal for England. Most of the reporters, wanting to catch an early train to London after the game, had written their reports as a draw of course. They had to do their work all over again. Many of them never caught that London train!

CHAPTER 9

SHUT OUT OF WEMBLEY

AND THE MOST EXCITING SEASON I EVER KNEW

Towards the end of the 1928 to 1929 season I saw one of the most freakish goals ever to decide an international match. It was scored direct from a corner kick at Hampden Park, Glasgow, and gave Scotland victory over England, and with it the international championship and Triple Crown. Scotland, who had lost the services of irrepressible Alex Jackson with a dislocated elbow just before half-time, forced a corner kick in the last minute. There was a strong wind blowing from goal to goal in Scotland's favour at the time. Alex Cheyne, Aberdeen inside-right, who soon afterwards was transferred to Chelsea, took the kick. He sent over a high ball that curled into the goalmouth. It looked to be going outside the far post but suddenly swerved into the goal with goalkeeper Jack Hacking looking on helplessly. Before the game could be re-started the final whistle sounded.

But the highlight of the season for me was the F.A. Cup final at Wembley between Bolton Wanderers and Portsmouth. During the previous week I had been reporting a golf tournament at Leeds. I went to Wembley expecting to collect my admission ticket at the main entrance. When I got there the commissionaire knew nothing about any ticket for me. He had strict orders that no one could get in without a ticket. I pleaded hard, but though he knew me, it was of no avail. There I stood, outside the Stadium wondering how on earth I was to get in. Right in front of me was a flaming yellow poster which said: 'READ CHARLES BUCHAN ON THE CUP FINAL ON MONDAY'. This was my first final as a reporter and it looked as though I would miss it. Minutes flew past until I heard a roar from inside which told me the teams had walked out onto the Stadium. I could see no hope of ever seeing the game. Just then the King's carriage rolled past. I ran behind it into the courtyard. I seemed to be no better off, but after talking persuasively to several attendants, I managed to squeeze a way onto the grandstand.

As soon as I sat down on the stone steps of a gangway the match started. I forgot the discomfort in the exciting exchanges. Bolton won the Cup for the third time at Wembley 2–0, but my sympathies went off to Portsmouth, who had the misfortune to have their full-back, Bell, injured about a quarter of an hour before the end with the score at 0–0. Although I have seen every Wembley final since that day, I shall always recall that 1929 incident as the most nerve-racking of the series.

Soon after the end of the season, I attended the League Annual General Meeting in London. There I saw Herbert Chapman secure from Exeter City the transfer of Cliff Bastin, the international winger. Cliff had just celebrated his seventeenth birthday when he signed for Arsenal. Before he was nineteen he had secured every possible honour in the game. Although he was neither fast nor exceptionally clever, Bastin was one of the greatest forwards of his generation. He had an ice-cool brain and always seemed to be in the right place at the right time, especially in front of goal.

In June, Chapman also got the signature of Alex James, Preston North End's Scottish international inside-left, for £9,000. So he paid out, within six months, nearly £20,000 to secure inside-forwards Jack and James. The League held an inquiry before James signed for Arsenal. They decided they had no objection to offer to the transfer. The reason for the inquiry was there were so many teams seeking James's transfer that it was thought there must have been some special inducement for him to go to the London club. It turned out that Arsenal were able to secure for James an appointment in a big London store. Nothing in the League's rules and regulations bans a club from placing a player in a job.

When he joined Arsenal, James was a brilliant individualist. He had scored many great goals for Preston after beating two or three opponents but his methods did not fit in with the Arsenal plan at first. After a few months he was dropped because Arsenal wanted a midfield schemer, not a goal scorer, however brilliant he might be. Before he put up the team sheet in the dressing room, Mr

Chapman asked James to come up to his office. After explaining why he had left him out, Mr Chapman said: "Alex, I want you to go on a fortnight's cruise. I think it will benefit your health and you'll come back a new man."

James thought the matter over carefully before agreeing. He had visions of a lovely Mediterranean trip in beautiful sunshine, but there was a shock in store. When he got down to Dover Harbour, in company with trainer Tom Whittaker, he was taken not to a luxury liner but to a trawler just about to start on its trip! Though James objected strongly, he was persuaded to go by Whittaker. James told me afterwards that he thoroughly enjoyed the experience. He certainly came back a new player and was the prime mover in Arsenal's upward rise. His perky Scottish humour helped the team out of many tight corners. He could be depended upon to produce his form no matter how tense the position.

Chapman certainly worked on very novel lines. If a player lost form temporarily, he often tried him in another position in the second, or even the third, team until he regained his confidence and touch. Joe Hulme, the international outside-right, was played at centre-half in the 'stiffs', the dressing room name for the reserves, for a few games. The change worked wonders.

Chapman also had many ideas about the game that have since been brought into being. He wanted to use a white ball twenty odd years ago. He also put forward the idea that each season six clubs should be relegated from the First Division and six clubs from the Second Division take their places. He thought that in this way the standard of play in the two divisions would be almost equal in a few years and relegation would not be the vital thing it is today. I wish it were in force now. The game lost a vivid personality when Mr Chapman died suddenly in the spring of 1934. Yet it was only a stroke of good luck that made him turn to management. Whilst Chapman was a player with Tottenham Hotspur, he was studying to become a mining engineer. One of his colleagues, an inside-forward named Archie Glen, had received an offer to take over the management of Northampton Town, then a Southern League club. After having a talk with Mr Chapman, Glen said to him: "Herbert, I'm not going to take the job. Why don't you put in an application?"

Chapman did so and became Northampton's manager. It was not long before he made them into a great side that won the

Southern League championship and brought off several notable F.A. Cup achievements. He was a strict disciplinarian. Every member of his staff had to give his best for the good of the team. They had to be sportsmen and good companions. During an F.A. Cup-tie one of his men deliberately fouled an opponent. Chapman said immediately after the game that the player would never kick another ball for the club. Within a few weeks he was transferred for a few hundred pounds.

Chapman's bold policy in the transfer line soon bore fruit. In the 1929 to 1930 season, less than twelve months after the James transfer, Arsenal won the Cup for the first time. It was a cute move by James that led to Arsenal's victory in the final, over Huddersfield Town, at Wembley. They were awarded a free kick about thirty yards from the Huddersfield goal. James took the kick quickly, before the Huddersfield defenders had time to take up position. He slipped the ball to Bastin, took the return pass in his stride and from the edge of the penalty area crashed the ball past the surprised Town goalkeeper. That goal, scored in the seventeenth minute, took a lot of confidence out of Huddersfield and a second goal, by centre-forward Jack Lambert early in the second half, completed their downfall.

There was another unorthodox goal in Arsenal's semi-final with Hull City, at Elland Road, Leeds. Goalkeeper Dan Lewis took a goal kick and 'half topped' the ball. It went straight to Howieson, the Hull inside-left, standing a few yards away from the centre semi-circle. He promptly hit the ball towards the Arsenal goal. It sailed high in the air and dropped over the goal line before Lewis had scrambled back into his goal. Arsenal were rather fortunate to survive. Only a masterly goal by Bastin in the late stages enabled them to draw 2–2. They won the replay 1–0 at Villa Park.

It was strange, though, that Arsenal had a very poor record in the League. They finished only four points better than Everton, who were relegated from the First Division for the first time. Sheffield Wednesday carried off the League championship in runaway style with ten points' margin over Derby County. Wednesday were a well-balanced side, brilliantly led by Jimmie Seed. They were unfortunate to lose the service of their international left half-back, Billy Marsden, who was injured when playing for England against Germany in Berlin. Marsden, who had been a colleague of mine when I was at Sunderland, never played again after this injury. As compensation in those days was trifling, he received little reward for serving his country. Now players are insured for international games up to £15,000. But of course his club, not the player, would collect this big sum. Just previously Marsden had been in the England team that gave one of the best exhibitions at Wembley, one that went a long way towards wiping out the memory of the debacle against the 'Wembley Wizards' two years before. England beat Scotland 5–2, thanks to a wonderful display by a forward line consisting of Crooks (Derby County), Jack (Arsenal), Watson (West Ham United), Bradford (Birmingham) and Rimmer (Sheffield Wednesday).

There was at least one record set up during this season. Joe Bambrick, Linfield centre-forward, scored six goals for Ireland in the international with Wales at Celtic Park, Belfast. Bambrick, who afterwards came to England and played for Chelsea and other clubs, scored ninety-four goals for Linfield and Ireland during that season.

One of the things I like to look back upon about this time was the birth of the F.A. coaching scheme. I happened to be there when it started on its career. Some sixty youths from public schools all over the country gathered at Highbury for the opening session, by invitation from the F.A. When I walked into the ground to interview Mr Chapman, all the youths were present but there were no instructors. Several prominent amateur players were there but not one had any experience of coaching methods. The Arsenal manager, temporarily at a loss, asked me if I could help him out. So whilst trainer Tom Whittaker gave the youths a talk on the care of their kit and the way they should prepare for a game, a scheme was improvised.

The youths were split up into classes. I took one class and put them through a series of exercises. It was not so difficult as I had written a book of instruction for the *News Chronicle* during the summer. The other classes went through the exercises in the same way. They were pronounced a success and certainly the lads and I enjoyed every moment. That was the start of a coaching scheme that has developed into a great business. The F.A. now runs classes at various colleges and there is an opportunity for every youngster to get the benefit of first-class coaching. I am a firm believer in coaching for the boys. But I am against coaches for professional League club players. You cannot teach an old hand new tricks.

Players should have the right ideas instilled into them whilst they are still novices at the game.

It is rather strange how some seasons are crowded with drama and exciting incidents. In League games, Cup-ties and internationals, events crop up that cause endless discussions. A season that stands out in my memory as an eventful one was that of 1930 to 1931. Records were smashed in face of fierce competition and there were incidents that are talked about to this day.

The best record of all was set up by West Bromwich Albion. They achieved the magnificent double of winning the F.A. Cup and promotion from the Second Division. No other club has equalled that performance even now. It was brought off by a team of young Englishmen, few of whom had established outstanding reputations. What is more, most of the side were local born. Albion defeated Birmingham in a first-class Cup final at Wembley and finished runners-up to Everton in the Second Division. No Second Division champions have succeeded in winning the F.A. Cup the same year. Albion were an eager, fast-moving side, with nothing new in the way of tactics but ever-fresh in their outlook on the game. Their team spirit and co-operation were a delight. They were somewhat fortunate that season in having so few of their players injured. Throughout the League programme of forty-two games, they called on only nineteen players.

The recognised team was: Pearson, Shaw, Trentham, Magee, Richardson (W.), Edwards, Glidden, Carter, Richardson (W.G.), Sandford and Wood. Outside-right Glidden is now a director of the club and a successful businessman in West Bromwich. He had been a colleague of mine at Sunderland although too young to command a place in the First Division team. The two Richardsons were not related in any way. The centre-forward was given the initials 'W.G.' to distinguish him from the centre-half. He was a Durham youth, with bright ginger hair. His energy was inexhaustible and, though not above average build, he never spared himself against the biggest defenders. No cause was lost whilst the game was on and he was about.

Albion's manner of winning the Cup is still fresh in my mind. They took the lead in the first half through a goal scored by centre-forward Richardson. Shortly after half-time, Joe Bradford, Birmingham centre-forward, who had been a doubtful starter until an hour or so before the game, crashed in a wonderful equaliser from twenty-five yards, the first equalising goal ever scored at Wembley. Straight from the kick-off, and almost before the Birmingham players had finished congratulating themselves, Carter, Richardson and Sandford took the ball straight through the defence for Richardson to tap the ball straight into the net for the winning goal. It was said afterwards that Albion's forwards had planned the move. At any rate, it caught the Birmingham defenders off guard, and must go down as the quickest Wembley goal. Birmingham however deserved sympathy.

Not only was Bradford handicapped by his injury, in my opinion he should not have played, but also they had what I thought a perfectly good goal disallowed. It happened early in the game. Birmingham were awarded a free kick near the touchline a few yards over the halfway line. The players lined up as usual near the Albion penalty area. All the Birmingham players were onside then. Cringan, the right-half, took the kick and sent the ball curling into the Albion penalty area. Not a defender moved. Gregg, Birmingham inside-left, timing his move perfectly, ran forward and headed the ball past goalkeeper Pearson. Unluckily for Birmingham, referee A.H. Kingscott decreed that Gregg was offside. From my place of view, high up in the stand, he was onside when Cringan played the ball. It was just one of those debatable decisions that cropped up in nearly every Wembley final round about that time.

I must say though that many bad decisions are still made regarding free kicks. No sensible player is likely to stand in an offside position when a free kick is about to be taken and there is a chance of his side scoring a goal. If he is onside when the kick is taken then he should not, according to the laws, be given offside in the subsequent movement, no matter what his position when he receives the ball. That is what often happens nowadays. A player runs forward after the kick is taken until he is in a clear position, but he is pulled for 'offside'.

Not only the Albion, but also Arsenal, set up records that have never been equalled. They won the League First Division championship for the first time in their history with a total of sixty-six points. The previous highest was sixty by Sheffield Wednesday, Liverpool and West Bromwich.

Arsenal's methods, started in 1925, and improved each year, certainly paid dividends that season. Their 'defence in depth' policy, modelled around that great centre-half, Herbert Roberts, and the fast 'smash and grab' raids of Joe Hulme, Cliff Bastin and Jack Lambert (mostly inspired by Alex James), had the rest of the First Division teams guessing. They had no answer to them.

Arsenal's record of thirty-three away points from twenty-one games still stands, and I think will remain for a long time. It is remarkable that their home and away results were exactly the same – fourteen games won, five drawn and two lost. There is no doubt that they owed a lot to the genius of Alex James. The Scottish international inside-left rarely played a bad game, whether at home or away. Winning or losing, he produced his inimitable style, beating the opposition with the 'fluttering foot' trick. Alex went on his way unperturbed and smiling. A player who, like James, can produce his real form on almost all occasions is worth his weight in gold to a team. His influence goes right through the side, enabling them to carry on in the most difficult situations.

Arsenal's tactics, of course, produced many imitators, though not with the same success. They are in vogue today but I fear are out-dated. Defences have developed counter plans to beat them. A new attacking system is urgently required.

Aston Villa, Blackpool and Manchester United also joined the record breakers during that 1930 to 1931 season. Villa, with a forward line consisting of Mandley, Beresford (or George Brown), Waring, Walker and Houghton, scored 128 goals, the highest ever in the First Division. Here again it was the generalship and scheming of inside-left Billy Walker that brought success in the scoring line. Blackpool, on the other hand, gave away 125 goals in the forty-two games. Yet they escaped relegation by a point. Leeds United and Manchester United finished below them. It was a bad year for Manchester United. They never recovered from a bad start, the worst start ever made by a club up to that time. They lost the first twelve games. Not until they beat Birmingham on 1st November did they get a point.

There were high jinks too in the international field. England and Scotland shared the championship, but the shape of things to come was shown when a team of 'Welsh Unknowns' drew 1–1 with Scotland at Ibrox Park, Glasgow. Until a day or two before that game, Ted Robbins, Welsh F.A. general secretary, did not know which way to turn for players to complete the team. The only regulars were Fred Keenor, Joe Bamford and Alf Robbins.

The rest were amateurs and young players taking part in their first representative game. And yet they put up such a spirited display that Scotland were hard pressed to get away with a draw.

Scotland later beat England 2–0 at Hampden Park in the only game Herbert Roberts, the 'Prince of Stoppers', played for his country. Roberts had that wily centre-forward, Jimmy McGrory of Celtic, up against him, and although he played well, the other defenders did not fully understand his style. Scotland's victory, however, was just a 'flash in the pan'. They embarked upon a Continental tour during the summer and suffered two humiliating defeats, 5–0 by Austria in Vienna and 3–0 by Italy in Rome. The defeat in Vienna was Scotland's first defeat abroad. The press at home had some scathing things to say about the performances.

Nor did England fare much better. They were beaten 5–2 by France in Paris. A team which included such stars as Cooper (Derby County), Blenkinsop and Strange (Sheffield Wednesday), Tate (Aston Villa), Crooks (Derby County), Waring and Houghton (Aston Villa) was overplayed by the superior skill and pace of the Frenchmen. One of the prominent forwards in the England side (he was not included in the Paris eleven) was Gordon Hodgson, the six-foot stalwart South African inside-forward of Liverpool and Aston Villa. He came over with a South African touring side about 1924 and signed on, together with goalkeeper Arthur Riley, for Liverpool. They established big reputations in League football, with Hodgson (a forceful player and strong shot) equal to anything in the country.

At the Annual General Meeting of the clubs in June 1931, it was decided to ban all broadcasts of League games. So the recent attitude of the clubs is nothing new. At the time, George Allison, Arsenal director and later manager, was making a big hit with his exciting commentaries on the games. He introduced a new technique. Attendances at the grounds showed a big drop because people stayed at home to listen to him. The clubs appealed to the F.A. to stop the broadcasting of all Cup-ties as well as League games. The F.A. agreed, with the exception of the final at Wembley.

At the next annual League meeting Newcastle United put forward a proposal to have the ban lifted. It was heavily defeated. In fact the ban remained until 1937, when it was agreed to allow broadcast to Empire listeners overseas only. There can be little doubt that broadcasting and television are going to play an important part in the future of soccer. Some better arrangement than the present one of putting over an 'unknown' game each week will have to be devised.

Continental football has made such enormous strides in recent years that I find it difficult to realise it is only twenty-four years since the first full international with a Continental side in the country. Spain provided the opposition at Highbury on the 9th December 1931. I shall never forget the game owing to the tremendous publicity it received. Only eighteen months previously Spain had beaten England 4–3 in Madrid, the first time we had been beaten by a Continental side. In addition, the Spanish goalkeeper, a chap named Zamorra, had been boasted as the best in the world, practically unbeatable. England were not given a chance. Events proved to be very different. England won by seven goals to one and the man who brought about the severe drubbing was the much-vaunted Zamorra. It was evident from the start that he had been warned about the rushing tactics of English centre-forwards and Bill 'Dixie' Dean in particular. He played throughout the game as if hypnotised by the Everton leader. A simple mistake in the opening minutes gave England a goal. Others followed until Zamorra covered his face with his hands in shame. It was a tremendous anti-climax. With the exception of Ellis Rimmer, Sheffield Wednesday outside-left, all the England forwards scored. Dean got only one, Sammy Crooks (Derby County) got two, Jack Smith (Portsmouth) got two and Tom Johnson (Everton) also got two. The Spanish invasion was routed!

A year later, however, England got a jolt from a Continental side. They were lucky to get away with a 4–3 win over Austria at Stamford Bridge after one of the best internationals I have ever seen. It was a magnificent match, with Austria supplying a brand of teamwork that had seldom been seen in this country. And they had in the fair-headed Sindelar the first of the roaming centre-forwards. He 'sold the dummy' frequently to our defenders and often had them wondering what to do. Fortunately, England had opportunist forwards who made the most of their chances. Goals were scored by Eric Houghton (Aston Villa), Sammy Crooks (Derby County) and Jimmy Hampson (Blackpool) two. Quick thinking on the part of Hampson saved England. He was a great little player. Blackpool and England suffered a grievous loss when he was tragically drowned in a boating accident whilst out fishing.

Earlier that year there was another Wembley F.A. Cup final incident that is talked about to this day. It was the equalising goal scored by Jimmy Richardson for Newcastle United that led to their 2–1 victory over Arsenal. Arsenal were leading at half-time by a goal scored by Bob John, Welsh international left half-back, who took the outside-left berth that day owing to an injury to Alex James. Then early in the second half, Boyd, Newcastle outside-right, sent a long pass towards the Arsenal goal line about fifteen yards wide of the goal. Richardson dashed for the ball. It looked a forlorn chase. The Arsenal defenders stopped, thinking the ball had crossed the goal line. Richardson got his foot to it and centred, then centre-forward Allen deflected the ball with his head past goalkeeper Frank Moss. Referee W.P. Harper, who, I am sorry to say, died a few months ago, immediately gave a goal.

Had the ball crossed the line? From my seat high up in the Wembley grandstand I thought it had. I could clearly see the white line with the ball beyond it. Press photographs and cinema shots showed likewise. But the linesman on the spot and referee Harper had no doubts. They were the judges. They gave the verdict in favour of Newcastle. From that point United were on top and Allen scored the winning goal about a quarter of an hour from the end. Newcastle were worthy winners on the day, but I have often wondered what were the effects of that equalising goal. Years afterwards I spoke to Richardson about it. He said: "I was concentrating so hard on reaching the ball that I couldn't tell you even now whether it was over the line or not."

It was a big disappointment for Arsenal, who were in the running for the League and Cup double. They won neither. Newcastle dashed the Cup from their grasp and Everton stole a march on them in the League championship. Arsenal finished in second place two points behind.

It was an exciting finish to a season that had opened with a tragedy. John Thomson, Glasgow Celtic's Scottish international goalkeeper, was so badly hurt in a game with Glasgow Rangers that he died the same evening. He dived at the feet of Sam English, Rangers' centre-forward, fractured his skull and lived only a few hours. Considering the fierceness of the exchanges it is surprising how few fatal accidents have occurred during the passing of the years. The first I remember was that of Bob Benson, Sheffield United and England left-back. He turned out for Arsenal during a wartime game in 1915, collapsed during the play and died in the dressing room. But he had not played for a year before.

Then there was Raleigh, a young Gillingham centre-forward. He received concussion during a game with Brighton in 1934 and lived for only a few hours.

Jim Thorpe, Sunderland's young goalkeeper, was badly hurt in a game with Chelsea at Roker Park. He died a few days later. At the inquest it was stated that his death was really due to diabetes.

Bury full-back Sam Wynne collapsed on the field during a League game with Sheffield United at Bramhall Lane and died in the dressing room. It was discovered later he was in the first stages of pneumonia although he was unaware of it.

Only a few years ago two Army players were killed by lightning, during the Army Cup final replay at Aldershot. Others too suffered from shock. In the circumstances, the list is small, thank goodness. It is to be ardently hoped there will be no others.

There were notable features of the 1931 to 1932 season. First Alan Morton broke a Scottish record by playing for the thirtieth time for his country. His record still stands. Morton, called the 'wee blue devil', was the outstanding outside-left of his generation. His ball control, swerve and pinpoint accuracy in centring the ball have rarely been equalled. His record appearance was against England at Wembley. Although Scotland were beaten 3–0, Morton showed that the years had not dimmed his artistry. It was not his fault that England won and took the international championship.

Morton is now a director of Glasgow Rangers, the team he helped to many of their triumphs. At one period he was the highest-paid player in the British Isles. He was an amateur with Queens Park, carrying on with his profession as a civil engineer. Before he was transferred to Rangers he turned professional. His share of the transfer fee was paid in weekly wages and, since there was no limit on wages in Scotland as there was in England, Morton was able to draw a big weekly packet, at the time reputed to be more than £50.

There are many people who still think that English professionals should be able to draw unlimited wages, like actors or variety artists. I do not think it would be possible. It could, perhaps, be done by several of the leading, crowd-drawing teams such as

Arsenal, Newcastle United and Aston Villa and probably by most First Division League clubs. But the majority of Second and Third Division teams could not carry on with a bigger wages bill. The League as a whole must be considered, for without the poorer clubs the competition would lose a lot of its appeal.

I think it is unfair to compare a footballer's wages with an actor's or a baseball player's. The weekly wages bill must be in proportion to the revenue of the club and even now it has gone beyond that in some cases. Actors play every night of the week, baseball players nearly every day during their season. The receipts from their performances are much bigger than those of a footballer who plays a home game only once every fortnight. Maybe if floodlit football gets a big hold on the public and players are called upon to play two or three times each week, they will get much higher pay than they do now. But whilst I agree that stars like Stanley Matthews, Tom Finney, John Charles, Jimmy Dickinson and Billy Wright are worth much more than the maximum wage, I am convinced that the modern player, on the whole, is well rewarded for his labours.

But to get back to Morton, the mighty little atom who led England defenders (and Scottish) a merry dance for a long time. It is interesting to hear how he became such a great player, and a lesson to the modern youngster who hopes to make a name for himself. I can do no better than quote Morton as he describes the stepping-stones to success. He said: "The three essentials are balance, ball control and quickness off the mark. They can come only from intensive practice – practice, mark you, that was never a labour, but a love. I well remember my days as a youth when I took a ball into a back garden and there, for hours, practised with an intensity, which didn't seem so at the time because I was seeking something, which was a challenge to my athletic ability.

"How did I set about my days of practice? Well, behind our house and in the back garden was a wooden door through which coal was emptied into the cellar. The door stood perhaps 4 ft from ground level and in its centre was an opening just sufficiently large to take a football. There then was my target. I aimed to put the ball through that aperture. Not always did it work out that way. Indeed I didn't altogether want a bull's eye every time. It was better when the ball came back at various angles. This meant that, as it shot back from the wall, I found myself compelled to meet the return with either foot. The upshot was I was continually pivoting to meet the capricious ball with right foot and left. Gradually, I found myself kicking the ball in the direction I wanted.

"Proficiency came slowly but in a way that became natural the longer I kept at it. In other words, at first everything was deliberate. Later it became almost automatic, like what the doctors call a reflex action. Time meant nothing. An hour and a half sped away without me giving thought to it. As an outcome of those days, I felt no difficulty when I became a player in meeting a running ball and sending it where I wanted with either foot."

What better advice could a youngster want from one of the game's greatest? It is advice, though, that is so often ignored. Too many of the present generation think they know all there is to be known already.

There was also the unusual occurrence in the League of a club retiring from the competition during the season. Wigan Borough were so badly off financially that during October they sent in their resignation. Their record was expunged and the Third Division North proceeded with twenty-one clubs instead of twenty-two. Lincoln City were the champions that year.

At the bottom, Rochdale set up a record that no other League club will want to equal. They went from November until the end of the season without winning a game. They lost twenty-five games, seventeen of them in succession, and drew one of the twenty-six games played. One could not help feeling sorry for the Rochdale players. As defeat followed defeat week after week so their confidence left them. They conceded 135 goals in forty matches, only one less than the record of 136 against Nelson in 1927 to 1928.

There is nothing harder than playing in a losing team. The ball always runs unkindly and the more you strive, the more things go wrong. It's different in a winning side. You have the breaks and expend far less energy during the course of the game.

One of the biggest shocks that the F.A. Cup had ever known came the following season, 1932 to 1933. Arsenal, of course, figured in a tie that has never been forgotten. They were beaten in the third round by Walsall, which was then a Third Division North club, by two goals to nil. Arsenal were at the top of the First Division when the draw was made. There were cries of 'lucky Arsenal' at being called upon to face such opposition. Manager

Herbert Chapman decided to bring some of his young players into the team for the game. Even so, they were reckoned to be odds-on favourites. But they were made to look very humble indeed. Playing with great determination and no little skill, Walsall beat them fairly and squarely on their peculiar sloping ground. They never allowed Arsenal to get into their stride. The First Division side became rattled long before the end of the game. It was a great sensation and although Walsall were knocked out in the next round by Manchester City, they had carved a niche in the annals of the competition.

It did not take Arsenal long to recover from the blow, however. They pulled themselves together so well that they won the League championship with four points' advantage over Aston Villa. That was a sure sign of their greatness.

CHAPTER 10

MY COLLEAGUE IS ARRESTED BY MUSSOLINI

I FIND AN 'ILLEGAL' PITCH; AND ADMIRE THE MAGIC OF STAN MATTHEWS

My first big job abroad as a reporter came in the summer of 1933, when I was sent to cover the England internationals with Italy in Rome and Switzerland in Berne. It brought many adventures. As I had not been given much notice I could make no definite arrangements, I just went out in a hurry.

England's visit to Italy had received tremendous publicity. Mussolini, Il Duce, was to meet them on arrival in Rome and they were to be given a terrific welcome. I travelled with the team and when we got to Rome not a soul was there to meet the party. The players went to their hotel in perfect silence. As this was so different from what was expected I thought it worth a story and wrote one of about 800 words, anticipating no difficulty in getting it through to the *News Chronicle*. So I went to my hotel, well away from where the team was quartered, and went to the phone. I was told there was a four hours' delay with all London calls. That was hopeless as edition time was less than two hours away.

After running round various newspaper offices in a taxi-cab, I came to the radio station. They were willing to send my message if I copied it out in block capitals. That would have taken hours, so I gave up in disgust and went back to my hotel. It was now around nine o'clock and I had failed in my job. In sheer desperation I picked up the phone in my bedroom and asked for the London number. I was through in less than a minute. My worries were over for the time being. But the taxi ride cost a little under £5. After a meal I went to contact our Rome representative. On reaching his address I found he had been arrested as an enemy of Mussolini! That meant that I had to make my own way for the rest of the trip and, once I had confirmed that the England team were to train the following morning in the Stadium where the match was to be played, I went to bed.

When I arrived at the Stadium the next morning there was no sign of the England team. I sought out the Stadium secretary only to be told they were training elsewhere. He gave me permission, though, to look over the Stadium and the playing pitch. As soon as I saw the pitch I thought there was something wrong. It did not look nearly big enough. I paced out the distance between the sideline of the penalty area and the touchline. It was only twelve paces, roughly twelve yards. This meant that the pitch itself was only sixty-eight yards wide. It did not come within the laws of the game which state that for an international game the width shall not be more than eighty yards nor less than seventy yards. No wonder our boys felt cramped when they got out there the following day. I think there is nothing worse than having to play on a narrow pitch like this.

The scene before the game started was one I shall never forget. When Mussolini arrived, the packed crowd rose to him waving white handkerchiefs and chanting in unison "Il Duce". It was like flocks of white doves hovering over the packed terraces. The nearest I have seen to it was during the 1950 World Cup competition in Rio de Janeiro.

The game is impressed upon my memory, too, for the wonderfully gallant resistance put up by England's defenders. Italy at the time were world champions, having won the World Cup competition. They started off like champions, raiding the English lines time after time. In five minutes they went ahead. Their inside-left, Ferrari, sent in a twenty-yard shot that goalkeeper Harry Hibbs got his hand to but could not keep out of the net. To make matters worse Tom White of Everton, England's centre-half, pulled a thigh muscle. For some reason he was kept in his position, hobbling about there and doing his best. As often as the Italians raided, the England defenders sent them back. Hibbs, Roy Goodall and Eddie Hapgood, the full-backs, and Alf Strange and Wilf Copping, the wing-halves, played the game of their lives. With blood streaming from a cut above the right eye, Goodall rallied his men. Occasionally the forwards broke away but made little impression on the Italian defenders until Cliff Bastin, Arsenal outside-left, equalised with a brilliant shot. In the main, however, it was all Italy. They attacked persistently but could not break down that superb defence. England were glad to get away with a 1–1 draw, a tribute to Goodall and his fearless colleagues.

The next day the England party went to the Palazza Vittorio for an interview with Mussolini. We were ushered into a tremendous room, where I manœuvred an end position, hoping I could get an interview with Il Duce. When Mussolini arrived, the F.A. official in charge said to him: "Do you speak English?"

He replied: "I speak English perfectly."

Then he went round the whole of the party in a very few minutes. I never got the interview.

Soon afterwards we were granted an audience with His Holiness the Pope. We kissed the ring. It was rather strange that he should chance to have a few words with Peter O'Dowd, Chelsea and England's reserve centre-half, who I believe was the only Roman Catholic in the party.

Later we went on to Berne to play Switzerland the following Sunday. There were changes in the team of course. The only forwards to retain their places were outside-right Albert Geldard and centre-forward George Hunt. Newcomers were Jimmy Richardson, Newcastle inside-right, and Eric Brook, Manchester City outside-left. Bastin moved to inside-left and formed with the dashing, roaming Brook a left wing that played a big part in a 4–0 victory. Bastin and Richardson each scored twice. Another big success was centre-half O'Dowd, who took the place of the injured White. But the whole England team gave a greatly improved display and outplayed a Swiss team that expected to do equally as well as Italy.

It was on this trip that the F.A. called in a team manager for the first time. Herbert Chapman, who travelled with the party on a 'busman's holiday', was put in charge of the players. I believe it was his influence that led to the great defensive exhibition against Italy. All England teams are now in the charge of Walter Winterbottom, F.A. coach and organiser. He has done a grand job of work.

In the following season, November 1934, Italy were given a return game. It took place at Highbury and turned out to be one of the roughest and toughest internationals I have ever seen. The game was given a lot of publicity. Italy were still regarded as the best team on the Continent and they meant to uphold their reputation at all costs. To make matters worse, they were offered a huge bonus for winning. I heard many sums mentioned but I believe the truth was that each player was to receive £50 if they won. It was a tremendous incentive to the Italian players. They were all out for victory from the start.

England's team included seven Arsenal players, a record for a professional club. They were goalkeeper Moss, full-backs Male and Hapgood, wing-half Copping and forwards Bowden, Drake and Bastin. The remaining four were Britton (Everton), Barker (Derby County), Matthews (Stoke) and Brook (Manchester City). The game had an unfortunate start. Monti, the Italian centre-half, broke an ankle after only three minutes' play and, as no substitutes were allowed, Italy played with ten men for the rest of the game. But how those ten fought! Nothing was barred. For twenty minutes England gave a wonderful exhibition of smooth, combined play. Although Eric Brook missed a penalty kick, they put on three goals (two by Brook and one by Ted Drake) during that brilliant spell. Italy were outplayed. Then the trouble started. The Italians, unused to being outclassed, went in for the man instead of the ball. In one case a defender seized hold of Drake around the neck and started to punch him. In another incident an Italian took a running kick at his opponent. Fouls were commonplace.

England were put off their game by these tactics. To their credit they never retaliated though Wilf Copping and Jack Barker rather shook their opponents with vigorous shoulder charges. But England never recaptured the glory of the opening minutes, and when Meazza, Italian inside-right, scored a breakaway goal, the picture changed. In the second half, Meazza scored a second goal and the fun grew more furious. The little dark-skinned Italian centre-forward, one of the best Continental forwards who ever played against England, came near to completing a hat-trick when one of his shots rebounded from the cross-bar. England, however, held out and gained the victory they well deserved, although it was a painful business. When I saw the England players at the banquet after the game, all had something to show, in the shape of bruises and cuts, for the experience. The war was not carried on during the banquet. Diplomacy gained the day, but the Italians were struck off the international list until 1939, a few months before the outbreak of war, when England played them once again, this time in Rome.

Meantime, in English football, Arsenal were ruling the roost. In 1935 they completed a hat-trick of First Division championships, emulating the record of Huddersfield Town nine years previously. They were given a special trophy in commemoration of the event by the Football League. It bore a golden emblem of H.M. King George V's Jubilee Year. It is strange, too, that in each season they finished with practically the same record. Their points totals read fifty-eight, fifty-nine, fifty-eight, and they had four points' margin over Aston Villa and Sunderland, and three over Huddersfield Town. They were the most feared, yet the most respected team during this period. Wherever they went they attracted record gates. Everyone wanted to see them beaten; yet I think that during this time they did more for the good of the game than any other club.

There was one F.A. Cup final I feel I must mention. It was between West Bromwich Albion and Sheffield Wednesday in 1935, one of the most thrilling and exciting finals seen in the famous stadium. Albion came with nine of the team that had won the Cup four years before. Sheffield Wednesday, under the astute manager Billy Walker, and, with the clever scheming of inside-left Ron Starling, were making their first Wembley appearance. The result hinged on one of the best referee's decisions ever made. With only five minutes left for play and the score 2–2, Albion had twice rubbed off a Wednesday goal, Bert Catlin, Wednesday right-back, was injured in a tackle. Realising that he was not seriously hurt, referee Bert Fogg, of Bolton, allowed play to proceed. The ball went straight towards the Albion goal. Outside-right Hooper sent across a long centre and outside-left Ellis Rimmer beat goalkeeper Harold Pearson to the ball and headed it into the net. Almost immediately afterwards Rimmer, who had scored in every round, added a fourth goal. Even now I can picture the scene that followed. The disconsolate Pearson allowed the ball to rest in the back of the net. But with only a couple of minutes left, Billy Richardson, Albion's dashing centre-forward, rushed back, retrieved the ball from the net, sprinted to the centre and restarted the game at once. He, and the Albion, were out to retrieve a forlorn hope. But Wednesday were on top and carried off the trophy for the first time in twenty-eight years by winning by four goals to two.

Early in the 1935 summer, on 18th May, I had the most unusual experience of flying to a match in Amsterdam and returning home the same day. England were playing Holland at the Stadium there. I left my home shortly before midday, embarked on a plane about 1.30 p.m. and had a two-hour tour of Amsterdam before the evening kick-off. Shortly after the game was finished, I telephoned my story to the *News Chronicle*, caught a plane about 9.00 p.m. and was back home before midnight. The whole journey did not take as much time as a trip to Leicester or Nottingham and was much more comfortable in every way.

England won the game by one goal to nil, scored by Portsmouth outside-right Fred Worrall. The Dutchmen put up a brave fight against a team which included such fine players as Harry Hibbs, Birmingham goalkeeper, George Male and Eddie Hapgood, Arsenal full-backs, Jack Barker, Derby County centre-half, Worrall, W.G. Richardson, West Bromwich, and Ray Westwood, Bolton Wanderers, in the forward line. The standard of play in Holland has deteriorated since those days. They were really amateurs and had a tough job trying to compete with their professional Continental rivals.

The following summer, 1936, brought one of the unhappiest Continental tours I ever had. England played Austria in Vienna and Belgium in Brussels and were beaten in both places. The 2–1 defeat in Vienna was bearable as Austria were just about the best team on the Continent at the time. They had great players like full-back Czestr, who was also well known as a boxer and wrestler, left-half Nausch, and forwards Sindelar and Bocan. Nausch afterwards became the one-man Selection Committee of the Austrian national side. He alone was responsible for the policy of the team. I think it is an example we might well copy. I am all in favour of one man being in complete control of our international teams.

After the Vienna game I went to phone my story as usual, but when I got back to the box to take my fixed-time call, I was told that somebody had already accepted it. I would have to wait at least an hour before another call came through. Whilst I was impatiently waiting, the banquet for both teams and officials and to which I had been invited proceeded. I had not eaten for several hours and was hungry. Finally the call came through. As I came out of the box after finishing my story, I ran into Tom Whittaker, the Arsenal trainer in charge of the party. We spoke a few words, and when I asked him why he was so late he said: "Haven't you heard? Harold Robbins is badly hurt internally and I have had to rush him to hospital."

He gave me the details and I dashed back to the phone and, after a little delay, got a call through to London. Then, my work done for the day, I went to the banquet hall. The sweets were being served when I arrived there. When the meal was over and the speeches started, the Austrian president gave out the news about Hobbis. The other reporters immediately got busy but, for once, I could sit back and enjoy my leisure time.

Luckily Hobbis was not as badly hurt as was at first thought. The Charlton outside-left made such a rapid recovery that he was able to take his place in the team against Belgium.

Changes were made in the team that was beaten in Vienna for the Brussels game. One of them saw Sam Barkas, the clever Manchester City left-back, introduced as Hobbis's partner at inside-left. Although Barkas began his career as an inside-left, he had built up a reputation as one of the best full-backs in Britain. An international was certainly not the time to experiment with him as a forward. It was no fault of Sam's, however, that England were beaten. The team played well enough to win most games but, in pouring rain, missed many easy scoring chances. The Belgians had fewer opportunities, but accepted three of them. For that reason alone they deserved their 3–2 victory, the only one they have ever gained over England. It was a sad party that made the journey home. I don't think I have ever enjoyed a Continental trip less.

But the next season at home soon made me forget the dismal summer tour. It abounded with sparkling football, and the best team in the League was undoubtedly my old Roker Park club, Sunderland. Although Arsenal won the F.A. Cup, beating Sheffield United at Wembley with a goal scored by dashing centre-forward Ted Drake, now a Chelsea manager, Sunderland were the team of the year, winning the First Division championship with a margin of eight points from Derby County and Huddersfield Town.

Sunderland gave some delightful exhibitions during the season. I saw them beat Brentford 5–1 at Griffin Park on a rain-soaked ground and cannot hope to see anything finer. The forward line, Len Duns, Raich Carter, Bobby Gurney, Paddy Gallacher and Jimmy Connor, made the ball do everything but talk. And the defenders, marshalled by Scottish right-back Bill Murray, were as safe as the Bank of England. Murray, of course, is now the manager of the club. He is a stickler for good, attractive play. This was Sunderland's best period for a long time. Some people compared them with the 'Team of all Talents' way back in the early years of the 20th century, others to the 1912 to 1913 team which nearly brought off the double, winning the League championship but beaten in the F.A. Cup final by Aston Villa.

Well, I cannot write about the early Sunderland. I can about the 1913 team as I played in it and I must admit that there was little between the two sides except physique. The 1913 team was much bigger and stronger but I think the 1936 team almost atoned by their supreme skill and combination. Raich Carter, the silver-haired, local-born inside-right, was the inspiration of the attack. His wonderful positional sense and beautifully timed passes made him, in my opinion, the best forward of his generation. Raich gained his first international cap against Scotland in 1934, and until he retired in 1952, stood out in every match in which he played. He was that rare combination of ball artist and marksman. Carter led Sunderland to their supreme triumph the following season, 1936 to 1937. They won the F.A. Cup for the first time in the club's history, beating Preston North End at Wembley 3–1.

When I first went to Sunderland the Cup was the great prize. Before each season started we heard 'this is to be Sunderland's year for winning the Cup'. Each year the good folk at Sunderland were bitterly disappointed until at last Carter and his men took the trophy to Roker Park. Yet there was a time at Wembley when it looked as though they were to be disappointed once again. At half-time Preston led by a goal scored by Frank O'Donnell. North End were the better side. Then early in the second half, centre-forward Bobby Gurney, that bundle of energy and loyal club servant, back-headed the equalising goal. From that moment Sunderland were on top. Goals by Carter and outside-left Eddie Burbanks brought a decisive victory.

There were big celebrations that night. One was by a band of enthusiasts who took a crate of beer to the 1913 final at Crystal Palace and, when Sunderland were beaten, swore they would not drink the beer until Sunderland won the Cup. I was told afterwards that no beer ever tasted as sweet.

At the end of that season in 1937 I went on a tour with the England party to Scandinavia. It more than made up for the bitter experiences of the previous summer. England won all three games played. Norway were beaten in Oslo 6–0, Sweden in Stockholm 4–0 and Finland in Helsinki 8–0. It was the happiest trip imaginable, not only from the playing point of view, but also from the many pleasant events that were included.

England's team had been re-organised completely during the season. The only one of the previous touring party who retained his place was George Male, the big, dependable Arsenal full-back who never played a poor game. Newcomers included Vic Woodley, Chelsea goalkeeper, half-backs Cliff Britton (Everton) and Alf Young (Huddersfield), forwards Alf Kirchen (Arsenal), Tom Galley (Wolves), Freddie Steele and Joe Johnson (Stoke), Len Goulden (West Ham United) and Joe Payne (Luton).

Steele, either at centre-forward or inside-left, was the big success of the tour. He scored seven goals in the three games and established himself as England's best centre-forward. His headwork was in the Bill Dean class. Now, of course, Freddie is manager of Port Vale. Their rise is mainly due to his foresight.

The Norwegian centre-half and captain in the first game was Jorgan Juve, a sports writer on an Oslo newspaper. He is now editor. We became firm friends. After the game he said to me: "As long as you beat Sweden by at least as big a score I am satisfied! England were a great team."

Although friendly countries, there is keen rivalry in sport between Norway and Sweden. I think Jorgan was quite happy after England beat Norway 4–0. The score was not so big, but the England team gave another fine display.

For the next match in Helsinki, the main party went by boat. George Allison, Arsenal manager, and soccer fanatic Harry Homer (who were both on a holiday tour) and I flew from Stockholm to Abo and on to the Finnish capital by rail. Homer was the world's greatest soccer fan. Wherever England played abroad – in Rome, Budapest, Vienna – he was sure to turn up!

When we arrived at Helsinki we made arrangements to meet the England team at the station. They were twenty-four hours late. They ran into fog during the Baltic crossing by boat and had an adventurous journey. I shall never forget reading the late L.V. Manning story with headline streamers:

£100,000 WORTH OF ENGLAND PLAYERS LOST AT SEA

By the way, the biggest fee paid before that summer was the £10,775 Aston Villa handed over to Portsmouth for centre-half Jimmy Allen in June 1934.

The Helsinki ground was one of the strangest I have seen for an international. It nestled under the shade of the present Olympic Stadium, but was open on all sides. It reminded me of a typical English village ground. The Finns were no match for the English side. They were fast, eager and wonderfully fit, but once Alf Kirchen opened the scoring the result was never in doubt.

When I look back on the year 1938, three players immediately jump to mind. They are Stanley Matthews, then with Stoke City, Willie Hall of Tottenham Hotspur and George Mutch, Preston North End inside-right. Matthews, of course, had already earned international honours, but during the 1937 to 1938 season he was at his best in outwitting the opposition and providing brilliant entertainment.

In one international against Czechoslovakia at Tottenham in 1937, Stanley took over the role of marksman. His three goals were mainly responsible for England's 5–4 victory. When Matthews goes out for goals he is the greatest player on two feet. On this occasion he streaked through the Czech defenders and finished off with great shots. There are days, though, when he is inclined to overdo the spectacular side of his play. The crowds love the way he leaves an opponent on one foot, but he often delays the final pass until the goalmouth is covered. Although it is lovely to watch, it does not bring goals.

There was another day, however, when his wizardry brought goals. It was for England against Ireland at Old Trafford on 16th November 1938. The score was 7–0 for England. Stanley made the most of the openings for these goals and the man to profit from them was Willie Hall, his partner. He scored five of the seven, three of them in the record time of three and a half minutes. Every time Matthews streaked down the wing there was Hall waiting for his pass. His shooting that day had to be seen to be believed. Personally I have never seen anything better. Three of the goals came from shots from the edge of the penalty area. They flew past Twomey (Leeds), the Irish goalkeeper. Yet funnily enough, Hall really had no great reputation as a goal scorer. He was a clever ball player who looked after his partner like a dear friend. There was no fear of a wing forward being out of the game whilst Hall was by his side.

Another thing I shall never forget about this game is the sportsmanship of Billy Cook, Ireland's left-back, who was unlucky enough to run up against Matthews and Hall at their best. Though he must have been hopelessly beaten scores of times, Cook never once brought his tantalising opponents down. He took his beating like the great fellow he is. Matthews was given a terrific ovation as he left the field. As they got near the exit, Cook put his arm around Matthews' shoulder. I do not know what he said but the memory of the grand gesture always remains with me.

The third player, Mutch of Preston, had the year of his life. He secured the two major honours of the game within three weeks. First he won a Scottish cap, and Scotland beat England 1–0 at Wembley. Then an F.A. Cup-winner's medal when Preston beat Huddersfield 1–0. Of course, Mutch's part in the Cup final victory is part of soccer history. He scored the winning goal from a penalty kick in the last minute of extra time. As referee A.J. Jewell was about to blow his whistle for the end of the game, Mutch wormed his way through the Huddersfield defence. Just as he passed the penalty line and was preparing to shoot, he was brought down by big, fair-haired Alf Young, the 'Rock of Gibraltar' Huddersfield centre-half. When Mutch got up he appeared to be limping. There was a few seconds' hesitation, and then Mutch picked the ball up and placed it on the penalty spot.

At the time I thought it unwise of the Preston captain to allow Mutch to make the kick. I need not have worried. The sturdy Scottish inside-right banged the ball hard into the net over the head of Town goalkeeper Bob Hesford. So North End avenged a sixteen-year-old defeat at Stamford Bridge, and by the same means, for in 1922, North End had been beaten by Billy Smith's penalty kick for Huddersfield. Every detail of that Mutch penalty kick was engraved on my mind – through anxiety. I had to get to the B.B.C. as quickly as possible to do a short broadcast so I wrote out my little piece for the air whilst extra time was being played. As the minutes went by, I made my way to the exit door of the Stadium press box ready to dart away as soon as the whistle sounded. I did so, but my story then was useless. I had to write another in the taxi on my way to the B.B.C.

One feature of that final was that it was the fifth in which Joe Hulme, my former Arsenal colleague, had taken part. Joe had been transferred to the Yorkshire club a couple of years previously. It was a long way from the day when Joe arrived at Highbury as a raw youth. He finished with everything the game had to offer. Also, he played cricket for Middlesex and thought nothing of a hundred break at billiards. A great all-round sportsman.

Soon after that final, England played a momentous match in Berlin, beating Germany 6–3 before a 120,000 crowd, one of which was the 'Great Dictator', Adolf Hitler. Although I did not see the game, I was told about it scores of times. The England players gave a wonderful display in nerve-racking condition. Most of the Germans expected their countrymen to win – they were the 'Super-race'! Instead they were given an exhibition by a much cleverer team.

Before the game the England players lined up and, under protest, gave the Nazi salute. It caused a lot of controversy. Why, I do not know! When you visit a foreign land you expect to pay tribute. All the visiting teams do when they come here. A salute is after all just an acknowledgment, and nobody then could but acknowledge that Hitler and his evil system were the ruling power in the country. It was certainly not the players' fault. The fault, in my view, lay with those who arranged the visit in the first place.

Soon after the match in Germany came a first-class sensation in England. George Allison, Arsenal manager, broke all transfer records by paying £14,000 for Bryn Jones, Welsh international and Wolves inside-left, in August 1938. Arsenal were slipping downhill at this period. The sparkle had gone from the forward line with the retirement of Alex James. They were prepared to pay the price, more than £3,000 above the previous record, to restore the team to pre-eminence. But Bryn, a great player with Wolves, did not completely fit into Arsenal's style. He was a forward ever looking for the quick burst through the defence and a lightning shot. Arsenal wanted a schemer and tactician on the James pattern. Not only that, I am sure than Bryn was worried by the tag of 'the most expensive footballer'. Whenever I saw him play, he lacked the confidence he had shown with the Wolves. Still, Arsenal, who had been headlined as the 'Bank of England' team, thought the money well spent. The gates at Highbury rose to their former big figures and they made a huge profit. At the time there was the usual controversy: 'Is any player worth £14,000?' In certain circumstances the answer is 'yes'.

There is no doubt that many players have been worth much more than that to their clubs. For example, Jimmy Seed, when he changed the fortunes of Sheffield Wednesday; Tommy Lawton, who played a big part in Notts County's promotion year; Trevor Ford and Len Shackleton, the Sunderland forwards. They have been worth more even that the present record transfer fee of £34,000. Ford has now moved to Cardiff and Lawson to Arsenal. Inspiring captains, too, such as Clem Stephenson of Huddersfield, Billy Walker of Aston Villa and Joe Mercer of Arsenal, were worth their weight in gold. Any First Division club would, I am sure, gladly push up the record fee if they could get players like them.

It was during this 1938 season that the Football League celebrated its Golden Jubilee. I went to the banquet given to mark the occasion and met a lot of old-time stars, former opponents and friends. The best thing that came out of it was the launching of the £100,000 Jubilee Benevolent Fund for needy players. This fund is still going on. It has done invaluable work in helping players who have fallen on hard times.

The same year marked the 75th anniversary of the Football Association. One of the celebrations was an international match, England v 'Rest of Europe'. It took place at Highbury on 26th October 1938 before a tremendous crowd, and England beat the scratch team 3–0. What chiefly remains in my memory of this game was the attitude of many of the European players. They were strangers to one another, except for four of the defenders who were Italian. Whenever a movement broke down, they stood in the middle of the field waving their arms or shrugging their shoulders. They were all great ball players, but they just could not get together. And, of course, could not speak to each other.

England's combined team took matters easily. The forward line – Matthews (Stoke City), Hall (Spurs), Lawton (Everton),

Goulden (West Ham United), Boyes (Everton) – gave them a lesson in combined play. Once more it was proved that something more than eleven brilliant players are needed to make a team and that the most important thing of all is teamwork. All the successful teams, like Arsenal, Manchester United, Tottenham Hotspur and Newcastle United, have developed teamwork to a fine art. The manager who gets his team working together for the common good is the most valuable man in the game.

One of the first managers who cashed in on this policy was Major Frank Buckley, who had the reputation of being the highest paid man in the game. Within a few years of joining Wolves he gathered a young team that threatened to run away with the honours and, at one period, looked like bringing off the League and F.A. Cup double, last performed by Aston Villa in 1897. He adopted new methods. He signed many promising young players and, if they did not develop as he expected, let them go to another club – at a price. In the course of a few seasons this policy enriched Wolves by something like £70,000. But he retained a team that was just about the best in the country. Amongst them were stars like Stan Cullis, England's centre-half at the time, and now Wolves manager; centre-forward Denis Westcott and inside-left Dickie Dorsett, whose interchanging of positions brought many goals; right half-back Tom Galley and full-back Bill Morris.

They were the complete team, one of the fastest I ever saw, who won most of their games in decisive fashion. Some people were convinced that much of their success was due to an innovation – the gland treatment. Before each game the players received gland tonic tablets that were supposed to speed up their thoughts and actions. Personally, I did not believe glands or any stimulant had anything to do with their grand play. It was due, in my opinion, to the co-operation of eleven young athletes who were great footballers. After I had interviewed Buckley about the gland business, I was more than ever convinced that the effect of the treatment was psychological, not physical. I felt they would have been as good a side without any medicinal aid. But glands or no glands, there was one occasion when this great side failed completely. It was the 1939 F.A. Cup final against Portsmouth at Wembley.

Wolves were the hottest favourites in years for winning. They were in the running for the League championship, full of confidence and playing like a winning team. Portsmouth, on the other hand, were in a very humble place in the First Division table. In fact, at one time they were in the struggle against relegation. Few people gave them a chance against the eager young Wolves. I must confess that I did not fancy them at all. But on the great day they gave the 'dismal Johnnies' a shock by outplaying and outstaying the gland-filled Wolves. There was no doubting Portsmouth were worth the 4–1 victory that gave them the Cup, which they held for more than six years as it was the last Cup final before the Second World War.

Portsmouth outside-right, Fred Worrall, had the best game of his life. He pranced round the Wolves' defenders and had a hand in the goals, two of which were scored by outside-left Cliff Parker, one by centre-forward Jack Anderson and one by inside-right Bert Barlow. Bert, by the way, is still on active service with the Third Division South club Colchester United. Jimmy Guthrie, now chairman of the Players' Union, was Portsmouth captain that day. He helped to expose the gland myth. It must be said too that Wolves did not last the season in winning style. They were overhauled and passed in the First Division championship race by Everton.

The new champions had, in nineteen-year-old Tommy Lawton, the greatest centre-forward of the time. Just over two years previously, as a boy of seventeen, he had been transferred from Burnley to Everton for the record sum of £6,500. Not only did he help considerably towards winning the championship by scoring thirty-five goals but also he played for his country against Scotland, Ireland and Wales. His great headwork, moulded on the pattern of 'Dixie' Dean, and his clever footwork stamped him as England's leader for many years to come.

Before Portsmouth's great Wembley triumph I had my first experience of television. I do not want another like it. On the eve of the match I had to give a fifteen-minute talk on the prospects of the two teams, and say which I thought would win. Needless to say I chose the Wolves. Having prepared my script I reported to the studio. It was in Selfridges, the big London departmental stores. I was sent to a room to be 'made up'. It was something new to me to have paint and powder put on my face, but I managed to get over that. Then, just as I was about to sit down to speak, I pulled out my handkerchief and blew my nose. So back I went to undergo the 'makeup' process again. It made me feel like a schoolboy who had done something wrong. That was not the worst. Sitting under arc lights, which blazed down on the nape of my neck from about a yard away, made me feel dizzy. I thought I was going to pass out. Somehow I managed to get through – but only just. It must have been one of the worst exhibitions ever given on television.

It was just before this that I saw England gain one of the most sensational victories in the series of internationals with Scotland. I was at Hampden Park in April 1939. Since 1927, England had not beaten Scotland at Hampden. Few of the record 150,000 crowd expected them to do so on this occasion. They braved the lashing rain hoping to cheer another Scottish triumph. When centre-forward Dougal, of Preston North End, gave Scotland the lead, the Hampden roar was at its loudest. It abated little when Pat Beasley, then Huddersfield outside-left, equalised for England midway in the second half with a wonderful eighteen-yards shot. Excitement mounted as the teams strove for a winning goal. England were having the better of the play, but it looked as though they would never score, until the last minute, when peerless Stanley Matthews sent over a lovely centre. Up rose the dark head of centre-forward Tom Lawton and flicked the ball past Dawson, the Scottish goalkeeper.

It was a tremendous finish. Sitting in the press box I glowed with satisfaction at a great victory, snatched in the closing seconds. Memories of previous defeats were wiped out. Never shall I forget watching Eddie Hapgood, Arsenal left-back and England captain, bursting with enthusiasm at the success of his team. He jumped up and down with arms outstretched like a Maori doing a war dance! He said afterwards: "I've played all these years and this is the win I've longed for. I could have jumped over the moon in delight."

And Lawton, describing the scene in the England dressing room as the happiest he had ever seen, remarked: "I'm glad I scored that goal. It made up for the one I missed earlier."

The winning England team, with the exceptions of George Male, Arsenal right-back in place of Morris, and Frank Broome, Aston Villa wing-forward, taking over from Beasley at outside-left, drew 2–2 with Italy in Milan about a month later. They were the victims of one of the worst decisions ever seen in an international.

When the score was 1–1, Piola, the Italian centre-forward, punched the ball past goalkeeper Vic Woodley into the net. Despite protests, referee Dr Bauwens of Germany, allowed the goal to stand. Although I did not see the game, I spoke to several England players on their return. All agreed that it was a clear case of deliberate handling. They told me how the crowd laughed. The referee, they said, was the only one who did not see the handling. All was well when Willie Hall got the equalising goal for England. It would have been tragic if they had been beaten in the circumstances.

During the 1938 to 1939 season, there passed over one of the greatest legislators in the history of the game, Charles E. Sutcliffe, President of the Football League. Most of the changes in the League rules and regulations came from his fertile brain during forty years' membership of the Management Committee. He was the man who compiled the fixture list each season, a tremendous job and one bristling with difficulties. Even now the copyright of the League fixtures is in the hands of his son. And it was this copyright that led to one of the bitterest struggles in the history of the game.

Sutcliffe, a lawyer by profession, was convinced that football pools, which were then taking a big hold on the public, though nothing like the big concerns they are today, were harmful to the game. His attitude was: 'we ought to stop them now'. He considered that pools were contrary to all football law and procedure. They were using football, and the League, for their private profit. So he went all out to smash them. First, the League fixtures were made copyright by law. Then a meeting of League club officials was called in Manchester, to discuss the Sutcliffe plan to smash the pools. It was a simple one. Scrap the League fixtures as they stood and substitute others arranged each week by Mr Sutcliffe. They were to be communicated to the clubs only in time for them to make the necessary arrangements. These new fixtures were not made known until the day before the games so the pools were unable to issue coupons. There was one incident during the meetings of the club officials where a bold reporter, and a photographer from a prominent newspaper, eavesdropped and took pictures through an open window. They were discovered in time, went into the meeting, apologised and handed over their notes and photographs, which of course were destroyed.

For three weeks the plan was put into action. The pools were badly shaken, but then the secret of the games began to leak out in some mysterious fashion. The clubs too became impatient at the disturbance of their fixtures, and the loss in revenue owing to the lack of publicity. The plan was called off. It was just in time as far as the pools promoters were concerned. One of them told me that they could not have held out for more than another week. If the clubs had carried on there would have been no pools as we know them today.

One result of the struggle was that the pools people offered big money for the fixtures copyright. It was refused. The League would have nothing to do with what they called 'tainted' money. It is the same today. Pools are making enormous sums out of football yet pay nothing to help the game because League officials will not take money from gambling.

In my opinion, they should accept at least enough from the pools to inaugurate a Central Fund that could be used to help needy players, improve grounds and accommodation, support coaching in schools and even build stadiums all over the country. A lot of money is made out of football. I can see no real reason why a percentage of it should not be put back into the game. It does seem strange that pools in various parts of the world should use English matches, and that the game abroad should benefit from the money invested in them.

I believe that in Norway, for instance, a State pool was started which devoted half the money invested to prizes, with a limit of about £250 for the first prize-winner, and the other half to improve facilities for the playing of games all over the country. When this scheme was begun, nearly a quarter of a million pounds of the million staked was used for the building of playing fields and for other worthy purposes. In one year in Norway one hundred and eighty requests from various places for equipping playing fields were granted because of money received from the pools.

With playing fields so badly wanted in this country (everyone is agreed that more pitches would cut down serious accidents) it is surely wrong that some of the millions gained from the pools should not be diverted to this worthy purpose.

CHAPTER 11

JACK STAMPS' CUP FINAL

AND THOSE
'FAST, FIT AND FEARLESS DYNAMOS'

No sooner had the 1939 to 1940 season started than the Second World War broke out. League football came to an abrupt end. Players' contracts were suspended and they were free to join the Forces or go into industry. The big majority chose the Forces. But the game went on. Regional Leagues were formed to reduce travelling, and the players were paid thirty shillings for each game in which they played.

Of course, the teams were more or less scratch affairs. The players were allowed to assist the teams nearest to where they were stationed, or were working. Clubs like Arsenal had their grounds commandeered. Arsenal, in fact, shared the Spurs' ground at White Hart Lane. Later, others, like Millwall and Manchester United, were bombed out. Some, like Sunderland, did not take part at all. It was very unreal and brought situations like that at Aldershot where the local team consisted almost entirely of internationals. Cliff Britton, Stan Cullis and Joe Mercer, England's half-backs, were in the middle line, and there were forwards like Tommy Lawton and Jimmy Hagan to make Aldershot the big shots.

Sometimes visiting teams arrived at the grounds two or three players short. Appeals were made to the crowd for volunteers to make up the number. There were queer results too. I once saw Leslie Compton, Arsenal full-back, converted into a wartime centre-forward and score ten goals in one game against Luton. Double-figure scores were common at the time. Norwich City beat Brighton 18–0, the highest score ever recorded in the League.

157

There were even League Cup finals. Arsenal met Preston North End at Wembley in 1941 and there I got the first glimpse of a great right-wing – Tom Finney and Andy McLaren. These two youngsters, totalling thirty-five years between them, put up a great show in a 1–1 draw. They were even better in the replay at Blackburn where North End won 2–1. They both became internationals, Finney for England and McLaren for Scotland. Tom is still England's outside-right, and an outstanding figure in present-day football. His quick acceleration, wonderful ball control and sense of timing made him the great rival to Stanley Matthews. In fact, so great an all-rounder was Finney that when Matthews took over the outside-right position, Finney moved to the other wing and played just as well there, for England.

There was always the danger of bombing of course. Every club had spotters on the roof of the grandstand looking out for the raiders. Often, when the siren went, the game went on. I recall one game at Stamford Bridge, when the dire wailing was heard during the second half. But as far as I could see, not a single spectator left the ground.

There was another occasion when, on my way to a match at Brentford, I passed a scene of complete wreckage. I was told it was a gas explosion. Actually it was the first V rocket to fall on London.

Many internationals with Wales and Scotland were played during the six years of the war. But the players were not awarded international caps. Nor did the results count in the international series. It was only fair because none of the countries had a representative team in the field. Many of their greatest players were abroad, fighting for their country. The teams were really chosen from Service men and workers at home. None of them had done hard football training of any sort.

England had at the time a wonderful team, including Laurie Scott (Arsenal), George Hardwick (Middlesbrough), Frank Soo and Stan Matthews (Stoke City), Raich Carter (Sunderland), Don Welsh (Charleton Athletic) and Dennis Compton (Arsenal). They served England well in both wartime and peacetime games. In one season, 1943 to 1944, they ran up eight goals against Scotland at Maine Road, and six at Wembley.

In another wartime international at Hampden Park, Tommy Bogan, Hibernian and Scotland inside-right, was injured in a collision with Frank Swift the England goalkeeper in the first minute. He was taken off the field and some minutes later I saw Les Johnstone, Stoke inside-forward, come on in his place. Bogan has never played for Scotland again since, so his career as a Scottish international (wartime) lasted only a minute. Johnstone scored Scotland's only goal on this occasion. England replied with six shared between Lawton, Carter, Matthews and two newcomers, 'Sailor' Brown of Charlton and Leslie Smith of Brentford, who formed the left-wing.

As I had been turned down by the authorities because I was over age, I joined the Home Guard for the duration. It was strange that whilst serving I got the worst injury of my life. In a field exercise, I rose from the ground very quickly. I felt something snap at the back of my right thigh. I had pulled a muscle rather badly. It kept me limping for six weeks. I had never experienced anything like it whilst playing. The longest I can recall being out of action through injury is a week. I was the luckiest fellow imaginable in escaping the really hard knocks and collisions. It must have been owing to my long legs, or awkwardness on the field.

As soon as the war in Europe was over the League Management Committee got down to the business of planning the future of soccer. After many discussions it was decided that the League should restart in August 1945, not on the pre-war standard but with the First and Second Division split into two sections to cut travelling. The Third Division too was made into two regional groups. There was neither promotion nor relegation at the end of the season.

As many players were still in the Forces, clubs were allowed to include up to six guest players in their teams. That is why relegation was waived for the time being. Everything in the garden seemed to be lovely – except to the players. They were paid only £4 for each game in which they played. It was a one-sided arrangement that, I am pleased to say, lasted only a few months. I remember the many squabbles that went on during what was called the transitional period. It was grand for the clubs, many of whom placed themselves on a very sound footing financially. Attendances turned out very much higher than expected.

Frankly, I do not recall very much about this season, though I do remember that the F.A. Cup started again in full force. It was played on the home-and-away basis, each tie consisting of two games, and was decided on the aggregate of goals. Derby County won the Cup for the first time in their history. They beat Charlton Athletic in the final at Wembley after extra time, by four goals to one. It was big, burly Jack Stamps' final. The County centre-forward, one of the most consistent players and scorers they ever had, that day scored twice during the extra thirty minutes, when his powerful physique enabled him to brush aside a rapidly tiring opposition. At the end of ninety minutes the score was 1–1 and the goals were both scored by the same man, Bert Turner, Charlton right half-back and Welsh international.

Midway in the second half, Turner had the bad luck to divert a shot from Stamps into his own net. A minute later, he took a free kick about thirty yards from the Derby goal. The ball was diverted past the Derby goalkeeper by one of his own defenders. As the goal was credited to Turner he thus performed a feat I do not think will ever be done again in an F.A. Cup final – to score for and against his team within a minute!

But the outstanding feature of that season was the visit of Moscow Dynamos from Russia. They set the country talking. People still eagerly discuss them to this day. It took place in November 1945 and created a sensation from the start. Remember, the Russians were our allies and helped us to a great victory over the Germans. Everybody wanted to give them a warm welcome and to see how they could play the game. There were, however, difficulties over hotel accommodation and they refused to play any other than club teams, and no more than one game in seven days. They could not understand why we would not put off our League games so that one of our teams could play them on a Saturday. They also stipulated many things to be carried out before they would step on to the field. Among them were:

1. The names of the teams to oppose them to be submitted and not changed without their consent.
2. Arsenal to be one of the teams.
3. Substitutes to be allowed.
4. That one of the games should be refereed by an official they had brought with them.

He did in fact have charge of the Arsenal game at Tottenham. But his methods were peculiar to say the least. He patrolled one side of the field whilst each linesman had one half of the opposite touchline to look after.

It was hard to 'pin point' the Russians; they would give no interviews. One morning I went down to Stamford Bridge to watch them training. They never turned up. Instead they went to the White City, where no arrangements had been made to receive them. Eventually the Russians did get down to the business of playing, at Stamford Bridge. The Pensioners included guest players Jim Taylor and Joe Bacuzzi of Fulham, and also Tommy Lawton, who had just been transferred to Chelsea from Everton.

That was another thing the Russians could not fathom. They thought Lawton had been specially brought in to play against them and did not like it one bit. With so much publicity and argument, the game attracted a tremendous crowd. The gates were shut at least half an hour before it was timed to start. There were 82,000 inside Stamford Bridge, overflowing the greyhound track right onto the playing pitch. When I arrived at the ground there was a milling crowd clustered around the closed gates. Many clambered over at risk of injury. As the minutes went past I almost gave up hope of getting inside. But somehow I was pushed through to a small gate and got to the press box just in time to see the start.

The Russians certainly could play football. They made the ball do the work, moved into position quickly and served up soccer of a kind that we had not seen in Britain for many years. They drew with Chelsea 3–3. Even though their equalising goal near the end had a strong suspicion of offside, they were a grand team, equal to anything we could put up against them. Immediately after the game, the Football Association received requests from many countries asking to be put in touch with the Russians. They played only in Britain, however.

There was one point that they introduced which some of our clubs copied. For about twenty minutes before each game, the players went on the field for practice so that they could get warmed up and accustomed to the conditions. We follow it now to a certain extent.

Dynamos' second game was with Cardiff City at Ninian Park. It was a match that never should have been arranged. Most of the City team were working lads, some in the pits and in other hard jobs, who came straight from their work to play. They provided a 'Roman Holiday' for the Russians, who won by 10–1.

I saw the game among 45,000 Welshmen, and whilst admiring the tremendous fitness and skill of the Dynamos I could only sympathise with the plucky but outclassed Cardiff team.

The third game was with Arsenal at Tottenham. Because Arsenal had so many players abroad, they invited guest players for the occasion, amongst them Stanley Matthews. As the Russians had not received his name amongst the list of players submitted to them they objected strongly.

After a lot of argument, the match was played in dense fog, which made the proceedings a farce for the 54,000 onlookers. The Dynamos won 4–3 but, like most of the crowd, I saw very little of what went on. If it had been a Football League game I am sure it would have been abandoned. But the Russian referee in charge (according to their stipulation) somehow managed to play full time. Many of the Arsenal players told me afterwards it was a tough game with plenty of obstruction tactics, especially against the hapless Matthews.

Dynamos took their unbeaten record to Ibrox Park, to play Glasgow Rangers in their last game. They had established such a reputation that a crowd of 90,000 turned up. They drew 2–2 and Rangers were, I was told, lucky to equalise with a penalty kick, taken by big George Young, Rangers and Scotland captain.

Before the Russians returned to their country, with a record of two wins and two draws (nineteen goals for nine against) there was a meeting between British and Russian officials to discuss the many problems of the tour.

I went to the meeting, but it was a one-sided affair. When any of the British asked a question about the Russian way they did not understand. All they wanted was our training methods and our technique: our plans in general. There is no doubt that the Russians were a great side. I would like to point out though that they had spent several weeks in the Caucasus Mountains training for the tour. They were fast, fit and fearless. They were up against players who were out of training, working hard for their living and very short of match practice. That, however, does not detract from their fine exhibitions.

When the Dynamos got home they were made the 'Heroes of the Soviet Union'. They received monetary payment, graded according to their performances and conduct off and on the field. Some of them, I understand, got more than £1,000.

The Russians have neither amateurs nor professionals! They are all players engaged in a trade or profession besides football. No player has a contract with his club for wages. Under the F.A.'s definition of amateurism, the Dynamos were professionals. But I think we in this country could follow their pattern to the improvement of the game.

CHAPTER 12

SOCCER'S POST-WAR BOOM

AND HAMPDEN STAGES 'THE MATCH OF THE CENTURY'

Before the end of the transitional period of League soccer, during which the change over from wartime to peacetime conditions was made, there came the biggest disaster in the history of the game. During an F.A. Cup-tie between Bolton Wanderers and Stoke City at Burnden Park on 9th March 1946, the crowd broke through the closed gates. Many people were crushed against the barriers and others trampled underfoot. Thirty-three were killed and more than 500 injured. The game was stopped for a while. Then the referee got the players onto the field and the game was finished. The referee came in for a lot of criticism, but I do not see what else he could have done. I understand he acted on instructions from the police, who were convinced that if the game had not gone on, the consequences would have been even more serious. There was a Home Office inquiry afterwards. The result of it was that, from that day onward, gates were limited in size and the accommodation at all League grounds overhauled. Nothing had been done to them for years in the way of repairs and reconstruction. They were put in order afterwards.

When the League resumed on a pre-war basis, in season 1946 to 1947, soccer entered on a boom period. Records were set up at several grounds and many of the clubs made hitherto unheard of profits. Charges for admission to the games were increased by seventy-five per cent and the only people who did not flourish were the players. True, their wages were increased to £12 per week maximum in the playing season, but this was only a thirty-three per cent rise. It was not enough for the men who provided the entertainment.

During the first post-war season, mid-week football had been banned so as not to interfere with production from factories, mills and shipyards. But for this first full season, the ban was lifted, at least for the games in the evenings during the early and late stages. It was also agreed by the League clubs to keep a Saturday clear for the F.A. Cup third round. To make up for this the season began a week earlier on 23rd August. And thus another week's encroachment was made on the cricket season. At the time it was thought to be only temporary but it still remains today and there are no signs of it being changed. It has made the season far too long. To start playing League games in summer heat and sunshine, when players have not got a proper touch of the ball, is certainly not in the best interests of the game.

It is remarkable how often the season has opened in a heat wave. I recall one season, many years ago, when it was so hot on the first day that players collapsed on the field. In one League game at Hyde Road, Manchester City finished with seven players and Woolwich Arsenal, their opponents, with eight. Yet the result went down as if nothing had happened. It is common talk among the players that if they could choose their time for a holiday it would certainly be the first fortnight of the Soccer season. One is almost certain of hot summery weather then.

With a return in 1946 to 1947 to the old knockout system, the F.A. Cup competition proved an enormous attraction. The winners were Charlton Athletic, the team that had been beaten in the final by Derby County twelve months before. They beat Burnley, after extra time, by a goal from little Chris Duffy, the outside-left who cracked a first-time shot past Strong, the Burnley goalkeeper. As soon as he saw the ball enter the net, Duffy took to his heels to escape the congratulations of his teammates. He ran back to the halfway line and jumped straight into the arms of left-back Bert Shreeve. It was just like an acrobatic turn on the stage. I have never seen anything like it before or since.

Shortly after the final came what was described as the 'Match of the Century', at Hampden Park, Glasgow, between Great Britain and the 'Rest of Europe'. It was to celebrate the return of the four British Football Associations to the F.I.F.A. They had withdrawn in 1928 owing to differences of opinion concerning 'broken time' payments; that is, payment for loss of wages to amateur players. Though the point has never been settled satisfactorily to this day, the home associations decided to return to F.I.F.A. hoping that eventually some agreement would be reached.

The match proved to be a splendid success. About 140,000 people lined the classic Hampden slopes and, although Great Britain won comfortably by six goals to one, they were rewarded with a great display, affording a striking contrast between two styles. The Continentals relied upon short, along-the-ground passing, which usually broke down because of a lack of understanding amongst the players, who came from nine different countries. Sweden and Denmark each had two representatives; the rest were from countries as far apart as Czechoslovakia and Eire. Yes, Eire was represented in the European team by Johnny Carey, the right-half. He was made captain and I did not envy him his job of trying to blend the team together when he could speak none of their languages.

Great Britain gave a great display, the forwards particularly being fast and progressive. They carved holes in the Continental defence, which included left-back Willi Steffen of Switzerland, who afterwards came to England for a few months and played many fine games in Chelsea's League side. There were great players among the Continentals. The two who impressed me most were centre-forward Gundar Nordahl of Sweden and outside-left Carl Praest of Denmark. They were amateurs in their own countries, but had joined Italian clubs as professionals. They were paid handsome fees (I was told £10,000) to change their status. Of course, that is not allowed in Britain. When an amateur signs professional forms here, he gets nothing except the £10 signing-on fee. This payment to amateurs has reached fantastic proportions on the Continent. Hans Jeppson, the Swedish international centre-forward, received £18,000 when he went from one Italian club to another less than two years afterwards – £36,000 in two years! This besides big pay and bonuses must have made the British professionals' mouths water.

Jeppson, a blond six-footer, and one of the best centre-forwards in the game, will be remembered as the man who played a big part in saving Charlton Athletic from relegation from the First Division.

He came to England to learn business methods and to perfect his English. He joined Charlton when they were practically halfway up the table. One hat-trick he scored, against the Arsenal, proved his greatness. I remember seeing him in the first international game against England at Stockholm in May 1949. I spoke to him for a minute or two and found him a shy, modest youngster. At the time he was the tearaway type of centre-forward, young and full of dash. He developed so rapidly that when I saw him again about a year later he was just about the best centre-forward in Europe, or anywhere else.

It was interesting to see who were considered the greatest players in Britain at the time. The team against 'Rest of Europe' was: Swift (Manchester City), Hardwick (Middlesbrough), Hughes (Birmingham City), Macaulay (Brentford), Vernon (West Bromwich Albion), Burgess (Spurs), Matthews (Blackpool), Mannion (Middlesbrough), Lawton (Chelsea), Steel (Morton) and Liddell (Liverpool). So there were five Englishmen, three Scots (Macaulay, Steel and Liddell), two Welshmen (Hughes and Burgess) and one Irishman (Vernon). Although I did not entirely agree with the selections, they put up a marvellous show that sent British prestige soaring on the Continent.

The game made the reputation of at least one of the Great Britain team – Billy Steel of Morton, the Scottish League club from Greenock. Though on the small side, he was exceedingly clever and following this fine display, which included the scoring of a great goal from twenty yards out, many English clubs were keen to secure his services. Eventually he went to Derby County, taking over the inside-left position from the Irish international Peter Doherty, who had been transferred to Huddersfield.

The County inside-right was Raich Carter, England's inside-right, and the finest inside-forward of his generation. Derby paid a new record transfer fee for Steel. The £15,500 for Steel eclipsed the old record, set up by Arsenal when getting Bryn Jones, by £1,500. It was the start of the sensational rise in transfer fees which saw tremendous sums handed over, like £26,500 for Eddie Quigley, when he went from Sheffield Wednesday to Preston North End; £29,500 paid for Trevor Ford by Sunderland to Aston Villa; and the biggest of all at present, £34,000 for Jackie Sewell, Notts County inside-right, by Sheffield Wednesday. Of course, there were outcries against what was called 'this foolish expenditure'. 'Clubs heading for bankruptcy' was the general theme of articles. But the clubs who paid out these colossal amounts are still flourishing.

Actually, the money expended was not as big as it looked. Most of these teams made huge profits during the boom years and nearly half of the fees would have gone to the Government in income and profits tax. Well, England's stock at this time was very high although the team did get a few shocks in the 1946 to 1947 season. It opened promisingly enough with a 7–2 victory over Ireland in Belfast, where Tom Finney, Preston outside-right, gave one of his most brilliant performances. He had taken the place of the injured Stanley Matthews. Finney provided most of the opening for the goals, three of which were scored by Wilf Mannion, the blond little Middlesbrough inside-left, a clever schemer and tactician who played a big part in England's revival after the war.

But only two days after this great victory, the England team let us down rather badly with a disappointing show against Eire at Dalymount Park, Dublin. It was the first time England had played in the Irish capital for many years. A packed house was prepared for a great show and a handsome beating. But England just scraped through by one goal to nothing. It was a game I shall always remember. The big crowd cheered from the start, trying to whip their team into a splendid fervour. As their men held their own with the Englishmen so the excitement mounted. It reached a crescendo in the second half when the Irish commanded a large share of the play. They were unlucky when their inside-left, Alex Stevenson of Everton, crashed a shot against the cross-bar. Almost straight away, England went into the attack and Tom Finney got the winning goal amid a silence that could be felt. From a wildly enthusiastic gathering, the crowd became as silent as the tomb. Still, the Irish boys had given a wonderfully plucky show. They gave the English team a really good one, their biggest fright – until they went to Switzerland the following May and were beaten 1–0!

On the way down from Belfast to Dublin with the England team, I had an embarrassing experience. When the train arrived at Dundalk, Customs officers came aboard. I did not think anything about them, sitting as I was in a compartment reading a book. I opened my luggage for inspection and carried on reading. Suddenly a Customs officer said: "What have you got here?"

I looked up and saw he had a parcel in his hand. Then I remembered I had put in my suitcase about a pound of tea that I was taking to give to a friend in Dublin. When I replied to his question: "Oh, it's only tea I'm giving to a friend," he then said: "Don't you know that carrying tea is one of the biggest rackets in Ireland? You're liable to imprisonment."

I did not know what to do or say. Just as I was getting really worried a fellow reporter, Ivan Sharpe, who was travelling with some of the players in the next compartment put his head round the carriage door.

"What's the matter, Charlie, having trouble?" he asked.

I answered: "Yes, it's about some tea I'd forgotten all about."

When he heard Sharpe, the officer said: "Are you one of the England party?"

I replied: "Yes."

So he just marked my suitcase with his green chalk and the episode ended. The tea happened to be part of our home rations; none of my family are tea drinkers, as we prefer coffee at all times after the breakfast meal. So we were able to save a little to pass on to friends occasionally. Sharpe is the doyen of English journalists. He played as an amateur in the early years of the century, gaining several international caps, and was a member of the England team that won the Olympic Games championship. He certainly got me out of a very tricky situation.

It was on this trip that I got into another of those arguments that were my lot through my football days. The England party had no trainer in charge of the team. I voiced an objection. There was a radiotherapist to attend to any injuries, but no one, except perhaps the twelfth man, to look after the players personally, or their playing kit. Every club is scared of an epidemic like influenza, eczema or itch sweeping through the camp. I have seen it happen in less than twenty-four hours. Raining gear and match kit are guarded very carefully to prevent anything like that happening. The argument against having a trainer was that if he 'mollycoddled' the players they would be slower in thought and action. If they looked after their own kit and themselves, their minds function more quickly on the field. My reply to this was that the slight mental benefit gained by a player looking after his own kit was more than often offset by the risk run in inviting trouble. I must have won the argument because since then a trainer has been in charge of England teams.

There was one amusing incident in which I was concerned. Before the game in Belfast, I played golf with Stacey Lintott, a noted journalist. He was a commanding personality, 6 ft 5 in. tall and built proportionately. He looked for all the world like a bishop. He turned out for the golf match in open-necked shirt and khaki shorts, like a scoutmaster. It was suitable gear for a warm, sunny day. When we finished the round and went back to the hotel, there was a message waiting: 'Mr W. C. Cuff, president of the Football League, who was in charge of the party, would like us to attend a little ceremony to be held in a private room.' We went to the room and sat down. As soon as we did so, Mr Cuff made a speech. He paid a grand tribute to Stacey and said he would like to make him a presentation on behalf of the League, the players and the journalists present. I thought he would hand over a trophy of some sort. Instead he went to the mantelpiece and groped behind a huge clock standing in the middle. He brought forth a child's bucket and spade and solemnly handed it over to Lintott. We all howled with laughter. Stacey took it like a sportsman and made a speech in reply that nearly brought the roof down.

The 1946 to 1947 season wound up in a blaze of glory for the England team. Only nine days after being beaten by Switzerland in Zurich, they trampled on the might of Portugal in Lisbon and ran up the colossal score of ten goals to nil. Although I did not see the game, being engaged in a golf game, every Englishman who saw it agreed it was the finest exhibition ever given by an international side. Portugal were, at the time, one of the best teams on the Continent. What Switzerland had done, they could do, and much better too. But they got the biggest shock of their lives.

The English forwards, Matthews (Blackpool), Mortensen (Blackpool), Lawton (Chelsea), Mannion (Middlesbrough) and Finney (Preston), simply ran riot. Lawton and Mortensen each scored four times and gave the Portuguese defenders the worst day of their lives. Even though the Portuguese brought on substitutes during the course of the game, they could not hold the English men in white. They were so demoralised at their utter rout that some of them did not turn up at the banquet after the game.

That was English football at its best, and I regret to say we have not seen many international exhibitions like it since.

Though I did see one glorious display given by Stanley Matthews that I shall never forget. It was against Belgium in Brussels in September 1947. Stanley was at the peak of his form and, thanks mainly to his wizardry, England soon set up a three-goals lead. Then the team began to indulge in fancy work, textbook play that, whilst it was pretty to watch, got nowhere. In fact it spurred the Belgians on and before we knew where we were they scored twice and were playing so well that at any time I expected them to equalise. Then midway in the second half, Matthews got the ball near the halfway line. He waltzed round one defender after another, evading their swift lunges with consummate ease. As he approached the goal, leaving four Belgians on the ground, he noticed Tom Finney standing uncovered in the goalmouth. With wonderful precision, Matthews placed the ball right on to Finney's head. Tom nodded it into the net. It was one of the best goals ever recorded and the beginning of a recovery that ended in a 5–2 win for England.

Then, about six weeks later, in November 1947, I saw one of the most dramatic goals of the international tournament. England (with only one change in the team that had beaten Belgium: Phil Taylor for Tim Ward at right half-back) were playing Ireland at Goodison Park. With only seconds left for play England were leading by two goals to one. Reporters were busy with their stories, describing a hard-earned England victory. I must admit I was one of them. Suddenly, Ireland broke away on the left wing. Tommy Eglington, Everton outside-left playing for his country on his own ground, received the ball near the touchline, about twenty-five yards from the England goal. Without hesitation, he sent the ball hurtling across the goalmouth about waist high. With superhuman effort, Peter Doherty, who was then the Huddersfield Town inside-left, threw himself at the ball, connected it with his head and sent it with bullet-like force past Frank Swift, the England goalkeeper. Doherty was at full stretch, some three feet from the ground, when he headed this great equalising goal. He must have jarred himself pretty badly when he struck the ground. Big Swift helped him to his feet and with his arm around his shoulder, walked towards the dressing room. The referee signalled full time before play could be restored.

Doherty, one of the greatest inside-forwards who ever wore the green Irish jersey, is now manager of Second Division team

Doncaster Rovers, and also has charge of Ireland's international teams. He took part in many great Irish successes. His auburn hair bobbed up all over the field. He was a real leader who got the best out of his men by his tireless example.

CHAPTER 13

THE GENIUS OF FINNEY

THE COURAGE OF MORTENSEN, AND FRANKLIN'S BOGOTA ADVENTURE

The season 1947 to 1948 was undoubtedly the peak season of League football. More than 40,000,000 watched the games with receipts of something like four million pounds. The aggregate was five million higher that in any previous season. One of the highlights that I can remember was England's 2–0 victory over Scotland at Hampden Park. And the man who set England on the road to victory was outside-left Tom Finney. Early in the second half Tom ran to a pass from Stan Pearson, Manchester United inside-left, cut inside Govan, the Scottish right-back, and hit a beautiful right-foot shot past goalkeeper Ian Black, now with Fulham. It spurred England on to great heights. Stan Mortensen added a second goal that completed the discomfiture of the Scots and gave England the international championship.

It was Mortensen, too, who was the central figure in the F.A. Cup competition that season. He played a notable part in putting his club, Blackpool, into the final for the first time. In the semi-final with Tottenham Hotspur at Villa Park, Mortensen saved his side when all seemed lost. There were only three minutes to play, and the Spurs were leading by a goal, when Stanley Matthews sent the ball through the middle of the Spurs' defenders. Mortensen ran on to the ball, worked himself clear, then with a clear opening he stumbled. In some miraculous way he recovered his balance and shot past Ted Ditchburn for the equalising goal. Then in extra time Mortensen scored two more goals that gave Blackpool a 3–1 victory and the right to meet Manchester United in the final at

Wembley. And to Stanley Matthews, his first chance of gaining a Cup-winner's medal.

But Matthews did not get the coveted honour. Though Mortensen had a hand in Blackpool's first goal, scored by right-back Eddie Shimwell from a penalty kick awarded when Mortensen was brought down and scored the second goal himself, Blackpool were beaten by four goals to two. The turning point in this classic game, admitted to be the best Cup final seen at Wembley, was a quickly taken free kick by Johnny Morris, the United inside-right. He placed the ball correctly onto Jack Rowley's head and into the net it went for the all-important equalising goal. After that, United took charge and won deservedly. The big crowd sympathised with Mortensen and Matthews. They wanted the great Stanley to get the winner's medal to crown a wonderful career. When they walked off the Wembley field, Mortensen waved to the crowd. They gave him a wonderful ovation. Mortensen said afterwards:

"I could not see my way to the Royal enclosure where the Cup and medals were to be presented. My eyes were filled with tears."

Yes, Stanley Mortensen was a wonderful character. During the war he was in an air crash and came out with terrible wounds that threatened to put an end to his career. But his wonderful spirit pulled him through that critical time and enabled him to become one of the finest inside-forwards in the game. His electric dashes through opposing defences have brought many goals and a name comparable with that of Steve Bloomer, one of the old immortals of England and Derby fame. He had the same sallow complexion, the same slight build and the same happy knack of scoring priceless goals. Mortensen will go down in history as one of the few men who have played for two countries. Born on Tyneside, he was, of course, qualified to play only for England. But he also turned out in the red shirt of Wales. During a wartime international between England and Wales at Wembley, Ivor Powell, the Welsh inside-left, was injured and left the field. A few minutes later, I saw a slight, red-shirted figure trot out onto the field. There was no mistaking who it was. I recognised at once it was Mortensen by his short-striding gait and the way he ran with his elbows bent and close to the sides. He had been sitting near the touchline, an England reserve who volunteered at once as soon as he learned that Wales had no twelfth man ready. It was Mortensen who, some months later, was responsible for one of the best and most dramatic goals ever scored by an England forward. It was against Italy in Turin in May 1948.

At the time Italy were recognised as the best team on the Continent. It was before the tragic air disaster that robbed them of the cream of Italian talent. They were confident they could beat England, and for the first twenty-five minutes of the game it looked as if their confidence was justified. By speed and cleverness with the ball, they made England look a second-class side. Only the brilliance of goalkeeper Frank Swift and superlative defensive play by Laurie Scott (Arsenal), Billy Wright (Wolves) and Neil Franklin (Stoke City) kept the Italians from piling up a winning lead. In the twenty-seventh minute Stanley Matthews got the ball near the halfway line. He cut inwards and sent a through pass to Mortensen. Stanley seized on the ball, flashed past Parola and Eliana, the Italian defenders, to the penalty area. There I thought he had lost control of the ball. He sent it ahead until it was on the edge of the penalty area and only four or five yards from the bye-line. But whilst going at full speed he crashed the ball hard into the Italian net when everyone, including the Italian goalkeeper, expected him to centre. It seemed an impossible angle from which to score. When I asked him about it after the game he said: "I saw the goalkeeper move out and leave a space in the goal, so I hit the ball hard. I took a chance and it came off."

That goal, out of the blue, transformed the England team. They proceeded to give a display that has rarely been equalled. They ran the Italian team off their feet by sheer skill, a blend of combination and punch that made them irresistible. Tom Lawton and Tom Finney added goals for England, who in the second half gave the Italians an object lesson in the way the game should be played. It made me proud to watch them, and also pricked the bubble of Italian invincibility.

Before the game in Turin, the England team – and I was with them – stayed in Stresa, a beautiful town on one of the Italian lakes. There I met with an awkward adventure. One day I had gone with the party on a sight-seeing tour. When I returned I wanted to send my story to the *News Chronicle* in London. I found there was considerable difficulty in getting my copy away and was thankful when an Italian journalist offered to send it to London from his office in Milan. You can judge my astonishment when I saw the headlines in one Italian paper the next morning:

'BUCHAN REVEALS THE SECRETS OF ENGLAND'S PLAN TO BEAT ITALY!' It turned out that it was a Communist paper to whose offices my story had been sent. They had converted it into a dramatic story, but it was nothing like the one I wrote.

One day I walked into a Stresa restaurant to have a meal. After I had finished the main dish I thought I would like some pancakes. I asked the waitress to bring me some. I'm afraid my knowledge of the language was not very good as she came back to the table with pen and ink!

Money was a scarce commodity on this trip. Journalists are allowed only a certain amount each day and with expensive meals and hotels to pay for it is usually not enough. It certainly was not in Stresa. I had miscalculated my funds so badly that I had to spend a day in my bedroom. That had been paid for but I had not enough in my pockets to pay for a meal.

Soon after the beginning of the 1948 to 1949 season I saw the passing of two great England players, Tommy Lawton and Jimmy Hagan, Sheffield United's scheming inside-forward. They were in the England team that drew 0–0 with Denmark in Copenhagen. It was a match that should have been won comfortably, but they were not the worst offenders by any means. I though both played well in midfield and deserved at least another chance for England, but it never came. Lawton was slower on the ball it is true, but he was still a great leader. He was dangerous in front of goal, especially with his head. A few months before this game he had been transferred from Chelsea to Notts County for a £20,000 fee and the player Bill Dickson, a half-back who has since played several times for his country, Ireland, and last year left Chelsea for Arsenal. Lawton's leadership took Notts County from the Third Division South to the Second Division in less than eighteen months. His presence added many thousands to the County gates.

After the game in Copenhagen, I was one of a party that went on a tour of the famous Carlsberg brewery. There I met John Hansen, who had been the Danish inside-right in the game. During our conversation he asked me for some advice: "I have been offered £10,000 to sign professional for an Italian team, what do you think I should do?"

John told me he had a junior appointment in the brewery and hoped to get an established position there before long. I suggested he should take the Italian offer and resume his business life on his return to Denmark. Either that, or start a business of his own with the money he would make in Italy. Hansen evidently took my advice for shortly afterwards he signed for the Italian club. He is still in Italy.

Vigo Jensen, a splendidly built left-back, was another member of the Danish team. He came to England and after qualifying (an alien has to live two years in the country before he can become a professional with a League club) signed for Hull City.

The unexpected draw in Denmark was not the only surprising feature of the 1948 to 1949 season. There were also the remarkable exploits of Portsmouth, who won the First Division championship for the first time in their history, and of Leicester City, a Second Division team who gallantly fought their way through to the F.A. Cup final. Portsmouth, under the captaincy of Reg Flewin, and with great players like Jim Scoular, Jim Dickinson and Len Phillips, had a wonderful chance of bringing off the League and Cup double. They did win the League but came a cropper in the Cup semi-final with Leicester. I saw this game at Highbury and there was no doubt the better side won. Leicester, who were more like League champions than Portsmouth, pulled off a great victory after being a goal down at half-time.

Then came the long five weeks' wait before the final. During that time Leicester ran into all sorts of trouble in the way of injuries to players. Two days before the final I went down to see them in their training quarters at Stevenage. They were awaiting hospital reports on the progress of Don Revie, their clever inside-right, who had a nose haemorrhage. He did not recover in time to play.

City made the mistake of gambling with putting Jim Harrison, normally a full-back, at centre-forward with Jack Lee, the regular leader at inside-right, in the final against Wolverhampton Wanderers at Wembley. The gamble did not come off and they were beaten 3–1. Even there I thought they were unlucky. Early in the second half, when they were 2–1 down, they had a goal disallowed, which I thought was a good one. Ken Chisholm, their big, burly inside-left, was undoubtedly offside when he received the ball before shooting into the net. But it seemed to me the ball struck a Wolves defender on its way from outside-right Mal Griffiths to the inside-left. An equalising goal then would have given City a fine chance of pulling the game out of the fire. Soon afterwards, however, Sammy Smyth, Wolves' Irish international inside-right, clinched the issue with one of the best goals ever seen at Wembley. Smyth picked up the ball from a clearance by the City left-back a few yards from the halfway line. He beat three defenders in a beautiful solo effort before slamming the ball past Bradley, the Leicester goalkeeper.

The Cup this season was also notable for the great deeds of Hull City, a Third Division Northern club. In turn they won at Blackburn, Grimsby and Stoke before falling at home to Manchester United by a single goal in the sixth round. Hull had as player/manager Raich Carter, the former England inside-forward. They not only did well in the Cup but also won the Third Division Northern Section championship and promotion. Raich was getting on in years but his astute generalship played a big part in the team's outstanding success.

The uncertainty of the game was exemplified by the case of Southampton. At Easter, with only six games left to play, they were leading the Second Division by eight points. Promotion seemed assured. I saw them beat Tottenham Hotspur, one of their strongest challengers at the time, at White Hart Lane. The only goal of the game was scored by little Charlie Wayman, their centre-forward. He pulled a muscle badly during the game and did not play again that season. His absence was so badly felt that Southampton got only two points from the six remaining games. They were beaten on the post by Fulham and West Bromwich Albion, who went above them on the very last day of the season. Now Southampton are in the Third Division, of course.

England met with mixed fortunes in the international tournament. After beating Ireland 6–2 in Belfast, Stan Mortensen getting a hat-trick, and Wales 1–0 at Villa Park, where they battled bravely with ten men, right-back Laurie Scott getting a knee injury that put an end to his international career, they were beaten 3–1 by Scotland at Wembley in the deciding game. Scotland were champions.

That defeat was bad enough, but worse followed during a tour of Scandinavia and France which was undertaken in May. The first game of the tour was against Sweden in Stockholm and England were beaten by 3–1. It was the first international for Spurs goalkeeper Ted Ditchburn. He made an error of judgement early in the game that cost the first goal. I fear the mistake had a marked effect on Ditchburn's international appearances for, although he was a member of the teams that toured Brazil and South America in later years, he has been overlooked for a long time by F.A. selectors.

The defeat at Stockholm, the first ever by Sweden, caused the selectors to overhaul the team before the second game with Norway in Oslo. There was a 'B' team match with Finland in Helsinki two days after Stockholm and players who were successes in that game, like Bert Williams, Wolves goalkeeper; Bill Ellerington, Southampton full-back; Jimmy Dickinson, Portsmouth left-half; Johnny Morris, Derby County inside-right and Wilf Mannion of Middlesbrough were drafted into the England team.

They came off, too, against Norway, winning four goals to one, all except Williams who stood down in order to allow big Frank Swift to make a farewell appearance. Swift, a great goalkeeper and strong personality, announced his retirement at the end of the season. The F.A. invited him on the tour so that he could play a last game. He put up a grand show and the Norwegian people gave him a wonderful reception. The place of Swift as a humorist and entertainer among England's touring team has never been adequately filled. There was never a dull moment when Swift was in the group. His antics with Lawton and Mortensen whiled away many long journeys and kept the players in splendid spirits. The nearest to approach him now is Bill Eckersley, Blackburn Rovers left-back, a born comic.

As the match with Norway did not start until the evening, I spent the afternoon at the home of my old friend Jorgan Juve. He lived about a quarter of a mile from the ground where the game was played. Just before we sat down to tea his wife said: "Oh, I would like to make a cup of tea like you get in England, but I can't."

So I volunteered to try. As I am about the worst man in the world around the house (everything seems to break in my hands) it was a bold attempt, but the tea turned out to be first class. I am sure I have never made a pot like it since!

As we left for the game I made arrangements with Jorgan to use his phone directly after the game. I wrote my report whilst the second half was on and dashed straight to the phone. My luck held good and my story was in the *News Chronicle* office less than fifteen minutes after the last kick of the game. This business of getting reports through from the games has given me more headaches than the many matches in which I played throughout the years. Many weary hours I have spent anxiously waiting beside the phone for calls to come through. The worst part about it is that you can do nothing about it.

The last stage of the journey was to Paris, where England were to play France four days later. We went by air, breaking the journey at Rotterdam, where we touched down for an hour. That trip from Oslo to Rotterdam was the most terrifying I have ever undertaken. Luckily most of the England team had left by an earlier plane and missed the worst part of it. We ran into a thunderstorm soon after leaving the airport and the plane dipped in such a way that I thought we must crash. Worst of all was the lightning. It seemed to go straight through the plane in front of me. I expected to be hit at any minute. I did not know then that planes were immune against lightning. I wish I had because I have never been so frightened in my life, not even during the First World War. When we landed at Rotterdam the tarmac was flooded. But I have never been so glad to step out into water. Luckily for me it did not lessen my love for air travel. I still look forward to any long trips by plane.

With the exception of Bert Williams for Frank Swift in goal, and Jack Rowley for Stan Mortensen at centre-forward, England's team against France was the same as did so well against Norway. England won by three goals to one, a well-deserved victory.

The match provided another example of the up-and-downs of an international career. In the first minute goalkeeper Williams ran out to intercept a centre from the French right-wing. He got his hands to the ball but only turned it into his own net. Williams hid his face in his hands in anguish. It was a worse mistake than the one made by Ted Ditchburn in Oslo, which nearly put an end to Ditchburn's international carer before it had really started. Williams, however, made a wonderful recovery. He afterwards brought off many brilliant saves and played a big part in the victory. He was England's first choice for many games after that unhappy beginning.

There was one other unusual incident during this tour. It concerned Eric Parsons, West Ham United outside-right now with Chelsea. Parsons played for England 'B' against Finland in Helsinki and was one of the outstanding figures in the game. When it was over, the players lined up on the field, and the crowd voted, by their measure of applause, for the best players. Parson was acclaimed England's best. He was given a silver statuette to mark the occasion. It was the only time I had seen such a ceremony after a game. Parsons was contemporary with Tom Finney, otherwise he might have been chosen as England's outside-right in other matches. But early next season he received a knee injury from which he took a long time to recover.

Just when it seemed that England's fortunes had taken a turn for the better, there came a severe jolt in the shape of a home defeat at the hands of Eire, the least powerful of the neighbouring countries. It happened at Goodison Park in September 1949; the score was 2–0 for Eire. It was the first defeat England had suffered on their own soil from a visiting country. Well do I remember watching the humiliating proceedings. England, with a strong team, started confidently enough and when Con Martin, the Eire centre-half, put his side ahead from a penalty kick nobody worried. We thought it was only a question of time before a forward line which included Peter Harris, Johnny Morris, Jesse Pye, Wilf Mannion and Tom Finney got cracking. But the Eire defenders had other ideas. They had little difficulty in holding England's attacks and when Peter Farrell (Eire's captain who, although he was normally a left-back, had taken over the inside-right position) added a second goal, the writing was on the wall. The Eire defenders thoroughly exposed the lack of ideas in England's front line. They fully deserved their victory. I sat in the Goodison grandstand thinking how ironic it was that where countries like Argentina, Austria, Italy, Yugoslavia and all the Continentals had failed, gallant little Eire had succeeded.

The England defeat was the first shock in what proved to be a most exciting season in which most of the championship, promotion and relegation problems were not settled until the very last day. For instance, Portsmouth won the First Division championship for the second year running, only because they had a superior goal average to Wolverhampton Wanderers.

Then there was a stirring three-cornered duel between Sheffield Wednesday, Sheffield United and Southampton for the second place in the Second Division promotion race. There, Tottenham Hotspur won the championship by a street. Their promotion companions were not decided until the last day. As I had a B.B.C.

engagement that evening I could not go out to watch any of the deciding games. It was almost as exciting, however, waiting for the results to come through.

I recall the Southampton affair. They beat West Ham by three goals to two. If they had prevented West Ham from scoring, they would have finished in second place; as it was they ended up fourth. Sheffield Wednesday, who drew 0–0 with Spurs, were second and Sheffield United third.

Arsenal won the Cup that year with a well-merited 2–0 victory over Liverpool at Wembley Stadium. Both goals were scored by Reg Lewis, a clever forward who had the happy knack of scoring goals when they were most vitally needed. But, although Arsenal fully earned their third F.A. Cup success, I thought they were the luckiest team in the world to have the opportunity. In the semi-final with Chelsea at White Hart Lane, they were two goals down in the first half. Roy Bentley scored twice and Chelsea looked to be certain winners. Then, as the referee was looking at his watch to signal half-time, Arsenal forced a corner on the right-wing. Freddie Cox took the kick. He hit the ball hard and just above head high. The Chelsea defenders stood as if spellbound and were thunderstruck as the ball, just as it reached the near post, turned at right angles and finished up in the back of the net. It was one of the most amazing goals I have ever seen. It did not seem possible for the ball to go into the net beside the near upright. It can only be described as 'a freak'.

That goal put new heart into Arsenal. It was no surprise when Leslie Compton headed the equalising goal in the second half from another corner kick, and Arsenal went on to win the replay on the same ground 1–0. The winning goal, I might add, was scored by Cox.

During the summer preceding this season, in 1949, the League was increased from eighty-eight to ninety-two clubs. Scunthorpe United and Shewsbury Town were admitted to the Northern Section of the Third Division, Colchester United and Gillingham to the Southern Section. Although they have held their own in the League since then, I still think it is a mistake to add to the number of League clubs. There were not enough players to go round the eighty-eight teams and additions can only lead to a lowering of the playing standard. I would much rather the numbers were cut down, not increased.

The following summer of 1950 was full of adventure and colourful incidents as far as I was concerned. First there was a Continental trip to Portugal and Belgium with the England team, then a short holiday in Dublin with Doctor Kevin O'Flanagan, the most versatile athlete of his generation, and finally the never-to-be-forgotten tour to South America to follow England's fortunes in the World Cup competition. It all began very promisingly. After a pleasant week's stay in Estoril, a lovely seaside resort a few miles from Lisbon, we went to the National Stadium for the game between Portugal and England. It is a magnificent achievement, this Stadium, nestling among the hills in countryside which resembles a typical English setting. With the exception of Rio Stadium, it is the best I have ever visited.

England, with a new forward line which had Jackie Milburn at outside-right (in my opinion his best and proper position), Roy Bentley at centre-forward and Tom Finney outside-left, beat Portugal by five goals to three. The victory was a triumph for Finney, who scored four of the five goals, two of them from penalty kicks. Finney always finds his scoring boots when playing on the left wing. Perhaps it is only natural as he is able to use his right foot more effectively when on the opposite wing.

On the Tuesday after the game we flew to Brussels for the match with Belgium on the Thursday. Shortly after I settled down in the Brussels hotel there came a telephone message for me. I was told to go at once to Amsterdam, where an England 'B' team were to play Holland the next day. The 'B' team had received a severe drubbing from Italy 'B' in Milan the previous Thursday and I had to report on their showing against Holland. This journey to Amsterdam sounded easy; actually it was a ticklish business. You see, no arrangements had been made for my visit and, owing to currency restriction, I had no Dutch money, nor had I permission to get any. So with just a little Belgian money in my pocket I set off with Clifford Webb of the *Daily Herald*. Neither of us could speak a word of Dutch. Neither had we the money to pay for a meal throughout the journey.

By sign language we got through the Customs and over the frontier. Luckily, towards the end of the trip we got into conversation with an Englishman who kindly treated us to a cup of coffee and a bun. It was really a dismal ride. Then to crown all, the England 'B' team gave another shocking exhibition. They were beaten hands down by the amateur Holland team by three goals to nil. There was no excuse for their second failure. All the side were up to international standard really. Laurie Scott, Bill Eckersley, Bill Nicholson, Billy Watson, Jesse Pye, Eddie Baily and Bob Langton had all played for England, yet here they could not pull together. I have rarely seen a side wearing England's colours so outclassed. There have been other 'B' team collapses, like the 7–1 drubbing from France 'B'. The only explanation I can put forward for them is that the players, in trying to play academic football, forsake their usual methods, overlooking the fact that drive and enthusiasm are required just as much in internationals as in League games.

We travelled back to Brussels the next morning low in spirits. We were heartened, however, by the performance of the England team against Belgium. They won comfortably by four goals to one. In the second half they gave a display worthy of a great England side. They had been somewhat disturbed in the first half by an early injury to Jackie Milburn, again at outside-right. Jimmy Mullen of Wolves came out as substitute. After a few minutes he changed places with outside-left Tom Finney. Mullen scored the first goal that restored the team's confidence and after that it was plain sailing to victory.

Soon after I got back to England I went to Dublin for a few days' holiday. But with a character like Doctor O'Flanagan, a native of the city, holiday is not the right word! His energy was inexhaustible and he nearly walked, or ran, me off my feet. But I enjoyed every minute of it. Neatly built, like all athletes, O'Flanagan had a unique record. He played for Ireland in both soccer and rugby internationals in the same season. He was also an even-time sprinter, which came in very useful in his position of wing three-quarter. He was the daredevil type of soccer forward who was never afraid to use his weight when the occasion demanded. Though not a polished soccer player, he was very effective. He gave great service to Arsenal in many First Division games. During the year 1946 the doctor set up a record that may never be equalled. In successive weeks he played rugby for Ireland against the Australians and soccer for his country against England. He was chosen for an international for the third week running, but missed the plane over and arrived too late to play.

When I got back from the holiday there came the first of many shocks that preceded England's visit to Rio de Janeiro for the World Cup competition. It was in the shape of a letter that Neil Franklin, Stoke City and England centre-half, had written to the F.A. In this almost unprecedented message, the great centre-half told the selectors that, for domestic reasons, he did not wish to be considered for the tour. Franklin, as a matter of fact, was the leading light in the now famous Bogota story. He signed on for the Santa Fé club in Columbia and was playing in that country before the England team left for the Cup tournament.

It proved to be a sensation. My paper, the *News Chronicle*, asked me to get in touch with Franklin at his Bogota address. For more than thirty-six hours, on and off, I tried to get him on the phone, but as soon as I got Franklin on the other end the line went dead. Somebody was very keen to prevent Franklin from giving a true picture of his life out there. I lost nearly two nights' sleep over this adventure, and got nothing for my pains. It was the same when I tried to contact Roy Paul and Jack Hedley, who had gone to Bogota but did not sign for any club there. I followed them on the phone all the way on their journey back to New York. Never once was I allowed to have a word with them although I occasionally got them on the line.

Franklin's withdrawal meant that England had to find a new centre-half. The choice fell on Laurie Hughes of Liverpool. He never let the side down in any way. In fact, if it had not been for an injury received in an F.A. Charity Shield game at Stanford Bridge, I think Hughes would have been England's centre-half for many years.

Another shock was the omission of the great Stanley Matthews from the party of eighteen players who made the trip for the World Cup. But before long the F.A. decided that Matthews was urgently required. They sent for him and he arrived with Jim Taylor of Fulham in time for the second game of the series, though he did not play until the final game against Spain. It was a bad beginning to a tour that brought the biggest disappointment in England's international history.

CHAPTER 14

A BURGLAR VISITS ME IN RIO

I SEE ENGLAND HUMILIATED BY AMERICA, AND STUDY BRAZIL'S FANTASTIC TRAINING METHODS

My first visit to South America, to report the efforts of the England team in the World Cup competition, will remain an outstanding memory, not only for the tremendous beating the team took but also for my own personal experiences.

The long flight to Rio de Janeiro, our headquarters for the tour, was a happy one, with the players singing cheerfully their favourite song, 'Barrer Boys', and four of us in a corner whiling away the hours with card games. For all the party, the first sight of Rio's fabulous harbour with the Sugar Loaf Mountain jutting out of the sea was a thrilling moment. Our eyes were wide open as we were driven from the airport to our hotels on Copacabana beach. This was the golden stretch of sand that later had to be placed out of bounds to the players because of the tiring effects of the sun's rays.

We had been there only a day when I had an unwelcome visitor. We had been warned by local journalists that all the undesirable characters in South America had gathered in Rio for the great games and one of them paid me a visit during the night. His way of working was to spray dope into the bedroom and, when the victim was nicely put away, ransack his room. I lost all my personal belongings, even down to my pipe and tobacco and a few cigarettes I had left out on the bed-table. Luckily for me he overlooked a small bag I had carried which contained my passport and travellers cheques. The rest of my money and effects just disappeared. Of course I reported the matter to the hotel manager. The police were called in and examined the room and the wardrobe in which hung my clothes with all the pockets trailing limply outside their proper place. As I could not speak their language I could not say a word to them. Soon after they had gone, the hotel manageress visited my room. She came from Sweden and spoke English perfectly. Almost her first words were: "Did you give them anything before they left?" When I answered "No," she replied: "You will never see your belongings again!"

Nor did I.

Once I had settled down I began to look around. One of my first visits was to the amazing training camp which had been organised for Brazil's own World Cup team. Seldom can a national soccer side have trained in such luxurious surroundings. A millionaire's home in the hills behind Rio had been taken for the twenty-two players chosen. Here, shut off from outside distractions, they were preparing for the World Cup with all-out enthusiasm and thoroughness.

By the time the English party reached Rio, the Brazilians had played many practice games. So thorough were their preparations that they even studied films of the England v Scotland game which had taken place at Hampden Park a few weeks earlier. Regarding England as their most dangerous rivals, they carefully analysed lessons taught by the films, and by the visit to Glasgow that had been made by their highly paid and efficient team manager Flavia Costa. I was told that the preparations were so careful that married players had not been allowed to see their wives during the training period. To prevent any jaunts into 'town', the training camp had been equipped with everything that could be required. There were complete medical rooms, billiard tables, and in the evenings stage artists visited the camp to entertain the players, who were considered national heroes. Costa's strict discipline kept the players in order. They were packed off to bed at ten o'clock each night after their cups of vitamin drinks!

Costa himself was a considerable character, probably the highest-paid football manager of all time. I was told that his monthly salary, paid partly by the Brazilian F.A. and partly by the club he managed, exceeded £1,000 a month. He also received from his club a signing-on fee of £4,000.

The camp certainly impressed me, especially the three resident chefs and the two doctors who were constantly on hand in case of accidents or injuries to the players. It made me wonder whether, in the future, England would tackle a competition with the same earnestness. I doubt it.

It was not long before I fell victim to 'Rio Tummy', a mild form of dysentery that is not only painful but leads to many delicate situations. Nearly every visitor to South America gets it at some time or other. Whilst I was suffering I had to attend a meeting at the hotel where the England party was staying, about half a mile along the Copacabana front from my own hotel. I went by taxi! On the hotel staircase I ran into Tom Whittaker, Arsenal manager, who was holidaying in Rio. He said: "What's the matter, Charlie?"

When I told him, he replied: "Oh, I'll soon put that right for you."

I thought no more about it for the time being. At the end of the meeting I dashed by taxi back to my hotel. No sooner had I got there than the telephone bell rang. It was the head porter who said: "Your doctor is waiting down here in the hall."

I thought there must be some mistake as I had not sent for a doctor, but he explained: "Mr Whittaker told him to call on you."

The doctor came into my room. First he examined my pulse as, unable to speak to him, I could not describe the symptoms. Then he brought out a stethoscope and after sounding me out in various parts of the body, patted me on the back and said: "Magnifico."

Vainly I tried to make him understand by sign that it was my tummy that was causing the trouble. He then proceeded with a blood-pressure test and again said: "Magnifico."

So I went through all the tests and all I could get out of him was 'Magnifico'. At the end I wondered about payment so, to bring the point to his notice, I pulled out all the money I had in my pockets and held it in front of him. He coolly took the equivalent of about £6 and departed. He did send round a phial of pills later, but by that time I had almost recovered from the inconvenience.

In the meantime the England players were quietly enjoying their stay in the hotel with its glass-sided restaurant. Walter Winterbottom, manager in charge, had wisely had a word with the chef about the cooking, pointing out that the excessive use of garlic would not suit his men. They had more or less English meals. In this and other details, Winterbottom took advantage of Tom Whittaker's experiences during Arsenal's visit in the previous year. Throughout the tour Tom's advice was invaluable.

On the following day I accompanied the players to the giant Rio Stadium, which had been built for the occasion. Shaped like a huge saucer, the ground, still uncompleted, was a few minutes' drive along palm-shaded avenues leading from the centre of the city. We were amused by the moat that, with a high wire fence, separated the spectators from the field of play. The moat, we were told, could be filled with water in the event of trouble. It did not have to be filled with water whilst we were there. The Brazilian fans were far better behaved than we had been led to expect. There was not one unseemly incident.

Much work had still to be done to the stadium dressing rooms situated under the stands. To reach the pitch from these rooms the players had to go along a concrete corridor and then climb twenty-three steps until they reached a heavy steel door. When this swung back, they emerged into the dazzling sunshine and saw the pale blue seats which circled the Stadium. With a capacity of 200,000, this Stadium dwarfed even Hampden Park. It looked particularly splendid at night when the 200 arc lamps were switched on.

At this stage, Brazil and England were the clear favourites for winning the World Cup. England's task in the preliminary group (in which they were drawn with Chile, United States and Spain) seemed well within their capabilities. Group winners went forward to the semi-finals. Spain had arrived in Rio before the England party. I was told they carried a banner which declared simply 'We have come for the World Cup', a degree of bravado which contrasted oddly with the modest bearing of the England players.

With £2-a-day pocket money the boys were finding that money did not go very far in fashionable Copacabana, especially with tea at one shilling and three pence a cup! I found it hard to get along on my allowance seeing that I had to pay approximately £3 for my bedroom, with breakfast extra.

All the time headlines in the paper were screaming: 'THE KINGS OF FOOTBALL ARE HERE!' Brazilian experts were highly impressed by the skill of the English players in training sessions.

When the team for the first game with Chile was chosen there was surprise at the omission of Jackie Milburn, Newcastle United centre-forward, from the attack. Roy Bentley was preferred as leader in a line-up which read: Williams, Ramsey, Aston, Wright, Hughes, Dickinson, Finney, Mannion, Bentley, Mortensen and Mullen. It proved strong enough to beat Chile comfortably. The 2–0 victory increased our hopes of doing well in the tournament. England were still favourites, with Mario, a leading commentator, remarking: "How tranquil are the English! After the first twenty minutes there was no danger for them . . . the result was certain because of the cold thinking of the English."

And yet I had a vague feeling of discomfort about the future. I thought the England team had put too much emphasis on 'copybook' football to the sacrifice of punch and finish in front of goal. Their midfield movements were perfectly carried out. But they were mainly across field, not direct enough to get the Chilean defenders in a panic. My doubts were not dispelled even by Mortensen's great first goal, nor by the superb shot with which Mannion increased the lead. It was exhibition soccer, not World Cup-winning stuff.

Conditions could not have been more favourable to the English. A downpour of rain just before the start soaked the pitch to their liking and in their favour. In the rainy atmosphere we might just as well have been in Manchester. Behind me in the stand, water cascaded through the roof onto the seat reserved for Sir Neville Butler, the British ambassador, and his party. Below me on the open terraces, other spectators huddled under black umbrellas. Apart from the weather, the crowd certainly did their best to make the English players feel at home. Their welcome was tremendous, cheers and whistles mingling with the explosion of hundreds of firecrackers, which sounded like a battery of machine guns. Before the kick-off, something like 5,000 pigeons were released and circled around the ground. But just as the President was delivering a welcome address and a gun salute was being fired, the game started. You see, three o'clock was the time scheduled for the kick-off and referee George Reader of Southampton had been instructed to start the game on time. He did so amid an indescribable din.

Immediately after the game, I had to broadcast a summary of the play to listeners at home. It was a big effort to get it done in time but somehow I managed it. Then I got into a friend's car and made for my hotel. On the way he turned on the radio and I heard my own voice coming over the air. It is the only time I have ever listened to one of my own summaries. I can't honestly say I enjoyed it.

So England, over the first hurdle, confidently set off for the interior of Brazil for the match with the United States, which was expected to be a walk-over for us. The team was unchanged. A mistake because I believe that the introduction of Stanley Matthews to the attack would have had an important psychological effect on the American defenders and the inclusion of fresh, new forwards would have added life and thrust to the most vital part of the team. Even so, no one in the worst of nightmares could have foreseen the humiliating experience that was to come.

As preparation for this game, the team stayed as the guests of the hospitable British gold-mining company at the little mountain village of Morro Velho. It was a British colony, a home from home, with British food and a whiff of home atmosphere. During the few days in this homely little community, I paid my first visit to a gold mine. I was told that I could carry away as much as I could lift. If you have ever tried to lift a block of gold you will understand how much I got away with.

The match itself was played in the flourishing new city of Belo Horizonte, reached from Morro Velho along a road twisting breathtakingly around the side of a mountain with a sheer drop on one side. It was clouded with a red dust that, even with the windows clamped shut, filled the cars.

Once again England gave a wonderful exhibition of 'copybook' football. The ball went from man to man with wonderful accuracy, but by the time the attack got to the American penalty area they ran up against massed defenders. Time after time England raided with perfect movements only to break down near goal. It was a one-team match really but I longed with all my heart for the first goal to come.

Then, in one of the American breaks-away, their centre-forward Gaetjens deflected a shot from Bahr (a half-back) with his head, past the surprised Bert Williams. Then I had qualms. After half-time, England's forwards interchanged positions, but they still went on with their exhibition play. So I became reconciled to defeat and began to write my story long before the game was over.

There was no excuse for England's 1–0 humiliation. I rated the American on a par with one of our Third Division teams, like Rochdale, yet by sheer guts and enthusiasm they humbled mighty England. At times, I admit England were a trifle unlucky, notably when a Mannion shot rebounded from a post and when a rugby tackle by the American centre-half stopped Mortensen when he had a clear run to goal. It is true that some of the Italian referee's decisions were unaccountable. True too that a header from Mullen looked like a perfectly good goal. But they were not responsible for the debacle. England's faulty tactics were to blame.

American officials danced along the touchline, joyful and triumphant for the time being. I spoke to one of the reporters from St Louis. He told me that, so sure had his bosses been of an American beating, they had forbidden him to cable his story. He had to send it by airmail the following morning. With the best football story of America's history, he was not allowed to spend twenty-five shillings on cabling it to St Louis.

It was thought that this victory would do American football a lot of good. But when I talked to U.S.A. officials when I was in New York three years later, they assured me the reverse was the case. Many American people got the idea that there could not be much in a game in which a team of amateurs and part-time professionals could beat the best in the world in a Cup competition.

Cable facilities were not available at Belo Horizonte for the British reporters. We could not wire our reports to London, they had to be telephoned to Rio, and with only two telephone lines between all the reporters present, there was a big delay. By the time the last message was through, the pitch was in darkness. When no one could find an electric torch there was the strange spectacle of half a dozen reporters grouped around the phone on an otherwise deserted ground, frantically making bonfires of newspapers so that the copy could be read to the cable office in Rio and thence transmitted to faraway Fleet Street.

I was not in this strange scene. I had rushed off to a little shed in the far corner of the ground to broadcast a summary of the game to England. It was a long and tiresome job. The line was so bad that little went over the air. I repeated the broadcast seven times and even then it was not satisfactory, but it had to do. When I was finished I found the outer gates of the ground were locked. I had to climb over them to get outside. There I stood in the darkness wondering what to do. I had no means of conveyance back to Belo Horizonte.

Perched on a high hill, I could see the lights of the city in the distance. It looked a terribly long way. I set off to walk hoping I would hit the right track. After walking for half an hour or so I was lucky to thumb a lift to Belo Horizonte. I was never more thankful when I got there and went into a restaurant for a meal.

My troubles were not over; the cars that had brought us from Morro Velho had all set off for the mining town. There I was, stranded in a strange city, unable to speak a word of the language. When I was getting worried, there walked into the restaurant a group of Englishmen. They were from the mining town, doing their best to drown the bitterness of an unexpected defeat. Naturally I joined in with them and had a riotous evening. Luckily for me they had a charabanc to take them home and I went with them, getting back in the early hours of the morning.

On the way back by plane to Rio the next day, the F.A. members in charge chose the team for the last group game with Spain in Rio. They remodelled the forward line, bringing in Stanley Matthews, Jackie Milburn and Eddie Baily of Spurs. There was still a chance that England could qualify for the final stages. A win over Spain would have brought a deciding game between the two for the right to enter the semi-final. The team that had the issue in their hands was: Williams, Ramsey, Eckersley, Wright, Hughes, Dickinson, Matthews, Mortensen, Milburn, Baily and Finney.

But the forward changes did not have the desired effect. Their failure to score against the fiery Spanish defenders was another pathetic example of weak finishing after grand midfield work. Spain won by the only goal of the match, scored in the fiftieth minute by Zarra, their bustling, tearaway centre-forward. And yet there could be no charge of 'lack of spirit' against the English. They fought magnificently and responded to Spain's tough tactics with a calmness that created anew the legend of British sportsmanship in South America.

The Spanish pushed and obstructed, they wasted time flagrantly, and once they fouled Finney in the penalty area, only for the referee to ignore the offence. All that has soon been forgotten.

Only the score remains important in the record books. I shall, however, long retain in memory the sight of the tired, sad English players as they left the field, knocked out of a tournament they quietly believed they would win. All around the ground spectators were taking out their white handkerchiefs and waving them at the disconsolate Englishmen as they went to the dressing room. It is the polite South American way of saying farewell to a beaten team.

This defeat brought a quick return home for the party. Within a few days they were booked for the plane journey. Even then their bad luck held, for the plane was delayed for twenty-four hours. The players were in no mood to enjoy the extra freedom.

It was learned afterwards that had the team won their way to the final, they would have earned some portion of the profits made in the final rounds. Being knocked out so early cost them something like £1,000 each in bonus money. The final between Brazil and Uruguay at the Rio Stadium brought world-record receipts of £125,000. It would have been no less if England had been one of the teams. It was a great opportunity lost.

And so we came to the end of England's first attempt to win the World Cup. It brought disappointment, though at the same time it provided enough excitement and thrills to last a lifetime.

CHAPTER 15

DOOLEY'S TRAGIC ACCIDENT

ENGLAND'S MAGNIFICENT FIGHT AGAINST THE SCOTS, AND THE TRIUMPH OF TOTTENHAM HOTSPUR

During the 1950 summer there was a lot of activity behind soccer scenes. First the League Management Committee inaugurated a provident fund for the players, which ensured that everyone on retirement received ten per cent of all the money he had earned during his playing days. It was a lovely 'nest-egg' and made me wish I were still playing. It gives a sense of security to the players knowing they have something to look forward to when they go out of the game.

They were granted an increase in wages by the Tribunal set up by the Ministry of Labour to settle the differences between the League and Players' Union. This Tribunal offered the suggestion that there should be a limit of £15,000 on transfer fees and that it should be divided three ways: between the club transferring the player, the player himself and a pool that would be used for the benefit of the game generally. This suggestion was turned down by the clubs at the annual general meeting. One reason for its rejection struck me as rather amusing. The president of the League said: "We have considered schemes to enforce limitation but with the tightening up of the country's financial position, there has been a reduction in the high level of these fees so we are not, at present, recommending any further action."

Yet during the next season, the record sum of £34,000 was paid by Sheffield Wednesday for the transfer of inside-right Jackie Sewell from Notts County. And since then there have been other transfer fees bordering on the £30,000 mark, like those for Tommy Taylor (Barnsley) and Trevor Ford (Aston Villa).

Sewell's transfer was almost like an auction market in which several clubs sought his signature. The proceedings dragged on until they became nauseating. Sheffield Wednesday were in danger of relegation from the First Division when they signed Sewell in March 1951, only a few days before the 16th March, which was the deadline for signing players eligible to take part in games affecting promotion and relegation. Sewell did not save Wednesday from relegation, but he played a part in helping them back to their First Division place in the next season, when they won the championship of the Second Division. He also helped in the remarkable rise to fame of giant centre-forward Derek Dooley, 6 ft 3 in. in height and wearer of size-twelve boots! This dashing, ginger-haired fellow, twenty-three years of age, and in his first League season, did not gain a first-team place until October and yet scored forty-six goals in thirty games and was a leading figure in the Wednesday's success.

There were hard words said about the robust methods of the dynamic Dooley. I thought he was rather clumsy, but scrupulously fair. I was sure that when the rough edges had been knocked off his play, with experience he would be England's centre-forward. Unhappily Dooley met with a tragic accident. He had taken part in only a few First Division matches when he broke a leg in a collision with Preston North End's goalkeeper at Deepdale. He was taken to hospital. Complications set in and Dooley had his right leg amputated a week or two after the accident. Within a few days of losing his leg Dooley received a cheque for more than £3,000 from a lucky gentleman who had just scooped a football-pool win. It was a wonderful sporting gesture. A fund was raised for Dooley. It helped to ease his burden financially, though it could not possibly compensate him for the abrupt termination of his playing career.

Newcastle United won the F.A. Cup in season 1950 to 1951 by beating Blackpool in the final at Wembley. On the road to the final they defeated Bristol Rovers in the sixth round at Eastville after a draw at St James's Park. I had to cover the match and intended to travel to Bristol by a morning train. There was a thick fog so I telephoned to Paddington Station asking for the time the train departed. On being assured that it would leave about eleven o'clock, I went to the station very early. When I reached it there was no train leaving for Bristol that would get me there in time. Others were in the same predicament. We dashed round to a garage, hired a car and reached Eastville with a few minutes to spare before the game started. The Rovers' ground was a mass of mud. I wondered how the players struggled through the ninety minutes. But all went well for Newcastle, who won by three goals to one. It was a tiring experience and it reminded me of one journey from Glasgow after an inter-League game. We left home a few hours after the match, which was played on a Wednesday, but did not arrive in London until Friday morning. Heavy snow had disorganised the traffic. We spent the Wednesday night at Carlisle, the train being unable to cross the mountains, and then sat through the next night in the carriage.

At Wembley, Newcastle owed a lot to the sharp-shooting of centre-forward Jackie Milburn. He scored both goals against Blackpool, the second being the best ever seen at the famous Stadium. Midway in the second half, Newcastle were attacking on the right wing. Little Ernie Taylor, who afterwards got another winner's medal with Blackpool, side-footed the ball back to Milburn. Without hesitation, the centre-forward hit it with his left foot. Though the range was about twenty-five yards, the ball flew into the net before goalkeeper George Farm had time to move.

A fortnight before this final I saw one of England's finest performances in an international. Although they were beaten 3–2 by Scotland at Wembley, they put up a magnificent fight against odds. After only seventeen minutes' play, England lost Wilf Mannion, the clever inside-forward, who fractured a cheekbone in a head-on collision with Billy Liddell of Scotland. With ten men, England fought gallantly. They scored first through Harold Hassell, only for Scotland to gain a 3–1 lead. Then we saw England at her best. Tom Finney, outside-left, moved across to partner Stan Matthews on the right wing and gave a wonderful show. Finney scored a second goal for England and four gallant forwards came very near to saving the game and sharing the international championship, won by Scotland. It was another point in the argument against substitutes. If England had been allowed to bring on another player in Mannion's place, we should not have seen an epic struggle that will never be forgotten by those who watched it.

The summer of 1951 was notable for the sweeping British

victories in a series of Festival of Britain internationals. Britain kept an unbeaten record against seven overseas national teams, amongst them Argentina, Portugal, France and Sweden.

I saw only one of the seven games, that against Argentina at Wembley. It aroused tremendous interest. Record receipts and attendance for a mid-week match in England were set up. England won 2–1 by scoring twice in the last quarter of an hour. The game provided a contrast in defensive styles and I can say with certainty that our method with the 'stopper' centre-half was much more the convincing of the two. England's forwards made many openings in the Argentine defence with its roving centre-half and a full-back covering the opposing centre-forward. But they missed many chances.

There was an exciting finish to the League that season, but not as far as the championship was concerned because Tottenham Hotspur won the title in a canter by a margin of four points. The previous year they had won the Second Division championship. Spurs were the most attractive team I had seen since the war. Their simple 'push and run' methods were carried out with great speed and accuracy.

It was at the bottom end where the excitement came. I went to Stamford Bridge on the last day of the season to watch Chelsea play Bolton Wanderers. Chelsea had to win to escape relegation. They were level on points with Sheffield Wednesday (promoted the previous May because they had a better goal average than Sheffield United and Southampton) and two behind Everton. And Wednesday and Everton were playing each other at Hillsbrough. When the half-time score came through from Hillsbrough, Wednesday were leading 4–0. Hurried calculations were made. They worked out that Chelsea had to score another goal to save themselves. They managed to do that with a quarter of an hour to spare and beat Bolton 4–0. Although Wednesday ended up by beating Everton 6–0 it did not save them. They were relegated with Everton.

It has always been a puzzle to me that goal average is still allowed to decide such vital matters as promotion and relegation. It is not a British characteristic to 'rub it in' to a beaten side. When a team is leading comfortably, they do not go all out for a mammoth score and yet at the end of the season, a single goal can promote or relegate a team. I think it would be fairer all round if the teams that finished level on points played a deciding game, or two games on the home-and-away principle.

Newcastle United took in the following season by winning the F.A. Cup for the second year in succession, a feat last accomplished by Blackburn Rovers in 1891. Their 1–0 victory over Arsenal in the final at Wembley again proved the point against substitutes.

Rarely have I seen better defensive play than that put up by Arsenal after they lost right-back Walley Barnes in the thirty-fourth minute. Inspired by captain Joe Mercer, the half-backs and full-back not only held the Newcastle attack but also gave their own forwards enough chance to worry the Newcastle defenders. They battled on until six minutes from the end when Chilean-born centre-forward George Robledo headed the winning goal. Newcastle went off with the Cup, their fourth success in four Wembley appearances, but Arsenal really took the honours.

This was also a great season for England's international side. They shared the international championship with Wales, drew with Austria and France at Wembley and rounded off with a successful Continental tour during which they drew with Italy in Florence, beat Austria in Vienna and Switzerland in Zurich.

After the game with Scotland at Hampden Park (where Stan Pearson, Manchester United inside-left, scored the two goals in a 2–1 victory) I had to dash away from the ground, immediately after the final whistle, to the B.B.C. Glasgow studio to give an eyewitness account of the game in the 5.30 p.m. 'Sports Report'. There was a car waiting outside for me. I reached it quickly, but that was as far as I got for quite a while. The car was held up in the traffic jam. The minutes went by. I asked the car driver to turn on the radio and almost the first words I heard were: "Come in, Charlie Buchan."

I was due on air. Eventually we got on the move. About five minutes later, again I heard: "We'll now go to Glasgow again. Are you there, Charlie Buchan?"

On we dashed and, arriving at the B.B.C., I rushed into the studio just as they were calling for the third time. Somehow I gasped out my little piece. It was the worst of many trying incidents that cropped up when hurrying to get from the matches to the studio. I shall never be as near missing a broadcast again – I hope!

The other extreme came after the 1938 Cup final won by George Mutch's penalty kick in the last minute of extra time. I got away very smartly but the rest of the speakers were stranded at Wembley. A few minutes before the time of the broadcast, I was the only speaker in the studio. It looked as though I would have to keep on talking for a long time. I was thankful when the others rolled in one by one as I did my own part of the programme!

The Continental tour in the summer of 1952 opened rather unfortunately for me. When I arrived at the Florence hotel I was stuck in a small box-room with a bed that was not long enough for my 6 ft 1 in. height. I got very little sleep that night. Matters improved when I moved to a bigger room the next day. But although we enjoyed seeing the sights of that great city, we certainly were not happy at the match with Italy at Florence Stadium, crammed with an excited 93,000 crowd.

Italy came very near to beating us that day. Although Ivor Broadis, the clever Manchester City inside-right, gave us an early lead, Italy equalised soon after the interval and almost snatched a winning goal during the closing stages. There was an unseemly incident near the close when a few bottles were thrown onto the field by the excited crowd. One fell near Nat Lofthouse, the England centre-forward, who had charged an Italian player in an effort to get the ball. A lot was made of this incident, unnecessarily I thought. As a wire fence separated the crowd from the field about twenty-five yards away, there was really no danger of a player being hit. It was, it seemed to me, the Italian way of expressing their feelings. They had expected a big defeat from the 'England Masters' and when their team held them to a draw they let themselves go in no half-hearted manner. At the end of the game, I had to hurry back to the hotel to send my report to London. Unfortunately the charabanc in which we went to the ground left without me. Eventually I got back to the hotel, but not a phone line could I get, so I went round to the General Post Office hoping to telephone from there. I got there about six o'clock. At half-past nine I was still waiting for my call to London. Luckily it came just in time for my story to catch the first edition, though I was something like a limp rag by the time I had sent it through. Although the draw with Italy in Florence had a sobering effect on the England party, it keyed them up for the splendid times that lay ahead.

The next few days were spent quietly in the little hillside town of Siena, world famous for its beautiful buildings and pictures.

The players trained hard for the next important stage, the game with Austria in Vienna on the following Sunday. It was a complete rest for us. Most of all I enjoyed the meals there, which for me consisted mainly of asparagus, grown profusely in those parts. From Siena we went by train to Rome, a four-hour journey, then on by plane to Vienna a few hours later.

On the morning of the Vienna game I was asked by the officers in charge of the British troops in Vienna to talk to the soldiers stationed there, mostly men of the Dorsetshire regiment. With two other journalists I went along to the barracks and explained why I was sure England were going to win. My main reason for such optimism was the rain that was falling at the time. I told them that on the wet pitch and with the ball skidding rapidly, our players would be in their element. Those soldiers certainly enjoyed the talk.

As soon as it was over, a corporal and two men marched quickly up to me. I was under arrest! They marched me over to the sergeant's mess, where I soon discovered the sergeant-major had been a guardsman. He said he could not let a fellow guardsman go out of the place without celebration. We celebrated for quite a while because I learned my talk had raised their spirits enormously. You see the British had been overpowered by the talk of the local people who rammed it down their throats that England had not a ghost of a chance of winning. Austria had drawn with England at Wembley a few months previously. They were the best team on the Continent at the time. They never lost an opportunity of telling them so.

The draw with Italy made matters worse. The Austrians were gloating over their coming triumph and the beating they were going to give 'the masters'. So my little talk raised their sinking morale. Before I left the mess, most of the rank and file had disappeared. They had gone to pledge their weekly pay packet to back England. I was more than glad my prophecy turned out correctly. I could not help but notice how silent the Austrian people were after England had brought off a great 3–2 victory.

Centre-forward Nat Lofthouse scored the winning goal midway in the second half. It was a superb goal that will always live in my memory. We were standing 2–2. Goalkeeper Gil Merrick threw the ball to outside-right Tom Finney, standing a few yards inside his own half. Tom moved forward a little way, saw Lofthouse standing unmarked just over the halfway line and sent him a long through pass. Lofthouse, with the ball under control, dashed through the Austrian defenders. The goalkeeper came out and fell on the centre-forward's leg just as he sent the ball unerringly into the net. Lofthouse was injured but he had won the game. Below me in the stand, a British soldier sent a tray of confectionery, carried by a white-coated seller, soaring high into the air with one vigorous sweep of his arm. Others danced a Highland fling.

After the goal and with Lofthouse limping, England outplayed the Austrians. They might easily have scored another two goals. There was no doubt about a well-deserved victory. No sooner had the final whistle sounded, than a khaki-clad crowd swarmed onto the field and carried the England players off the field shoulder high. I stood there with a lump in my throat. I have rarely been so moved at a football match.

The next game with Switzerland at Zurich proved something of an anti-climax. With Ron Allen, the West Bromwich Albion forward, at outside-right and Tom Finney outside-left England romped to a 3–0 win. Lofthouse again proved the 'match winner', scoring twice. Jackie Sewell of Sheffield Wednesday got the third goal.

Before the game started we had our spirits dampened by an unsportsmanlike display by a team of Birmingham and District youths who were playing a local team as a curtain raiser. I know that the tactics of the locals provoked them but that was no excuse for their behaviour, which culminated in one of their players being ordered off the field. It was the only black mark in a tour which went a long way towards restoring England's prestige on the Continent.

CHAPTER 16

MATTHEWS' HOUR

*I MEET PERON, ASSESS THE TRUTH ABOUT THE
HUNGARIANS, SEE BOTH FINE AND DISGUSTING
FOOTBALL IN THE 1954 WORLD CHAMPIONSHIP, AND
SELECT MY GREAT FOOTBALLERS OF ALL TIME*

The excitement of that tour was followed by more at home in
the following season 1952 to 1953. The top note of all was
Blackpool winning the F.A. Cup at Wembley and thirty-eight-
year-old Stanley Matthews getting the Cup-winner's medal he
had striven for twenty years to obtain. It was the most dramatic
and sensational final ever seen at Wembley. Bolton Wanderers
were leading by three goals to two with only three minutes left
to play. Then Blackpool were awarded a free kick just outside
the penalty area. Stan Mortensen took the free and sent the
ball crashing past Stan Hanson, the Bolton goalkeeper. With
the seconds ticking away, Matthews got the ball. He beat
two opponents with his body swerve, and then sent the ball
low across the Wanderers' goal to outside-left Bill Perry, who
promptly hit it into the net for the winning goal. Perry is the
only South African ever to secure a winner's medal. He played
a big part in the victory.

It was thrilling to listen to the great ovation Matthews got
when he walked up the Wembley steps to receive his award from
Her Majesty the Queen. Matthews told me afterwards he was
so excited he could not hear what the Queen said to him. It was
thought this was the crowing moment of his wonderful career. But
the next season Matthews was recalled to England's international
team and put up more brilliant performances.

Blackpool were worthy of their first ever Cup triumph. They overcame adversity in the shape of injuries by grand teamwork. It seemed when Allan Brown, their Scottish international inside-left, broke his right leg scoring the winning goal in the sixth round with Arsenal at Highbury, their Cup chance had gone. They rose to the occasion magnificently. It was the second time Brown had been deprived of his Cup chance by injury. Two years before he had been kept out of the final team with a knee injury. And besides two Cup final medals, Brown also lost two international caps. He had been chosen to play for Scotland before each game and had to cry off.

Nat Lofthouse, Bolton's centre-forward, also deserved sympathy. He scored in every round of the Cup, including the final tie, and yet he finished on the losing side. But the dashing leader had a wonderful season. He led England in all the internationals and equalled a record by scoring six goals in succession for the Football League in a game with the Irish League at Wolverhampton. He might have set up a record but when the League were awarded a penalty kick, it was taken by full-back Alf Ramsey. The crowd howled for Lofthouse to take it but captain Billy Wright carried out the pre-arranged plan.

By the way, the Cup final was played on the last day of the season. It was not only broadcast on radio but televised too. Television kept many of the people who would have gone to the League games that day in their own homes. The clubs suffered financially, but it was their own fault. Months before, the F.A. had advised them to put forward any League fixtures arranged for that day. Many of them did so, but those who did not paid the price. To prevent that happening again, the F.A. gave permission for the League season to be opened a few days earlier so that matches could be played during that period and the last day of the season kept clear for the Cup final.

The Cup final was not the only dramatic event at Wembley early in 1953. Only a fortnight before, Scotland had drawn the international with England by a goal scored with the last kick of the game. Laurie Reilly, their 'quicksilver' centre-forward, enabled his country to share the international championship with England. Once again we saw ten gallant men fighting against the odds. Scotland lost left-back Sammy Cox with a knee injury twenty minutes before the end. Yet they battled on courageously and got no more than they deserved when Reilly pulled the game out of the fire.

There was also a thrilling wind-up to the League campaign. Arsenal and Preston North End were running a neck-and-neck race for the First Division championship. Preston completed their programme by winning at Derby three days before the season ended. On the last day Arsenal had to beat Burnley at Highbury to carry off the title. They won by three goals to two and set up a record by winning the championship for the seventh time. But it was only because they had a better goal average than Preston that they took top place.

Although the season was exciting, it was not entirely successful. Attendances at the games dropped by nearly two million from the previous season, a serious five per cent drop. I put that down to the increased price of admission to the League games, raised from one shilling and six pence to one shilling and nine pence at the Annual Meeting in June. I think it is too much to expect the public to pay for their afternoon's entertainment. The standard of play had not improved to justify the increase. In most of the Third Division games, the fare provided was not worth it. Soccer has to compete with other attractions like the cinema, where there is more comfort for the onlookers. Unless the price is competitive it will be on the losing side. I fear there will be more slumps in League attendances unless the price is reduced very soon.

As soon as the season was over, England embarked on one of their most ambitious tours, a 25,000-miles trip to the Americas that lasted thirty-four days. I went with the party. The first part of the tour was in Argentina, in the capital Buenos Aires, where two matches were played. The first, labelled Argentina XI against England XI, proved how wrong F.A. officials were to arrange such a fixture. It was supposed to be a warming-up game before the international between the countries four days later. Each country was to put in scratch elevens so there would be no mistake. England's XI was made up of seven players who, it was believed, would not play in any of the internationals and four from the recognised England team. But when the opposition turned out it was the full Argentine side. Of course Argentina won by three goals to one. Even to do that they played a substitute inside-right throughout the second half. He was the man who inspired the victory, easily won in the last forty-five minutes when two goals were scored. The people of Argentina were so jubilant over their team's victory that the day of the match was made 'Footballer's Day' by decree of President Peron. The 14th May to be celebrated every year. The players were rewarded too. An expensive motorcar was raffled and the proceeds divided among them. It was a hollow victory really, but it put the England players who saw it right on their toes.

They determined to avenge the defeat in the international. They were disappointed. It rained the day before and during the morning of the match and it was still raining when the teams took the field. Referee Arthur Ellis rightly decided to make a start. England were so much at home in the conditions that they threatened to run away with the game. The rain fell heavier still. Soon the ground resembled a miniature lake. Players could not kick the ball more than a yard or two. So referee Ellis had no option but to call a halt after seventeen minutes 'water-slogging'. It was a pity. England, I am convinced, would have wiped the black mark from their record with a resounding triumph.

We stayed for eleven days in Buenos Aires. We had been warned that there might be trouble as just before we arrived there had been bomb outrages. One destroyed the famous Jockey Club with its priceless collection of pictures. We experienced nothing of this kind. The city was calm, the inhabitants hospitable and everything possible was done to make us happy, but we could not forget the beating.

During our stay I received no fewer than eighty-seven books, all propaganda for the Argentinean government. I had the impression they were doing their best to make us feel that Argentina was the best run and happiest country in the world. However, we could not overlook the policemen who were on guard at the wonderful River Plate Stadium, where from the stand one could see the River Plate delta in which the pocket battleship *Graf Spee* took refuge during the war years. Nor the fact that as we went into the Stadium, police inspected us, even to opening my typewriter (my 'two-finger exerciser') in case there were hidden bombs.

One of the events of our stay was a reception given by President Peron at his city residence. He talked to us over a cup of coffee and jokingly remarked: "If you want the ground wet for the match, I will order it for you."

No one anticipated that it would turn out as wet as it was on the big day. I was told that rarely has it rained so much or so heavily in Buenos Aires.

Soon after the reception I made the journey to the Olympic Village a few miles outside the city, to watch the Argentinean team in training. I was greatly impressed by the whole surroundings. They are soccer crazy in South America. In Buenos Aires there are four colossal stadiums, each capable of holding more than 75,000 people. The government advanced the money for these to be built at a low rate of interest so that the youth of the country would have every opportunity for training and development. I wish we had some like them in this country. They would be a boon to our young athletes.

From Buenos Aires, we went on to Santiago, the capital of Chile. When we drove from the airport I had the impression I was taking part in some Wild Western film. I expected, as we drove through dirty unpaved streets and past one-storey shacks, that Red Indians would come galloping after our bus. But when we turned a corner into the outskirts of the city, we jumped straight into modern times. There were traffic lights at the first crossroads. Really, it is a beautiful city, and nothing is more modern than the National Stadium where England played their first ever international in Chile. England won more comfortably than the score of two goals to one suggests.

It rained practically throughout our ten days stay. We might have been in Manchester in dreary November. Unfortunately the players went down with 'Chile tummy', a mild type of dysentery. Some of them, like Nat Lofthouse and Tom Finney, also had influenza.

The plane journey from Santiago to Monte Video, where England had the big match of the tour against world champions Uruguay, was not without its thrills. We ran into bad weather on approaching our destination. Over the loud speakers the aircraft captain told us that visibility at the airport was so bad that it was impossible to land. We might have to fly to Cordoba, an up-country town about two and a half hours away, or to Porto Alegre, a port in Southern Brazil. He added: "There is no need to worry. We have enough fuel in the tanks for five hours more in the air."

After cruising around for a while, the pilot saw a break in the clouds, dived through and landed us safely in Buenos Aires. We went on to Monte Video the next day.

Our players, however, had not fully recovered from the effects of 'Chile tummy'. It had its effect on their play during the match with Uruguay. We were beaten by two goals to one after a magnificent fight. Tommy Taylor, Manchester United's twenty-year-old inside-forward taking part in his first trip, scored the England goal. He was one of the successes of the tour. So grand was the show put up by the England team that thousands of Uruguayans waited outside the ground to cheer them as they left by charabanc. It was an unforgettable moment when the players responded to the ovation given them by singing lustily 'Land of Hope and Glory'. It wiped away the bitterness of defeat.

Although we stayed only three days in Monte Video, they were beautiful days. I thoroughly enjoyed the walks along the seafront in English-spring-like weather. We looked out across the Atlantic Ocean with nothing between us and the South Pole except the Falkland Islands. It made me wish that Monte Video had been the headquarters throughout the tour. It would have been ideal, within a few hours journey by plane of all the South American countries visited.

Then we made the long trek to New York. On the way we touched down for an hour at Port of Spain, capital of Trinidad, in the British West Indies. There we were met by Mr Gomez, a West Indian cricketer and president of the local F.A. It was Coronation Day. We sat beneath a spreading palm tree and drank the health of Her Majesty the Queen. It was a most impressive little ceremony. We were entertained by native calypso singers before embarking for the final stage of the flight. A happy interlude.

It was hot in New York. So hot that when I stepped out of the hotel each day, it was like walking into an oven. But during the night before and in the early hours of the morning of the game with the United States at the Yankee Stadium it rained heavily. Despite the fact that the rain ceased some four hours before the game was due to start and the sun shone brilliantly, Yankee Stadium officials declared the match off. It was incredible.

You see the Stadium is a baseball field. They were not going to have the precious turf churned up by such a secondary game as soccer. Matt Busby, Manchester United manager, who was out there to coach the American clubs, offered to demonstrate that a soccer match would do the turf no harm, but they were adamant. Eventually the game was played the following evening, the first time an England team had played under floodlights. So little publicity did the game get that there were only 7,000 spectators.

England won by six goals to three and avenged the World Cup defeat three years previously. It was a walkover, really, with outside-right Tom Finney the man of the match. He was generally voted the 'best player ever to play in America'.

Soccer is not popular in the U.S.A. I tried to get some photographs of the play but not a single New York newspaper or free-lance photographer had bothered to go to the match. Baseball is the game over there. It seemed to me that they are determined to stop the American people getting the soccer bug.

A few days later we flew we home. It had been a wonderful experience and England had made new friends in all the places visited by their grand sportsmanship and skill. Though beaten by Uruguay, there were no regrets. You cannot win all the time. That is a point to be remembered by players, spectators and all officials connected with the game. You can give your best in all circumstances but you cannot command success. You take the good with the bad.

During the summer months that followed, there were many searching inquests held over the performances of the England team. The displays of the Argentine and Uruguay teams made it plainly apparent that England were no longer masters of the world. There has been such an improvement in the standard of play abroad that the time has come when we must change our tactics if we wish even to hold our own with other countries.

Whilst our League system, with its constant urge for winning points regardless of the way they are won, remains as it is, I fear we shall not be able to match the precision passing, the quick positional movements and the combination of the teams from the Continent and South America. Until we have a team trained together for international games, we shall always be struggling against opposition that puts internationals first and prepares as a national team. For years now we have been complacent. We have been saying: 'If only the Continentals could finish off their midfield work with good finishing, they might give us a shock. But they just cannot shoot.' Well, the shock has come. England has been beaten on her own soil by a foreign team for the first time in her ninety-one-years history. It was Hungary, Olympic Games champions, who rubbed our noses in the dust to the tune of six goals to three at Wembley Stadium on 25th November 1953.

Only five weeks before this great shock, England were given a taste of what was to come. A team selected by the F.I.F.A. to play a game to mark the 90th birthday of the F.A. drew 4–4 with England at Wembley and really deserved to win. Though the selected team had played together for only a few hours, they gave an exhibition of controlled ground passing, sweet movement and masterly ball control that made England's hard-working efforts look commonplace. It is to England's credit they battled on bravely against wonderfully clever opponents. At half-time they were only a goal down. Soon afterwards Jimmy Mullen, Wolverhampton Wanderers outside-left, equalised. Hope was born anew. But when Kubala, Hungarian born, and a naturalised Spaniard, put the F.I.F.A. ahead with a glorious shot (he was the best inside-forward in the game) it looked all over until the last minute, when Stan Mortensen, Blackpool centre-forward, was brought down when going full tilt for goal. A penalty kick. Alf Ramsey, Tottenham Hotspur right-back, moved forward to take the kick. There was dead silence as he placed the ball. Then a mighty roar as he sent it straight into the net. Before play could be restarted, the final whistle blew. England were saved in a dramatic finish. But everybody who saw the game was uneasy at the prospect ahead.

Hungary, the next team England had to meet, were really a national team, not a scratch side like the F.I.F.A. eleven. They had played together for three seasons and had got through something like fifty internationals without defeat. They were a complete team, working together in harmony. And they rounded off their midfield movement with powerful and accurate shooting. Although England put up a spirited resistance, and at one period just before half-time looked like making a fight of it, the speed, fitness and finish of the Hungarians took them to a great victory. They had superb inside-forwards in Puskas and Kocais, a grand centre-forward, Hidegkuti, who scored a hat-trick, and a brilliant right half-back, Bozsik, an M.P. in his own country.

The thing that impressed me most about the Hungarians was their supreme fitness. I watched them in their training before the game when every exercise was done as though it was in an actual match. There were no slipshod methods. Players tackled, moved into position and combined during the practice game as they would in match play. And their shooting was designed to make the most of 'half chances'. The Hungarian victory (I almost said 'rhapsody'!) caused a flutter in official circles. It made them realise the England team was not good enough for the commitments ahead, a Continental tour including matches with Yugoslavia in Belgrade and Hungary in Budapest followed by the World Championship in Switzerland, in the summer of 1954.

In a few months between the Hungarian disaster and the Continental trip, the F.A. selectors set about building an England team. They introduced new players, recalled old ones like Stanley Matthews and did their best in the circumstances.

It was thought when England beat Scotland 4–2 at Hampden Park and won the home international championship which gave them a place, with Scotland, in the World Championship, that we would put up a bold show both against Hungary and the other world competitors. But it was not long before we realised that England were lagging behind.

On 16th May 1954, Yugoslavia beat England in Belgrade by a goal scored by their inside-right Mitic in the last three minutes of the game. It boded ill for the future. Then the following Sunday, 23rd May 1954, came the crowning blow. Hungary gave England the biggest hiding of her international history by winning 7–1 in Budapest. It was a humiliating disaster because Hungary were so much the better side in all respects; they deserved every goal they scored. England fought pluckily to the end but were outclassed. I had to give summaries of the game for the B.B.C., and as I sat in the cabin from which the broadcast was given, I could not help passing remarks and groaning every time something went wrong. I did not realise that there was a double microphone in the cabin. Every one of my asides went over the air and was heard in Britain. I have not heard the last of it yet.

Despite the defeat, we had some pleasant times behind the 'Iron Curtain'. A major sensation was caused by Mr Needler, Hull City chairman, who arrived in a gleaming Rolls Royce car. Crowds gathered round it everywhere it was parked. They had seen nothing like it for nearly twenty years. Many times we were stopped in the street by local people who felt the texture of our clothes and then pointed to their own. But it was expensive in Budapest and nothing like as beautiful as when I previously visited the city in 1913 and 1926.

When the England party returned, there were only three weeks left in which to set about revitalising the side for the World Championship. The selectors had already chosen their players for Switzerland and could not add to their number. So they called the players together for two three-day spells of training in England. I thought they should have kept the players together for the whole time. The little they trained together, however, did a lot of good. England set out with new hopes.

Scotland were, with England, among the sixteen nations who took part in the World Championship. England did as well as expected by reaching the quarter-finals, but Scotland were knocked out in the preliminary stages. They lost 1–0 to Austria and then were trounced 7–0 by Uruguay, who won the championship in 1950.

England drew 4–4 with Belgium after extra time. They really threw the game away, for after leading by two goals midway in the second half, they eased up and let the Belgians gain control. Stanley Matthews put on one of his great shows. He should have finished on the winning side.

Then Switzerland were beaten 2–0 in the second game and England won Group IV of the competition. Each group had four teams, the fourth in this case being Italy.

The quarter-final game with Uruguay at Basle was played in terrific heat, 104 degrees. It was so hot that Uruguayan officials told me that if the match had been in their country it would not have been played until the sun went down. As I sat in the broadcast cabin at the back of the grandstand I could hardly breathe, the heat was so oppressive. It must have been a grim ordeal for the players. Yet, inspired by the great efforts of captain Billy Wright at centre-half, and by the artistry of Matthews, England put up a tremendous fight. With more efficient goalkeeping, they might have got away with a draw. But bad defensive mistakes brought about their defeat 4–2, in the second half.

The World Championship, though not a financial success (the grounds in Switzerland were not big enough to house huge crowds), produced two games that will be talked about for a long time. The first was the quarter-final between Hungary and Brazil at Berne. It was a disgrace to the name of football. Three players, two Brazilian and one Hungarian, were sent off the field by British referee Arthur Ellis and two penalty kicks were awarded, one to either side. The Hungarian player sent off was right-half Jozsef Bozsik. There was so much vicious tackling and indiscriminate kicking in this game that it is a wonder to me several legs were not broken. I have never seen a more disgraceful exhibition. Hungary won four goals to two.

Worse followed after the game. There were free fights, with boots and bottles used, on the way to the dressing room. Some heads were gashed, including those of a Brazilian player and a Hungarian official. Police were called to the scene and three of them were also injured in the scuffle. I tried to get into the dressing room after the game. I got as far as the door, which was barricaded by policemen; the glass panel was smashed by a boot thrown by one of the players. One incident was really revolting. A player went up to an opponent with arm outstretched to shake hands. The hand was gripped but with his free fist the opponent struck the player forcibly on the chin. One of the policemen had his legs swept from under him with a vicious sweep of a player's leg.

The second match was between Hungary and Uruguay at Lausanne. It produced the best game I have ever seen, a real classic with both sides playing as near perfectly as possible. It could rightly be called the 'match of the century'. Hungary won by four goals to two after extra time but it was a pity that one of these great sides had to be beaten. Even in continuous rain, both Hungary and Uruguay lived up to the reputation of World Champions. Yet neither of them won the title. That honour went to Germany, one of the outsiders of the sixteen nations taking part in the tournament. They beat Hungary in the final at Berne by three goals to two. On the day's play, again in heavy rain, they deserved their triumph. They were fitter and faster than the Hungarians, who, it seemed to me, had had the edge taken off their speed and stamina by their tremendous exertions against Brazil and Uruguay.

As the reigning World Champions, Germany must be given No. 1 in the world soccer ranking list, but I rate both Hungary and Uruguay above them because their defences are superior. My ranking list compiled from the championship games is: Hungary, Uruguay, Germany, Brazil Austria and England. Yes, England for the time being cannot be given a higher place. Unlike the other nations we have no settled national side. Only a few of the team are certain of their places from one game to another.

Our hope of future progress lies, I am sure, with the League clubs and their managers. Once they can introduce styles of play similar to, and even better than, those of the Continentals, and improved by British vigour and direction, we shall forge ahead. There are young managers like Matt Busby (Manchester United), Andy Beattie (Huddersfield Town), Stan Cullis (Wolves), Frank Hill (Preston) and Vic Buckingham (West Bromwich Albion) who I am sure will soon put their teams on the right lines, and think out new attacking methods.

It is strange how a manager can make or mar a team. There are some who can get the best out of their players by their own personality, men who do not try to teach their players how to play but make the most of their talents. They fit the style of the team to the accomplishment of their players. Others seek to mould the style of the men under their charge and this, I am certain, is a mistake. It has led to the downfall of many League clubs. The first type of manager quickly sums up the ability of his men. He has faith in them and keeps them in the team when they strike a bad patch. The second continually makes changes hoping to hit upon the right blend, usually without much success.

Luckily for me I came under two of the best managers the game had known. The first was Bob Kyle of Sunderland, who signed me on from Leyton and kept me in the Sunderland team, despite a lot of criticism, until I had settled down in new surroundings. I shudder to think what might have happened to me if he had not been such a shrewd judge. I should most likely have plodded along in the reserve side for a while, them moved along to a Third Division or non-League team. There are many young players who have been wasted in this way. If they had been persevered with in their youthful days, they would probably have made the grade. Bob Kyle had the happy knack of commanding loyalty. I know I would have done anything in my power, both on and off the field, to back him up.

Herbert Chapman, having been a player himself, knew exactly what to expect of his men. He was a great psychologist and instilled confidence in every player on his staff. That is the way he built up the Arsenal club spirit. He encouraged every one to think for himself and not to be afraid to express his opinions before his colleagues. He also employed the best men he could find as scouts, trainers and for looking after the welfare of the players. And, above all, his great flair for publicity made Arsenal the most talked-of team for many years. It did not matter if the team were doing well or badly. Arsenal were always in the news.

Many times I have been asked why I did not take a manager's job after I gave up playing. The reason is because I think it is the most worrying position in the game. Even if he is in charge of a good team, a manager is worrying how to keep it good, or improve it. If his team is a poor one, he worries how to turn it into a successful one that will attract the crowds. I am not the worrying type. I should have been out of my element as a manager. Not only has a manager to worry about his team, he also has his staff and directors to consider. Unless he has a board of directors who have faith in him, he is likely to run into all sorts of difficulties. There are too many managers who are little more than glorified office boys. The directors run the team and, I must say, not too well in many cases. It has always been a wonder to me why some club directors pay a manager a big salary to run the playing side and then do it themselves. It is a strange way to run a business, and a League club today is really big business.

There is a story of the directors of a club insisting upon signing a player contrary to the judgement of the manager. One of the directors went to sign the player the day before a League match so that he could take part in it. There was little time to spare. Immediately the form was signed, the director said: "Come on lad, we'll have to run."

Whereupon the player gasped: "Not so fast sir, my rheumatism's killing me!"

It is my firm opinion that a manager should be in sole command of the players, the directors taking care of the business side. The manager knows the little fads, the strengths and weaknesses of the players and is better qualified to hit upon a winning combination. There is no reason that I can see why he should not work smoothly with the directors, taking advantage of their experience and using, to the extent he thinks is advisable, their knowledge and judgement. I have always found that a happy atmosphere in the boardroom spreads to the dressing room and the players. Where you find a happy club, you find a successful one.

Selecting a team, whether for a League game or an international, is a job for specialists. There should never be more than three having a hand in it. If there are more, usually the strongest personality, not the best judge, gets his way. No two people sum up a game or a player in the same way. The bigger the selection committee, the greater the divergence in opinion and the less likely they are to agree upon a balanced side.

The days have gone in international circles when there were two or three players of equal class for each position in the team. Now, the selectors find it almost impossible to hit upon a settled and combined team. Outstanding personalities, such as there were in days of old, are few in number. They have been sacrificed in the craze for streamlined teamwork. There are just as many good players today as ever there were. They are, however, lost in the pattern of the modern League side. I think any comparison between old-timers and the present players is a waste of time.

The game changed with the alteration of the law in 1925. I believe the 'old-timer', with a few weeks to get used to the new conditions, would stand out just as prominently now. And the modern, given more scope to play his own game, would have held his own with players to whom the passing years have added extra qualities. It is usually a practice to select teams from olden days and say there will never be anything like them. I am not going to do that but choose what I fancy would be the ideal team for the years between 1910, when I started playing in first-class football, and 1925, when the offside law was changed.

There is no doubt about the defence. Sam Hardy, the 'prince of goalkeepers', Bob Crompton and Jesse Pennington. They served England well in many internationals and were the perfect blend, the vigour and resourcefulness of Crompton dovetailing with the clever covering and general-like qualities of Pennington at full-back.

My half-backs are Colin Veitch, the music teacher with an ice-cold soccer brain; Charlie Roberts, expert at bringing the ball under control and a great general; and Arthur Grimsdell, powerful in defence and attack. Three different types, but three of the finest half-backs I met.

Then in the front line, I place Jockie Simpson, the opportunist, with Harold Fleming, unorthodox but a marvel with the ball on the right wing. In the centre, Albert Shepherd, fast, fearless and a born leader. On the left George Holley, one of the greatest all-round forwards of my time, and Billy Smith, the Huddersfield Town 'flier' with the raking stride and dainty ball control.

Here it is then, my eleven old-timers to tackle any team in the world:

Hardy (Aston Villa), Crompton (Blackburn Rovers), Pennington (West Bromwich Albion), Veitch (Newcastle United), Roberts (Manchester United), Grimsdell (Tottenham Hotspur), Simpson (Blackburn Rovers), Fleming (Swindon), Shepherd (Bolton Wanderers), Holley (Sunderland), Smith W. (Huddersfield).

Yes, a great side, but who is to say that it would prove better on the field than eleven of post-1925 players who, in a few years' time, will be spoken of in the same breath as the men who preceded them?

For example, a team that has Harry Hibbs, the immaculate little goalkeeper with the safe pair of hands. Fair-haired Tom Cooper, a clean kicker and sure tackler, and Eddie Hapgood, positional play expert. As full-backs: Willis Edwards, sturdy and precise in placing the ball. Stan Cullis, described as the last of the attacking centre-halves, and Sam Weaver, of the long throw-in and skilful feet, as half-backs. The great Stanley Matthews, Bob Kelly, noted for his swerve and quick burst. Bill 'Dixie' Dean, the record goal scorer. Billy Walker, schemer-in-chief and Jimmie Dimmock, in his day, the finest individualist in the game, as forwards.

Here they are with their clubs:

Hibbs (Birmingham), Cooper (Derby County), Hapgood (Arsenal), Edwards (Leeds United), Cullis (Wolverhampton Wanderers), Weaver (Newcastle United), Matthews (Stoke City), Kelly (Burnley), Dean (Everton), Walker (Aston Villa), Dimmock (Tottenham Hotspur).

Even the old die-hards who can see little good in present-day soccer must admit this is a grand side, capable of meeting the best opposition. Even now we are beginning to ask: 'Where are players like them today?' We shall be saying the same in years to come.

Of course, it is impossible for two teams such as I have selected to meet and settle the argument. Perhaps it is a good thing. The spice of football is in the arguments it creates and which go on continuously for years. They will never be settled.

Yet it is a fact that soccer, unlike other sports, has not produced a mass of literature. There have been passages in novels by great authors like Arnold Bennett and J.B. Priestley, and mystery stories by various writers. Surely the game is popular enough to be worthy of the attention of our present leading writers.

For many years after the old *Athletic News* closed down, there was no paper or magazine devoted exclusively to the game. It was in a bid to fill this gap that in 1951 I started *Charles Buchan's Football Monthly*. It has caught on so well that it was obvious something of the kind was badly needed. It is a new field for me and I am getting as much pleasure from it as I did from my playing days. One is never too old to learn. In life, just as in football, there is always something new and exciting round the next corner.